A Minister's Handbook of Mental Disorders

 *Integration Books*

STUDIES IN PASTORAL PSYCHOLOGY, THEOLOGY, AND SPIRITUALITY
Robert J. Wicks, General Editor

also in the series

A Minister's Handbook of Mental Disorders

Joseph W. Ciarrocchi

Integration Books

paulist press/new york/mahwah

Acknowledgments
Pages from the Mini-Mental State Examination are reprinted with permission of New England Medical Center, Department of Psychiatry. Excerpts from THE FARTHER REACHES OF HUMAN NATURE by Abraham H. Maslow, copyright © 1971 by Bertha G. Maslow, are used by permission of Viking Penguin, a division of Penguin Books USA Inc.

Library of Congress Cataloging-in-Publication Data

Ciarrocchi, Joseph W.
    A minister's handbook of mental disorders/by Joseph W. Ciarrocchi.
        p. cm.—(Integration series)
    Includes bibliographical references and index.
    ISBN 0-8091-3403-9 (pbk.)
    1. Pastoral counseling. 2. Pastoral psychology. 3. Psychotherapy.
4. Psychopathology. I. Title. II. Series.
BV4012.2.C518 1993
253.5′2—dc20   93-11092
                                                                    CIP

Published by Paulist Press
997 Macarthur Boulevard
Mahwah, New Jersey 07430

Printed and bound in the
United States of America

Contents

DEDICATION

To Jim and Linda Ryan

Acknowledgments

I wish to express my gratitude to those who helped me with this project. Sister Dolores Pfeiffer typed early versions of the first five chapters. My son, Michael Ciarrocchi, typed original versions and revisions of the remaining chapters, and designed the figures in Chapter 5. His collaboration demonstrates how computers create role reversal between parents and children. Pamela Milhouse May typed references and assisted in manuscript preparation.

The Loyola Pastoral Counseling community supported me in multiple ways. Bob Wicks, the Series Editor, was infinitely patient and encouraging throughout. I cannot thank enough the hundreds of graduate students enrolled in my course on Psychopathology for Ministry over the past ten years whose insights, questions and experience shaped the presentation of this material. My only goal for this book is that it become a practical guide for ministry, and if it succeeds it will be the result of my listening to their issues. No teacher could ever hope for more mature, thoughtful, intelligent, and committed students.

Finally, I thank my wife, Terri, and our children, Michael, Laura, Katie, Jennifer, and Daniel, for their many sacrifices while this book has been in preparation. My apologies to the younger ones who do not understand its unsuitability for their bedtime story.

Joseph Ciarrocchi
St. Valentine's Day, 1992

Foreword

Understanding adult psychopathology is an important part of ministry. To avoid learning about this topic or to "do nothing until the doctor comes" is unnecessary and may be dangerous. In this book Joseph Ciarrocchi recognizes this reality and provides a serious yet practical treatment of the subject. He also brings the material to life for persons in ministry by providing clear pastoral situations and moral issues that are related to the major psychological disorders being covered.

In addition to special sections on the major theories of abnormal behavior and how to assess and interview persons experiencing and manifesting (observable) signs and (reported) symptoms of psychopathology, this book contains detailed chapters on: anxiety and mood disorders, stress, addiction, schizophrenia, sexual problems and dysfunction, and personality disorders.

A Minister's Handbook of Mental Disorders fills a void then that has long been present: the need for a serious book on adult psychopathology by a person familiar with ministry who can present relevant psychological information along with related implications for persons involved in pastoral care. Consequently, this is a book that I hope will find its way into the hands of both experienced ministers as well as those persons preparing for helping roles in the church. It is certainly a timely resource for which to be most grateful given the stressful world we live in today.

Robert J. Wicks
Series Editor

Chapter 1

Pastoral Care and Abnormal Psychology

I. Introduction
II. Definition of Mental Illness
III. Scope of the Book
IV. Personal Values
V. Learning Objectives
VI. Consultation

Introduction

Every clergy person can describe some eventful encounter with the mentally ill. Whether the encounter concludes humorously, poignantly or tragically, it often begins with bewilderment. The person may ring the rectory doorbell or capture the rabbi after services and start a philosophical discussion that Socrates could not follow. At other times the experience provokes grief as in suicide. Clergy normally feel uncertain and ill-at-ease in such situations, as do most people. The expectation placed on clergy is to know how to handle such incidents with the wisdom of Solomon and the patience of Job.

Ordination, vocation or religious commitment does not automatically confer skill in recognizing or relating to the mentally ill. This book takes the view that these are skills to learn. The crucial point here is that *a knowledge of abnormal psychology, the science of mental illness, is essential for ministry.*

The frequency alone of these interactions dictates this. National Institute of Mental Health researchers Anne Hohmann and David Larson reviewed surveys of Americans seeking help for personal problems (Larson *et al.*, 1988). They note that 40 percent first consult clergy, 29 percent consult a psychiatrist, and 21 percent a physician. Clergy themselves spend anywhere from 10 to 46 percent of their time counseling.

A major difficulty, as this study points out, is that 50 to 81 per-

3

cent of the clergy report feeling unprepared by seminary or professional training to handle mental health problems. Furthermore, clergy refer less than 10 percent of their clients to mental health professionals, and many (45–56 percent) confess no training in the criteria for a proper referral, in how to make a referral, nor in how to help the transition to a mental health professional. What makes this all the more startling is that *the number of psychiatric symptoms has no influence on whether people consult clergy or mental health professionals.* In short, pastoral ministers deal with what the authors term "a vast array of mental disorders." This situation would be less troubling were it not for evidence that the deficits for clergy are real and not just perceived. A recent study of clergy's knowledge of psychopathology indicates that clergy know significantly less than college undergraduates as well as graduate students in counseling psychology (Domino, 1990). Surely, front line pastoral ministers require as much information in abnormal psychology as college undergraduates.

Whether the clergy will help or hurt depends on their expertise in a) recognizing mental disorders, b) assessing the person's level of impairment, c) knowing when to refer, and d) knowing how to relate pastorally to the mentally ill and their families. This book's goal is to increase pastoral ministers' expertise and confidence in each of these areas.

Definition of Mental Illness

The American Psychiatric Association defines mental disorder as "a clinically significant behavioral or psychological syndrome or pattern that occurs in a person and that is associated with present distress (a painful symptom) or disability (impairment in one or more important areas of functioning) or with a significantly increased risk of suffering, death, pain, disability, or an important loss of freedom" (American Psychiatric Association, 1987, pp. xxii). This definition encompasses persons with acute illness, chronic illness, or personality disorders.

Chronically impaired persons have problems related to brain diseases which severely limit the person's adaptation to life. These disorders include schizophrenia and disorders of aging. Some ministers spend significant time caring for such persons. Hospital chaplains and those involved with the homeless also meet this population regularly. To use the homeless as an example, effective one-to-one intervention is only possible with some understanding of the various illnesses within this group. Although political advocacy certainly has its place, ministers involved in primary care need to understand the symptoms of these disorders and what intensifies the symptoms. They also need to appreciate the limits of rational persuasion, and be aware of current treatment methods and resources. Workers often feel frustrated when shelters and economic opportunities become available but the homeless themselves do not use the resources. How should one respond to a client who refuses to enter a shelter because the wooden benches are made from "a living organism," or who refuses to eat because someone poisoned the food?

Acute mental illness involves disorders such as depression, manic-depression, anxiety, stress disorders, and the addictions. These disorders represent those most commonly encountered in congregation, parish, or synagogue. They also represent the bulk of mental disorders covered in this book.

Mood disorders, for example, are so common that the field has dubbed depression the "common cold" of mental illness. The symptoms of these disorders interweave with religious beliefs and come to the attention of the clergy. Depressed persons often obsess about past failings and do not benefit from the usual form of spiritual guidance. The client may simply give up or, perhaps worse, experience more guilt. "Look how sinful I am: I can't even accept forgiveness," would be a common distortion.

Individuals suffering from anxiety disorders represent a similar challenge. Their excessive standards generate self-doubt which spills over into the spiritual arena. Some become scrupulous and constantly seek spiritual reassurance. For others personal doubt grows into religious doubt. Often they doubt the worth of all they are or have accomplished and repeated spiritual advice provides little relief.

Addiction problems are at the root of many pastoral aggravations. A large percentage of marital conflicts, spouse and child abuse, sexual dysfunctions, parent-child conflicts, and financial and legal problems are the result of addictive behavior. The addicted person's own denial and that of family members make these disorders difficult to recognize and therefore treat. Ministers may waste valuable time on surface problems that divert attention from the core issue. Alcoholism, drug abuse, and compulsive gambling are pervasive yet hidden, and ministers often labor in vain without identifying the cause of the person's problems.

Personality disorders are particularly troublesome because of their interference with ministry. They sabotage the creation of community and frustrate the mission of pastoral care. Too often clergy invest time, energy and sparse parish resources in trying to rehabilitate someone who needs "a second chance" only to find out that they have been manipulated and conned.

How often does the work style of the following personality types burden a parish or synagogue committee? The compulsive perfectionist whose rigid adherence to "going by the book" infuriates other committee members; the brilliant technician whose good advice is difficult to take because of his or her total indifference to the feelings of others; the passive aggressive member who never voices a complaint at meetings about policy, yet who procrastinates, makes negative comments outside the group, or "forgets" assignments and is unavailable to help; the member with excellent work habits but who suspects that committee decisions are aimed at outmaneuvering him or her.

The effect of personality disorders on ministry is like hiking with a stone in your shoe. They irritate, slow down the journey, and eliminate personal satisfaction. Too often ministers try to influence these persons through rational discussions as if the disorder is a momentary lapse. Unfortunately, they are pervasive, enduring styles which frustrate even the most skilled clinicians.

Scope of the Book

This volume resembles yet differs from a course in abnormal psychology or psychopathology. Introductory chapters focus on models of mental disorders, their classification and assessment. The remaining chapters describe specific mental disorders with each chapter explaining symptoms, theories of causality and current treatment methods.

There are, however, notable differences. The range of disorders is narrower in scope than standard texts. The book details only adult disorders because other volumes in this series focus on children, adolescent and family issues. Also, the book discusses the more common mental disorders while excluding those that ministers are less likely to encounter (e.g. multiple personality).

More substantive differences result from the book's attempt to speak directly to problems in ministry and pastoral care. The author has tried to tie in each disorder to the context of ministry using examples from pastoral situations. While this volume will not attempt to teach pastoral counseling skills or advanced pastoral care methods with the emotionally ill, each chapter offers guidelines for developing pastoral care plans.

Another major difference centers around the question of values. A general text in abnormal psychology or psychopathology aims for neutrality about values. That approach is sensible as a method for the behavioral sciences. This book requires some divergence. Clergy often mistrust the advice of mental health professionals when they suspect conflict with their own value system. To avoid such misconceptions we will address value issues related to pastoral care on an issue-by-issue basis. The chapter on depression, for example, will distinguish between the guilt accompanying that illness versus moral guilt as understood by church and synagogue.

Personal Values

In this context, the reader may wish to know the author's own value system and how this influences the presentation of material. In brief, my viewpoint assumes the Judaeo-Christian concept of the person including human freedom, belief in a personal God, and a belief that transcendence gives ultimate meaning to our life. Nevertheless, I further maintain that no ultimate conflict exists between the scientific method of psychology and the value system just described. Abnormal psychology holds many insights with direct, practical relevance which the minister can apply respectfully.

Such a position is risky and open to misinterpretation. Some may feel a need to reconcile every fact in psychology with a particular religious position. Others may feel discomfort with any talk about values. This has not been my clinical experience. In teaching, supervising, and practicing psychotherapy I have learned to speak openly about values when they appear as *client issues,* and to remain silent when they are not. Value discussions sometimes take ironic twists: I may remain silent with a perfectionist, self-demanding, guilt-ridden client but challenge others who appear to have little or no social conscience.

Learning Objectives

The learning objectives for pastoral care workers are several-fold: 1) to recognize the more common mental disorders seen in ministry; 2) to determine when referral to other resources is necessary; 3) to understand standard treatment for the specific disorders and their relative effectiveness; 4) to develop support strategies for the pastoral care of the mentally ill; and 5) to increase consultation skills for interacting with mental health professionals.

Consultation

It is no secret that an aura of mistrust has existed in many quarters between mental health professionals and pastoral ministers. Some behavioral scientists explain away religious experience through psychological reductionism. Others view religious values as causing emotional dysfunction. Only gradually is this climate changing. Clergy voice complaints that after referring a client some mental health professionals do not treat them as colleagues. If not totally ignored, the religion professional may be viewed as contributing to the problem.

Psychologist Allen Bergin (1991) surveyed mental health professionals and found that only 29 percent rated religious content as important in treatment. He suggests that a "religiosity gap" may exist between clients and treatment professionals. This may explain why the general public turn first to clergy for personal problems. Also, 76 percent of the public agree with the statement, "My whole approach to life is based on my religion," but for mental health workers only 46 percent agree. The gap may be even wider for certain disciplines in mental health. For example 31 percent of psychologists and 24 percent of psychiatrists identify themselves as non-religious versus only 9 percent of the general public. Bergin points out that mental health training programs need to sensitize professions to religion as an important content area in treatment in the same way that race, ethnicity and gender are.

In the meantime, one solution is for the clergy to educate themselves regarding mental health issues and interact assertively with mental health professionals. Clergy should take advantage of changing conditions in health service delivery which give the referral sources considerable influence. From a purely economic standpoint competition among private health care providers has increased and private practitioners depend on referral sources for their livelihood. The public sector as well, pressed by shrinking resources, has strong incentives to collaborate with the community resources pastoral ministry can provide. This sets up a situation where referring clergy may expect and even demand dialogue with the treatment provider in much the same way that a surgeon communicates openly with the referring physician. Clergy need some technical background for sensible dialogue to occur and also to feel self-confident enough to act assertively. Providing this background is a major goal of this book.

Clergy today have additional reasons to wield influence besides economic leverage. First, we need to take the offensive in communicating research which identifies the positive role religious belief plays in mental health as well as adaptive life functioning. Empirical studies conclude, for example, that religion relates in a modest but significant way to positive mental health (Bergin, 1991; Gartner *et al.*, 1991). Other examples include data which point to regular church or synagogue attendance as a preventive factor in adolescents staying off drugs and alcohol (Bry, 1983). In the past clergy might have hesitated to proclaim such information for fear of appearing puritanical. A society which loses over 273 billion dollars annually from the costs of mental illness, drug and alcohol abuse, however, is grateful for support from any quarter (Keegan, 1991, p. 26).

Data are also accumulating that religiously committed persons view negatively therapists with secular values and who are unsympathetic to client spiritual values. They view most positively therapists with similar religious backgrounds (Keating and Fretz, 1990). Furthermore, empirical studies now indicate that pastoral counseling may be as effective as traditional cognitive-behavioral therapy in the treatment of moderate depression in outpatient settings (Propst *et al.*, 1992). The implications of these findings for the field of pastoral counseling are extensive. As these authors note, ". . . a large portion of the public is religiously oriented, and there are far more pastors than therapists" (p. 102).

These issues highlight both the usefulness and the limitations of the material presented in this book and, by implication, the role of the social sciences in matters of faith. A religion professional may feel encouraged that active church/synagogue participation promotes a drug free youth culture. Yet increasing attendance at services is not the ultimate goal. The religion professional ultimately values depth of faith, personal commitment to faith, and a faith both that informs the individual and provides personal meaning. These goals are distinct from even positive social ends. Science has no methodology to handle these issues.

The task I have outlined for this volume, therefore, is complex. The position maintained here is that a knowledge of psychopathology will aid clergy and pastoral care workers in ministry. At the same time I acknowledge the limits of behavioral science in answering questions of ultimate meaning.

Chapter 2

Theories of Abnormal Behavior

Role of Theory in Abnormal Psychology

The role of theory in science is to provide causal explanations and the role of abnormal psychology is to provide causal explanations of mental disorders. When theories are productive they generate hypotheses which predict the causes of abnormal behavior and help develop methods for treatment and prevention. Empirical methods are the ordinary means for testing theories. These methods include objective observation and measurement. Experiments either verify or falsify hypotheses, which, in turn, affirm or alter the original theories.

No single unifying theory holds sway in abnormal psychology to the degree found in the material sciences. Scientific progress in psychology is limited both by the complexity of the subject matter (people) as well as ethical constraints on research. Since no one theory dominates, this book will explore the dominant theories, their applications to psychopathology, and their potential utility for pastoral care.

Biological Theories

Overview. These theories maintain that biological sources cause abnormal behavior. Biology can influence behavior in several ways.

11

Through *heredity* faulty genetic development results in abnormal conditions. *Infectious diseases* may create an abnormal condition such as brain disease resulting from syphilis. *Physiological abnormalities* may lead to abnormal conditions through structural, endocrine or neurotransmitter irregularities. In structural irregularities an organ is damaged from birth (congenital) or as the result of trauma. Endocrine dysfunction results in hormone irregularity, thereby influencing behavior. Finally, neurotransmitters are the chemical messengers of the nervous system and irregularities affect a range of moods and feelings.

Implications for Psychopathology. Genetic errors account for disorders such as Down's Syndrome. An extra chromosome causes this condition which results in mental retardation, characteristic facial features, and physical problems such as cardiac conditions. Infectious diseases at first heralded a key to solving many mental disorders. For example, general paresis is a severely debilitating psychotic condition which filled mental institutions over a century ago. When the microscope revealed the syphilitic spirochete as the agent of this disease, many hoped all mental illness would have a similar source. This has not happened and likely never will.

Endocrine disorders are also well known to generate behavioral syndromes. Thyroid disorders, for example, mimic psychological conditions such as depression and anxiety. Newer psychiatric uses of endocrine tests suggest that subtle irregularities in this system may be responsible for many clinical syndromes. Some researchers and clinicians now maintain that depression is a *sub-clinical* form of thyroid disease. In this case sub-clinical means an endocrine irregularity that is less than a full-blown endocrine disease, yet can still generate significant psychiatric symptoms.

As neuroscience—the study of the nervous system—has developed, much of its focus is how the nervous system communicates. The electrical and chemical modes of communication provide a rich source of hypotheses and data about mental disorders. Some biological researchers maintain that depression, severe anxiety disorders, and schizophrenia, to name but a few, result in neurotransmitter imbalances, the chemical messengers in the nervous system.

Structural damage to the biological system itself also creates behavioral problems. Organ abnormality, whether congenital or from trauma, affects behavior. Some neuroscientists believe that certain forms of schizophrenia result from abnormal brain structure as revealed by sophisticated neuro-radiological procedures—e.g. C.T. Scan and Position Emission Tomograpy (PET Scan). Loss of brain cells is implicated in certain structural diseases such as Parkinson's and Alzheimer's. Furthermore, structural damage sometimes results in irregularity of electrical impulses in the brain, thereby leading to various forms of epilepsy which frequently creates behavioral problems.

Treatment Methods. Biological researchers search for *biological markers*—the biological correlates of mental illness. The discovery of biological markers, such as the genetic factors in Huntington's chorea, permits rapid assessment, provides clues for treatment and makes genetic counseling possible. One biological marker—the DST test—identifies certain sub-types of depression. For some depressed persons their DST test is abnormal when they are depressed and returns to normal when non-depressed (cf. Chapter 5 on Depressive Disorders).

Until now biological theories have had their greatest impact on the development of biological or somatic therapies. These range from diet to electroconvulsive therapies. Medication for psychopathological conditions is the most common of this type and provides symptom relief for anxiety, depression, mania, schizophrenia, alcohol and drug withdrawal.

Evaluation of Biological Theories

Limitations. Biological theories assume that abnormal behavior operates like a medical illness with similar organic processes. While this model has strong appeal for explaining some disorders, its cogency appears weak for others. Schizophrenia and mental retardation appear to have biological sources, but some disorders relate to environmental sources (e.g. post-traumatic stress disorders). Some theorists (e.g. Bandura, 1969) maintain that calling certain groups of abnormal behavior "diseases" ignores social factors. When we label a rapist or gang member who brutally assaults an elderly couple "sick" we are only saying that we find this behavior repulsive. So-called "sick" behavior appears purposeless. No evidence indicates that diseases influence purposeless criminal behavior, but other factors influence purposeful behavior such as theft.

Critics also hold that biological models imply that individuals lack responsibility for their behavior. This leads to legal defenses which appear to mock science and common sense. An example of this is the so-called "Twinkies" defense in the murder case of San Francisco city councilman John Moscone. The defense used psychiatric testimony to demonstrate a lack of homicidal intent due to the defendant's high consumption of junk food. Others argue that biological theories are counter-therapeutic in that clients may take a passive role wanting to be "cured" instead of helping themselves through insight and self-discovery.

Contributions. As noted, biological theories have led to many effective therapies relieving the suffering of countless numbers. These theories also suggest many avenues of future research. Advances occur continually in neuroscience which may lead to cures for serious mental illnesses such as schizophrenia and manic-depression.

Implications for Pastoral Care. Pastoral care workers need to consider the importance of social influences even for biologically influenced problems. Medication plays an important role in preventing relapse in schizophrenia but environmental factors are also crucial. Some depressive episodes appear to have biological influences as well, yet the lack of an intimate confiding relationship is a high risk factor for women to develop depression (cf. Chapter 5).

Pastoral care, then, means avoiding the mentality of "do nothing until the doctor comes." Some biological treatments are so effective initially that the importance of social influences are downplayed or ignored. The client's participation enhances the effectiveness of all forms of healing, including biological interventions, and the minister can augment this process through active participation. At best, medications work for only a sub-population of any particular disorder, and pastoral ministers need to engage the other social factors which aid recovery.

Psychoanalytic Theory

Sigmund Freud (1856–1939) is the single most influential theorist in psychopathology from an historical perspective. His theory grew clinically rather than in an academic setting. He developed his theory as an outgrowth of treating the mentally ill rather than in a formal scientific manner.

Basic Concepts. In Freudian theory the structure of personality involves three psychological processes which mediate the demands of external-internal forces impinging upon the person and shape behavior. The *id* is the first structure to emerge and represents the person's basic instincts. The id is the container of the various instinctual impulses such as hunger, thirst, sex, aggression and safety. The unbridled expression of these instincts is so threatening to the person that

they are repressed, that is, buried out of awareness into the unconscious. Although hidden, these forces shape the bulk of behavior. The
id operates on what Freud calls the *pleasure principle*. The motivating
dictum of the id is, "I want what I want when I want it." Infants and
small children act on this principle frequently and disregard the
rights of others in search of instant gratification.

Gradually a second structure develops, the *ego*, which operates
under the *reality principle*. The id urges the person to get what it
needs immediately, but the ego appreciates the role that external
reality plays. For example, the five year old may desire her three year
old sister's luscious dessert, but if she reaches for it her sister may stab
her hand with a fork. Such reality factors influence the ego to operate
via planning, so the little girl takes the dessert when her sister looks
the other way or asks daddy for a second helping.

The *super-ego* emerges as the voice of social standards and represents the third structure in personality development. The super-ego
incorporates the demands of cultural expectations, customs, rules and
mores. The super-ego represents two aspects: *ego-conscience* is the
experience of guilt from rule transgression; the *ego-ideal* is experienced as positive values to strive for. If my parents teach me to be an
honest citizen, then I feel guilty if I swipe my neighbor's juicy garden
tomatoes without asking. This negative feeling represents conscience. On the other hand, I can live alone and yet feel uneasy about
the messy condition of my apartment if my parents emphasized clean-
liness and orderliness. In this latter situation, I violated no ethical rule
but failed to achieve an ideal. Later theorists call shame the emotional
reaction to violations of the super-ego's ideals. In Freud's system, the
super-ego as well as the id operates in a largely unconscious fashion,
and creates as much conflict for us as our baser drives.

The individual personality develops through the interaction of
the three structures of personality. External factors, in conjunction
with the three psychological structures, determines the personality
style around the age of five. Freud's system is deterministic, with the
individual having little choice over the resultant conflicts.

The ego's *defense mechanisms* play an important role in maintaining the system's balance and harmony. The defense mechanisms
prevent disruptive anxiety and tension from emerging and destroying
the individual. There are many defense mechanisms in psychoanalytic thinking, but some of the most prominent ones include
repression, displacement, identification, reaction formation, and
sublimation.

For Freud the basic mechanism is repression which forces the object choice out of awareness when too threatening. If I am attracted to my neighbor's wife and am a church-going individual with high community status, one way to deal with the conflict is simply to press it out of existence. Displacement handles the threat through disguising the target. If I am angry with my boss, I come home and yell at my kids which is infinitely safer. Identification handles anxiety associated with an object choice by taking on the characteristics of the feared person. One way for minority groups within a culture to cope with an aggressive majority is to adopt the dress, speech and hair styles of the majority while discarding their own. Reaction formation handles a threatening situation by acting out its direct opposite, so that a parent who really did not want to have a baby becomes over-protective of the baby's welfare. Finally, sublimation represents shifting psychic energy from a primitive instinct to a more noble one, such as refocusing one's aggressive instincts and becoming a world-class athlete.

Stages of Development. Developmental theory such as the psychodynamic approach involves "critical periods." The critical period in developmental theory suggests that the organism must accomplish certain tasks at a particular stage. Failure to accomplish this causes arrested or retarded development. In physical development, if certain metabolical processes do not occur during certain time periods within fetal development, physical abnormalities occur. Some psychological theories such as psychodynamic approaches make similar assumptions.

In psychodynamic thinking five stages of development occur: oral, anal, phallic, latency and genital. In the *oral stage*, lasting from birth until roughly two years of age, the baby derives its basic instinctual satisfaction through the mouth. The infant reduces tension by sucking when it is hungry or in distress and biting when it is frustrated. The *anal stage*, lasting from two to three years of age approximately, indicates that the primary source of gratification is from elimination of feces. This represents the child's first major confrontation with cultural realities and the need to conform behavior to external rules. Depending upon the toilet training procedures of a given culture a child may exert power during this stage either by withholding or by messing.

The *phallic stage*, ages three to six, sees a shift to the genital area for the source of gratification. This stage witnesses the *oedipus conflict*, an essential feature of Freudian theory. In classical Greek drama Oedipus was the ancient king who, without awareness, murdered his father and married his mother. Freud uses this myth to explain a universal tenet of personality development. During the phallic stage the male child develops sexual fantasies for his mother during periods of masturbation and wants to possess her completely. However, the reality factor of his father interferes with this desire. The child fears that the father will discover his secret rival and end the rivalry by castrating the boy (*castration complex*). The boy eventually resolves this conflict through the defense mechanism of identification, wherein he identifies with his father, thereby possessing his mother vicariously.

For girls the process is more complicated. At first the girl has a strong love for her mother as the primary care giver who satisfies her basic needs. Gradually the youngster discovers that males have a penis and she has "only a cavity" (Hall and Lindzey, 1970, p. 52). This leads her to believe that her mother has castrated her. This information weakens her attachment to her mother and generates stronger attachment to her father. She remains ambivalent in her attachment to her father and regrets that she lacks a penis, a condition Freud labeled *penis envy*. She can resolve this deficit in later years when she has a male baby. The super-ego emerges during the phallic stage, and the various defense mechanisms mediate these incestuous and aggressive instincts.

The *latency stage,* ages five or six to puberty, represents a period of relative quietude in preparation for puberty. Finally the *genital stage* at puberty represents the reawakening of sexual feeling and satisfaction which results in opposite sex union.

Implications for Psychopathology. According to Freudian theory disorders result from a person's inability to resolve conflicts within one or more of the psychosexual stages. Over- or under-gratification at any stage leads to *fixation* in that state. For example, weaning an infant too soon leads to aggression in the form of fighting, and as the person ages, anger shifts to sarcasm or even physical violence. Too strict toilet training may lead to an anal retentive personality—a compulsively neat individual who might line up the pencils on his desk in a north-south direction or else experience intense anxiety. A mental disorder according to this way of thinking represents the ego's inability to cope with some major conflict whether internally or externally generated. Abnormal behavior represents a continuum with normal behavior and is not qualitatively different.

Treatment Methods. Freud was the leading force in the development of the so-called "talking cure." He observed and treated patients through hypnosis where the therapist, but not the patient, became aware of the underlying conflict. To reveal the unconscious conflict to the patient he developed the techniques of free association in which the person speaks whatever comes to mind. The therapist interprets the meaning of these associations along with other clues to the unconscious revealed through dream analysis and behavioral events. In this system the patient actively collaborates with discovering the source of the conflict. In classical Freudian analysis treatment is long term and intense. The patient may meet with the therapist from one to five times a week and treatment might last several years.

Evaluation. The major limitation of Freudian theory from a scientific standpoint is that many of its concepts are untestable. That is, it is very difficult to design an experiment which could either verify or disconfirm the theory. Second, as other authors have noted (Sarason and Sarason, 1984, p. 54), Freudian theory is much better at explaining than predicting. Progress in science only happens when a theory predicts, since almost any theory can explain current or past behavior (Bandura, 1986). Finally, the theory often takes a "damned if you do, damned if you don't" approach. The old joke about the person going to see his analyst illustrates this aspect. When the patient arrives late it means he is hostile; if he arrives early he is anxious; and if he is on time he is compulsive. A theory that explains everything explains nothing.

Psychoanalytic thinking has made a variety of contributions to psychological theory and treatment in psychopathology. Freud developed a treatment method for at least some individuals with a range of mental disorders. Furthermore, it has shaped modern culture through the arts, cultural criticism, biography, child rearing practices and even how we define personhood. Freudian theory goes beyond the practice of psychology and psychiatry and is an integral part of the western intellectual tradition. Although only a small percentage of therapists today practice classical psychoanalysis, the clinical theory remains influential. Clinicians have modified its treatment methods in the interest of practicality and cost-effectiveness. They have developed short-term models for crisis intervention and brief therapy.

Implications for Pastoral Counseling. Pastoral counselors often feel at home with psychoanalytic thought since it acknowledges the "dark" side of human nature. The domain of the unconscious with its "messiness" is comfortable to the pastoral counselor through the analogous concepts of sin and redemption. In addition, Freud's literary style is elegant, and his frequent references to the arts and humanities also resonate to the cultural humanism of those in pastoral care and ministry.

Yet it is also wise to note that Freudian thinking does not easily fit into the Judaeo-Christian tradition. In the final analysis his system is deterministic, a philosophical dimension which is opposed to a tradition of human freedom and individual responsibility. Although some religious thinkers believe that Freud's system is not inherently opposed to acceptance of a transcendent and personal God, the most obvious interpretation of his position is one that opposes such beliefs. In Freud's framework theistic beliefs are projections of the person's own dependency needs. In this sense Freud's theory is more akin to German materialism of the nineteenth century (e.g. Feuerbach) than to a biblical view. Many theistic intellectuals have grappled with Freud's view of religion to explore his reductionism and to see if his psychological constructs can allow an integration of belief and psychological health (e.g. Küng, 1990).

Learning Theories

Overview. Learning theories in general make the assumption that human behavior is lawful in consistent, predictable ways. In this model people learn abnormal behavior through the same laws that govern normal behavior. While not denying the impact of biology, these theorists are more interested in environmental influences on our behavior. Learning theory today includes many ideas beyond the earlier behaviorists and encompasses at least three major schools.

The first school involves that of classical conditioning which emphasizes that humans learn through associations with automatic, unlearned responses. First systematized by the Russian Ivan Pavlov, any introductory psychology text outlines the basic concepts in his theory known as *classical conditioning*. Briefly stated, Pavlov noted that some responses are automatic (unconditioned) or unlearned. Loud noises will create a startle reaction in an infant regardless of gender, race, or culture. When other events (stimuli) are associated (paired) with these unconditioned events, they also become capable of eliciting fear. In classic behaviorist fashion an early American psychologist —John Watson—conditioned fear in a toddler to a rabbit by presenting a loud noise each time the child saw the rabbit. Gradually the child became frightened of the rabbit even when the noise was no longer associated with it.

Operant conditioning describes learning that results from the consequences of behavior. Behavior followed by pleasant outcomes or those which eliminate an unpleasant experience will be strengthened (reinforced). Behavior followed by unpleasant consequences or which turns off a pleasant event will be weakened (punishment). If parents scold, criticize, or even physically punish a child's natural exploratory behavior, the child learns to avoid such experiences and the resulting skill deficits will leave him or her timid, shy and fearful. B.F. Skinner is the psychologist who is most associated with this learning approach.

A third form of learning theory was developed by Albert Bandura (1969, 1986) and is termed *observational learning.* Bandura noted that many forms of learning do not require either reinforcement or punishment and occur through simple observation. This form of learning he termed modeling and is clearly evident when a child observes a parent become terrified of a thunderstorm and now he or she becomes afraid. Another example of observational learning is racial prejudice wherein a child learns to become afraid of certain racial groups even though there has never been a direct unpleasant interaction with that group. Bandura's major contribution is that he extended learning theory to include not just environmental events but cognitive processes as well. His theory is a strong plea to focus on thinking as equally important to the learning process as external events.

Implications for Psychopathology. Learning theory emphasizes social-environmental influences in the development of abnormal behavior. Although it does not deny biological or genetic influences, it maintains along with the song lyrics that "you've got to be carefully taught." Abnormal behavior is on a continuum with normal behavior. In this model much of what passes for psychopathology is the product of learning. For example, people learn to be afraid or fail to learn skills to satisfy their social needs and hence become depressed. Learning theory sees no need to postulate "disease" processes in emotional disorders. Treatment methods, therefore, have an educative thrust. Maladaptive behavior which is the result of either unpleasant experiences (e.g. phobias) or deficient skills (e.g. shyness) can change as the result of structured retraining experiences.

This optimism regarding human change potential along with the development of technical methods has led to a host of practical therapeutic strategies with multiple populations. Learning theory influences most teacher strategies through the concept of reinforcement. The theory has derived strategies for teaching the retarded self-help skills to enhance their quality of life. Many institutionalized patients have achieved greater independence as the result of learning theory applications. In treatment of adults it has tackled problems as varied as anxiety, depression, sexual dysfunctions, eating disorders, addiction, and chronic pain, often providing significant relief from these conditions.

Implications for Pastoral Counseling. Many pastoral ministers find learning theory an alien model. The terminology of learning theory is probably a barrier to most and its strong empiricism also puts off those trained in a humanistic tradition. Philosophical determinists such as Skinner probably also alienate many in ministry. However, this theory has much to offer pastoral ministry. Learning theory principles can be applied to the spiritual realm as well as to the material realm. A counselor or spiritual director can use behavioral strategies to increase the frequency of "God thoughts" (prayer, meditation) in the same way a coach uses them to establish an exercise program. It is also useful to distinguish between philosophical versus methodological behaviorism. In methodological behaviorism one maintains one's own philosophical system but applies the principles of learning theory to a given problem. This avoids throwing out the baby with the bath water.

Humanistic Theories

Overview. Humanistic theories grew in reaction to psychoanalysis and behaviorism by clinicians who believed that the former was too pessimistic and the latter too cold (Hall and Lindzey, 1970). While a variety of theorists refer to themselves as humanistic, we will concentrate on that strain of humanism which is represented by Abraham Maslow and Carl Rogers.

The American psychologist Abraham Maslow broke with traditional observational methods in psychology by focusing on the especially healthy personality rather than the so-called common man or the mentally ill. Maslow believed that the best contribution psychology could make is to examine the very healthy and use them as role models for self-improvement. He called such individuals self-actualizers. In contradistinction to psychoanalytic thinking, which probes the dark human side, the humanistic approach unveils the full human potential—the heights we can achieve.

> If you want to answer the question of how tall can the human species grow, then obviously it is well to pick out the ones who are already tallest and study them. If we want to know how fast a human being can run, then it is no use to average out the speed of a "good sample" of the population: It is far better to collect Olympic medal winners and see how well they can do. If we want to know the possibilities for spiritual

growth, value growth or moral development in human be-
ings, then I maintain that we can learn most by studying our
most moral, ethical, or saintly people (Maslow, 1971, p. 7).

How, then, do self-actualizers behave? Why are they different?
"Self-actualizing people are, without one single exception, involved
in a cause outside their own skin, in something outside of themselves"
(Maslow, 1971, p. 43). To explain this behavior, Maslow's theory of
motivation discusses needs at two levels. First, we have basic needs—
food, thirst, safety, sex, etc., those which are central for survival itself.
The more important human needs are *metaneeds,* which are truth,
goodness, beauty, justice, order, etc., the seeking of which leads to
self-actualization.

Implications for Psychopathology. In Maslow's model, mental
health represents "full humanness" and neurosis is "human diminu-
tion" or a failure of personal growth. Such a model directly contradicts the biological and medical model described earlier.

But by now we have learned very well that it is better to
consider neurosis as rather related to spiritual disorders, to
loss of meaning, to doubts about the goals of life, to grief and
anger over a lost love, to seeing life in a different way, to loss
of courage or hope, to despair over the future, to dislike for
oneself, to recognition that one's life is being wasted, or that
there is no possibility of joy or love, etc. (Maslow, 1971,
p. 31).

Intervention Methods. Humanistic theory opposes the process of
labeling and diagnosis. Adherents are critical of standard diagnostic
categories. In this model, putting a label or diagnosis on an individual's behavioral pattern (e.g. hysteria) loses the uniqueness of the
person and the inner world which gives life meaning.

Therapeutic methods emphasize respect for the growth potential
of each client. Carl Rogers emphasizes non-possessive warmth, positive regard, and accurate empathy to the client's world view as the
essential ingredient for growth in counseling. This therapeutic stance
sees growth as a process in which the client gradually uses his or her
freedom to overcome the natural fear we all have of self-
actualization. Maslow refers to this as our "Jonah complex" after the
biblical figure to describe how many of us fear our fate to become
fully human, just as Jonah was afraid of his call. The therapist's role is
to be non-directive or client-centered and to avoid advising, admon-

ishing, or interpreting lest the client's own inner-dynamic toward growth be derailed.

Evaluation. One limitation of humanistic theory focuses on its restricted range of application. While it is reasonable to conceptualize mild anxiety and depression as rooted in the meaning of existence, it is difficult to see how this would trigger severe disorders such as acute schizophrenia or manic psychosis. Maslow, others would argue, confuses facts with values. If some individuals self-actualize, why does this become the *norm* for what is fully human?

On the other hand, humanistic theory has made many contributions. Maslow and Rogers without apology advocate concepts which had received too little emphasis in psychology. These concepts include values, particularly the so-called "higher" values such as the search for meaning, altruism, faith and hope. They also spoke directly about human freedom when rigid determinism from psychoanalysis and behaviorism dominated the field. Rogers' work led to renewed interest in psychotherapeutic research. He stimulated research in which therapist variables facilitate growth in the client and, perhaps more importantly, how these qualities could be taught to counseling trainees. Thanks to the work of Rogers and his colleagues, systematic training in counseling techniques is now standard practice (e.g. Egan, 1975; Truax and Carkhuff, 1967).

Implications for Pastoral Counseling. Humanistic-existential theories attract many pastoral counselors with their affinity for the issues raised in these theories, e.g. spiritual needs and "higher needs." This model accommodates the concerns of those in ministry with human freedom and self-determination, and also discusses the issue of values openly. A religious framework can easily incorporate many of the concepts espoused in humanistic theory as the following quote suggests:

> [The deprivation of metaneeds] breeds certain currents of pathologies which have not yet been adequately described but which I call *metapathologies*—the sickness of soul which comes, for example, from living among liars all the time and not trusting anyone. Just as we need counselors to help people with the simpler problems of unmet needs, so we may need *metacounselors* to help with the soul-sicknesses that grow from the unfulfilled metaneeds. [These metaneeds] are the meanings of life for most people, but many people don't even recognize that they have these metaneeds . . . ultimately, some professionals will come to think of themselves

as philosophical or religious counselors (Maslow, 1971, p. 44).

Pastoral care workers can readily assimilate such a model as part of their self-identity.

Cognitive Theories

Overview. Cognitive theories represent the views of psychiatrist Aaron Beck and psychologists Albert Bandura and Albert Ellis. While there are commonalities in each one's theory, their theories developed independently and in specific settings. Beck's theory evolved as a specific treatment approach for depression. Ellis formulated his theory as part of an overall therapeutic strategy which he calls Rational-Emotive Therapy (RET). Bandura's developed from experimental psychology which isolated the importance of cognitive factors in learning. From laboratory studies he then applied these principles to behavior change.

The historical roots of cognitive theory can be traced back to the Stoic philosopher Epictetus and the aphorism "people are not distressed by things but the views they take of them." In this theory internal beliefs, attitudes, expectations, plans, and strategies are the major influences on behavior and emotion. To use Ellis' ABC Schema, A is the activating event, C is the emotional or behavioral consequences, and B is the intervening belief which results in how a person behaves and/or feels in reaction to A (Ellis and Grieger, 1977, p. 6). For example, if someone hands me two hundred and fifty dollars as a lottery winner I would expect to have a joyful reaction, but not if I am asleep or unconscious. I must comprehend the money's meaning and translate it into positive expectations. From the perspective of Bandura's notion of self-efficacy, a world class athlete in his prime faces each new challenge or event knowing "I can handle this." One would expect such an internal belief system to leave the person confident and alert as the event approaches.

Cognitive assessment methods analyze the irrational beliefs or distorted cognitions which are behind the emotional upset. For example, if a counselor is working with an individual who is over-possessive in relationships, one likely irrational self-statement the client is making is "I can't survive without him/her." Therapeutic intervention would revolve around changing these irrational statements which typically lead to emotional upset.

In one form or another treatment strategies based on cognitive theory entail modifying what clients say to themselves. Once the client identifies the irrational or negative beliefs, change involves catching oneself reacting to situations with these beliefs. Once the client identifies the self-defeating cognitions, the next step involves restructuring or relabeling the events or experience in a more realistic/positive manner. Cognitive theory maintains that altering these beliefs will lead to a positive emotional state. To use the example of over-possessiveness noted above, one could challenge the irrational belief by making statements such as: "Do I *really* need my partner to survive? What skills, talents, resources are truly available to me?" The therapist might direct the client to make the following self-statement when upset: "She is not essential to my survival. I was self-sufficient before the relationship and will be so afterward."

Evaluation. A limitation of cognitive therapy is that some treatment populations and conditions are non-responsive. Individuals with obsessive-compulsive disorders increase their ruminations when they attempt to apply these methods. Also, as Beck and his colleagues themselves admit, severe forms of depression respond more rapidly with a combination of cognitive therapy and antidepressant medication (cf. Chapter 5). Some depressed individuals seem unable to mobilize enough energy intellectually to work at the cognitive assignments.

In a positive vein, cognitive therapy has developed treatment methods for certain disorders such as depression, anxiety conditions, sexual dysfunctions and personality disorders. Further, therapists have extended its application to impulsive children for training in self-control and creativity.

Implications for Pastoral Counseling. Although a relatively new theory, creative efforts to integrate pastoral counseling and cognitive therapy have already begun. Cognitive theory represents a potentially fruitful area for exploration since the individual could use religious beliefs to dispute irrational beliefs. For example, a highly stressed, workaholic executive, despite an abundance of worldly goods, might see this behavior as necessary due to his financial insecurity. Using Ellis' ABC method, one could substitute the biblical notion of "what does it profit a man if he gains the whole world but loses himself?" as a corrective belief to the "irrational" one emphasizing unlikely financial ruin. Pastoral counselors attempting such an integration do not seem bothered by Ellis' notion that belief in God and immortality is "irrational." Indeed, psychologist Rebecca Propst found that depressed patients who focused on positive religious statements recovered more rapidly than patients who focused on the traditional "rational" self-statements used in cognitive treatment of depression. In addition to Propst (1988), psychologists William Miller (Miller and Jackson, 1985) and William Backus (1985) represent attempts to integrate cognitive approaches within Protestant liberal and conservative traditions respectively.

Interactive Models

One approach to avoid accepting any of the foregoing models is to say yes to all of them. Although that statement may sound glib, there are at least two ways to accomplish this. One approach to accepting multiple models is the *interactive* model. An interactive model acknowledges the influence of several forces in the manifestation of abnormal behavior, such as dynamic, biological, and learning. An interactive model also recognizes the reciprocal interaction of various factors. For example, in biological models the assumption often is that biological abnormalities influence maladaptive behavior. An illustration of this would be biochemical factors which result in the clinical syndrome of major depression.

An interactive model maintains that the reverse is also possible. For example, animal research with monkeys proves that maternal separation in infancy results in metabolic irregularities and behavior change in the infant monkey. It would be absurd to say that the physical changes in the infant monkey caused the mothers to abandon their charges. Rather, this is an instance of an environmental event (maternal deprivation) leading to physiological changes. This illustration shows that either-or explanations are inadequate.

A second approach involves a *diathesis-stress* model. Diathesis refers to a "congenital, often hereditary predisposition to a disease, group of diseases, or structural or metabolic abnormality" (*Webster's New Collegiate Dictionary*, 1973). In this model the person has a diathesis factor which combined with a stress factor results in a disorder. For example, if one identical twin develops schizophrenia there is an extremely high probability that the other twin will also develop the disorder, and this rate is significantly higher than the rate for fraternal twins alone. Despite this high probability it is not an absolute certainty that one twin will also develop the disorder. These facts point to the importance of both heredity and individual influences. Many researchers and clinicians in the field believe that science will gradually uncover the various predispositions to mental illness which will result in their early identification and prevention.

Models of Psychopathology and the Pastoral Counselor

A model of abnormal behavior provides for the pastoral counselor a systematic method to unify different facts of psychopathology. Armed with a reasonable model the counselor approaches individual encounters with greater self-confidence instead of seeing a "blooming, buzzing, confusion." If a counselor meets a grieving widow, age 46, three years past her husband's death, the counselor may find the psychoanalytic concepts of attachment and loss particularly fruitful. Models provide a framework for ministerial brainstorming. This process is one way that the pastoral care worker remains interested and excited about the helping enterprise.

Are there guidelines to adopting a theory in pastoral care? At the risk of sounding anti-intellectual, the selection of a model in psychopathology often is a matter of taste. The counselor may use a theory as long as it works, that is, makes the minister feel comfortable, generates ideas which pay off, and keeps the minister fresh. If pastoral care becomes stagnant, this may be a signal to explore other models.

Some theories have appeal because of their depth of reflection on ultimate values. But often these same theories lack practical implications. On the other hand, theories which frequently lend themselves to practical counseling approaches and intervention strategies often appear superficial in concept. Pastoral care workers by background, interest and training often prefer the grander theories while the technology appropriate to practical theories alienates some (e.g. the behavioral therapies).

There is probably no ultimate harm in theory selection since the jury is still out on a consensus model in psychopathology. Nevertheless, great harm may occur from applying any theory inflexibly as the following case illustrates. Throughout the centuries various theories have explained alcoholism. A moral model viewed this disorder as stemming from a lack of will power, and the intervention techniques were prayer, resolution and self-discipline. A psychodynamic model emphasized the arrested development of the alcoholic stemming from conflict in the oral stage. In this model, drinking is a symptom of exaggerated dependency needs. Through psychoanalysis the alcoholic resolves the underlying conflict. Once the alcoholic develops insight into the nature of the conflict, the expectation is that the drinking will cease.

Learning theory maintains that the alcoholic behavior is learned from poor role models or from the reinforcing tension-reducing effects of the alcohol. Just as this behavior is learned, the alcoholic can unlearn it. In such a model controlled drinking is possible for the alcoholic. In a medical model alcoholism is a disease, treatable but not curable. The treatment of choice is abstinence and the causes of alcoholism are seen as multiple, i.e., an interaction of biology in heredity, abnormal metabolism and/or physiology.

The model one selects for alcoholism appears crucial. Certain models, for example, psychodynamic and moral, were tried for years in the laboratory of human experience and proved ineffective. Alcoholics cooperated with such regimens and many died. Pastoral care workers and counselors cannot be totally indifferent to theory. Various models sometimes suggest radically different treatment strategies, so that the usefulness of a particular model is a relevant decision. However, no theory explains all disorders, but some theories provide better models for treating specific disorders. Ironically, effective treatment may explain nothing about the cause of a disorder just as headaches are not the result of aspirin deficiency.

In summary, the challenge to the pastoral minister is selecting a theory which a) provides guidelines for understanding abnormal behavior, b) suggests effective intervention strategies, and c) allows the minister to remain interested and involved in the helping effort. By implication this selection process is an ongoing task for the minister requiring periodic revision and updating as new facts emerge in the discipline of abnormal psychology.

Chapter 3

Pastoral Assessment

I. Introduction
II. Relationship Skills
III. Organizing the Pastoral Assessment
IV. Assessment Outline
V. Conclusion

Introduction

Assessment is a technical term for getting to know your client. The process of assessment may occur either formally or informally, in an efficient or haphazard manner depending upon the skills of the interviewer. A proper assessment properly conducted provides the counselor with a working diagnosis completed in a time-saving manner. Too often a pastoral interview resembles the following: Mrs. Smith asks to speak with the pastoral counselor and spends the bulk of the session complaining about her husband. She notes he is never around, doesn't help with the children, is unaffectionate, criticizes her all the time, doesn't give her time to herself, etc. The counselor begins the second session with "And how are you and Mr. Smith doing?" which launches a continuation of her litany. By session's end the counselor determines that the major issue is a marital problem. The intervention may involve several options: marital therapy, adjusting to a bad situation, finding supportive outside relationships, or even divorce counseling. This assessment could be wrong on at least half a dozen counts, and, if wrong, any therapeutic intervention is futile. Or, as my speech teacher was fond of saying, "If you aim at nothing, you're bound to hit it." In addition to a working knowledge of abnormal psychology, an efficient assessment interview requires relationship skills and the ability to organize interview data.

29

Relationship Skills

Personal relationship skills are as important for assessment as for the counseling process itself. Two types of relationship skills can be distinguished. The first involves basic helping skills taught in all introductory counseling courses. They involve traditional listening skills described by Carl Rogers and his associates (Rogers, 1951; Truax & Carkhuff, 1967) which involve communication of warmth, positive regard, and accurate empathy. These skills create a climate which allows the client to develop trust and rapport with the pastoral minister and share personal information.

Reflective listening plus questioning helps the interviewer transition from topic to topic. "Losing your father at such a young age sounds as if it were horrible for you. I wonder what was going on between you and your mother at that time." Non-directive counselors need to desensitize themselves to asking questions. Even direct questions such as "Do you have any medical problems?" are seldom seen as intrusive. Indeed clients feel comforted when the interview is thorough.

Skillful questioning is an equally important part of pastoral assessment. A common mistake in ministry particularly for those well-trained in client-centered techniques is to misapply non-directive strategies. Those of us who supervise trainees in this approach sometimes parody this with fanciful dialogues:

> Client: My house is on fire; please come and help me.
> Counselor: You're extremely upset; your house is on fire.
> Client: Please, you fool, I need water.
> Counselor: You're very angry that I'm not helping you.

Assessment similarly requires some direction to the interview via questioning. Clients typically avoid discussion of certain content areas. In the case example above for the woman with marital problems consider the following responses to the question, "Have you ever sought help before, Mrs. Smith?" If the answer is, "Yes, I've been in psychiatric hospitals six times and I'm on three different medications," the counselor might radically alter the original conceptualization of her problem.

Open-ended questions gather information in a non-invasive manner. "Could you tell me a little about how it was growing up in your family?" is more effective than "Were your parents warm or harsh?"

Organizing the Pastoral Assessment

Preliminary Considerations

The diagnostic interview may take place in a variety of settings—office, home, or institution. In all settings the goal is to derive a comprehensive description of the person's problems, strengths, support systems, and personality traits. The purpose of the assessment determines the degree of comprehensiveness required. Some circumstances—for example, a brief non-repeated hospital visit—require a relatively brief assessment interview, while a request for individual counseling may require an interview of considerable length and complexity. The setting also determines the degree of formality and structure to the assessment. A pastoral care visit to a sick person may be quite informal in structure, whereas an intake interview in a mental health agency demands a strict interview format with coverage of required content areas.

Some clinicians also find it helpful to establish an assessment contract with the client.

> It will probably take a few meetings for us to get to know each other before I have a clear picture of how to best help you. Why don't we spend the first three to four sessions putting all the facts together as best we can? At that point I'll tell you what I think is going on and some ways to deal with it. Then you can tell me your opinion.

This represents a low-key approach to assessment and communicates the ultimate purpose of initial assessment as well as alerting the client to its probable structure. This also enlists the client's support in the initial assessment process.

Assessment Outline

Mental health professionals follow a traditional outline for summarizing their interview data. This outline is also recommended for formal pastoral counseling settings since it represents a time-honored model for reporting a large body of information concisely. It represents a system familiar to mental health professionals who can easily understand and interpret the pastoral counselors' written communication.

Each interviewer develops a personal style in conducting the assessment interview. Whatever style the counselor adopts, using the formal outline ensures that important content areas are covered. Some counselors keep the outline on hand during the interview, perhaps on an index card or a clipboard attached to the interviewer's own notes. Despite conducting fifty to seventy-five diagnostic interviews annually I am still quite capable of missing relevant information during the initial interview more often than I care to admit. An example of this is forgetting to inquire about the living arrangements of a single person. Obviously psychological issues differ if the client lives alone, with parents, or is cohabitating.

My own introduction to the assessment interview is to state simply: "Maybe we could begin by you telling me what it is that brought you here today," or "What is it that made you decide to seek help— or suggested that it might be helpful to talk to someone?" An open-ended question such as this allows clients to describe in their own words their presenting problems. They control the initial flow of the interview while at the same time the counselor facilitates appropriate responses. At some point most interviewers will need to decide when to intervene to cover essential content areas. No client spontaneously covers each content area of the formal diagnostic assessment, and this necessitates some questioning. Some clients are quite verbal and cover many details on their own initiative such as marital status or family background. In these cases the interviewer may need to ask only a few questions toward the end of the interview. In any event transitional statements may be useful: "You have told me a great deal about your current difficulties and I really appreciate how hard that can be. I wonder if we could take some time to answer some background questions. Could you tell me a little bit about your parents? Are they still alive . . . ?"

The length of the assessment interview will also depend upon the skill and style of the interviewer as well as the pastoral setting. An agency setting may require a relatively complete assessment after a single sixty to ninety minute session, but a private office setting may need two to four sessions to obtain the required information. The former will necessitate structured questioning and taking control of the interview after the initial problem clarification stage. The latter situation allows both client and counselor to proceed at a slower pace.

What follows is a formal assessment outline with content areas explained in each instance. Each section will include a clinical example for purposes of illustrating the content of a final report. Beginning counselors should not confuse the structure of the formal outline with the actual conducting of the interview. The interview itself should follow the flow of the client's issues. Once the major presenting problems have been identified, the interviewer gathers background information through relevant questioning. The outline assumes that the counselor will organize a rambling client narrative into a coherent framework.

Identifying Data

This includes identifying characteristics such as the name, age, gender, race, religion and marital status of the client as well as demographic data, including address, telephone number and referral source. Many counselors have clients fill out an intake form at the time of the first visit so that interview time is not wasted. A summary paragraph will follow each subsection to illustrate the clinical assessment of a fictitious client.

> John Doe is a 39 year old, white, Episcopalian, married male who was referred for counseling by a friend who is also in counseling with this therapist. He lives at 901 East Riverdale Road, Midtown, Pennsylvania. His phone number is 555-2121.

Presenting Problem(s)

This section describes what is the immediate precipitant to seeking help. The focus here is on surface conflicts and not on what some systems might conceptualize as the dynamic issues, for example unresolved oedipal conflict. Rather it refers to the proximate cause of help-seeking.

> Mr. Doe has been feeling rather despondent for the past six months. Over the weekend while feeling particularly worthless he reacted angrily toward his wife's comment that he should stop sitting around feeling sorry for himself. He pushed her away, resulting in her falling backward and twisting her ankle. Both he and his spouse report this is his first act of physical aggression in fourteen years of marriage. He feels ashamed and realizes he needs some type of help.

Often more than one problem is identified in the assessment interview; in such cases each problem is described, for example, depression and alcohol abuse.

History of Presenting Problem(s)

Each problem identified has its own history. Answers to the familiar journalistic questions of who, what, when, where, why, how, how often and how long can serve to flesh out this section succinctly.

> Mr. Doe observed that the onset of his despondency coincided with the death of his twin brother from a cardiac condition. John was close to his brother when each of their spouses stopped talking to each other as a consequence of an inheritance dispute over the estate of Mr. Doe's parents. Although his parents had died over five years ago, due to poor estate planning their sizeable financial holdings were now tied up in probate. When his brother died after only one week of hospitalization Mr. Doe felt intense guilt. He had not visited his brother, fearing his own wife's wrath (each had heard initial medical reports that the brother's condition was a minor one). Gradually his intense grief subsided but a host of dysphoric symptoms remained. These include intense feelings of sadness, guilt, loss of energy, work retardation, difficulty in falling asleep, increased irritability, loss of appetite with concomitant weight loss of fifteen pounds in the past two months, loss of satisfaction for normally pleasurable events, pre-occupation with his own health (despite medical assurance he is convinced he has inherited his brother's cardiac condition), and nearly total loss of interest in sex. These symptoms have interfered with his parenting in that he has withdrawn from all but the most essential parental duties. Furthermore there is evidence of occupational dysfunction through increased use of sick days and relatively frequent tardiness at work.

Previous Therapy/Counseling History

This information may provide crucial clues regarding the degree of chronicity of a problem. It may also suggest what previous treatments helped or failed, thereby saving precious time when people are hurting. The counselor inquires about all mental health contacts—psychiatry, psychology, social work, pastoral and general counselors. Both inpatient and outpatient mental health contacts are included.

Mr. Doe's only history of previous treatment occurred at age twenty-five after completion of his Master's degree when he suffered what he called "Post-thesis blues." He saw a psychiatrist for a period of three months and was treated with an anti-depressant whose name he does not recall. His symptoms subsided and therefore he ceased the medication and his visits.

Family History

This section may be as brief or extensive as the interviewer desires. Family systems-oriented clinicians expand the information contained here while others record sparse details. Essential information includes first degree relatives, their ages, occupation, and cause of death if deceased. An important task in family history-taking is "shaking the family tree" for histories of substance abuse, mental illness and suicide. This information is vital due to the familial basis of many of these conditions. Whether one assumes a genetic or learning influence for their transmission, the presence of such disorders may predict their occurrence with the identified client.

Both of the client's parents are deceased. His parents were married to each other for thirty-two years and died within six months of each other five years ago. His mother was fifty-five and died of breast cancer while his father was seventy-two and died of a heart attack. His mother was a homemaker since her marriage but had completed a nursing degree before marriage. His father was a land developer and had acquired a considerable fortune in real estate prior to his death. A severe depression following his wife's death led to his not adequately declaring his will and this resulted in probate problems. The patient has no other siblings beyond his fraternal twin brother who is also deceased. His brother had been employed as a pharmacist. Aside from his father's depression the only other identifiable, significant emotional problem relates to a paternal uncle who died of an alcohol related illness.

Personal/Social History

Early developmental history includes birth history, early childhood separations, significant caretakers and number of moves by the family. The interviewer investigates the level of conflict through parental separation and divorce as well as general dimensions of warmth/hostility in the home. A matter-of-fact inquiry regarding physical or sexual abuse is also desirable although early responses to this question are often inaccurate. Some clients open up to the therapist only after establishing trust.

Educational history encompasses grades, learning difficulties, school failures and behavioral problems such as suspensions. When the client admits to suspensions or school difficulty the interview attempts to delineate the cause whenever possible. Suspensions for minor infractions such as truancy or smoking in lavatories have one meaning while suspensions for physical violence may suggest antisocial tendencies.

Occupational history focuses on types of employment, stability, and level of employment. This latter refers to the fit between the person's background education or training and current employment. A person with an advanced graduate degree working in a semi-skilled occupation may signal therapeutic issues from the standpoint of underachievement. Similarly, work patterns may provide useful data such as frequent periods of unemployment or "workaholism" which may disguise a bad marriage.

Marital/relationship history starts with dating history, sexual orientation, number of marriages with length of time for each, number and ages of children, current significant relationships and living arrangements.

Legal history summarizes number of arrests, criminal charges, convictions, incarcerations and pending legal charges. Counselors frequently overlook parole or probation status but this may have a significant impact on the client's motivation for therapy.

Religious history includes faith of family of origin and level of religious commitment during developmental periods. It includes current religious practices at both a public and a personal level with a subjective estimate by the client of religion's importance in his or her life.

Mr. Doe's birth and delivery were normal. He was raised by his parents in the Boston suburbs. He describes his family environment as subjected to "normal" ups and downs but felt his parents generally cared for their children and each other although they were not particularly demonstrative with expressions of affection. He denies any sexual abuse but admits he was spanked "often enough" when he was little though not with brutality. He attended public schools, achieving above average grades, graduated high school and completed a bachelor of science degree in accounting from Tufts University. He earned an M.B.A. from Harvard immediately afterward.

Following college he worked for several major accounting firms while earning his C.P.A. and started his own firm with parental financial assistance. This work has been quite successful, with the patient gradually building up to a company employing fifty workers. He dated in high school and college and married his wife of fourteen years during graduate school where they met while she was completing her education degree. She worked as a high school teacher for several years, then resigned when she became pregnant with their first child, and has been a homemaker since. The couple has two boys ages nine and six. Mr. Doe has never been arrested or legally charged. His religion is Episcopalian but his parents were described as not regular churchgoers. Mr. Doe's spouse is quite devout and he has experienced a genuine interest in his faith as a function of their relationship. They attend church regularly as a family and are involved in educational and social activities of their congregation.

Past Medical History

The rationale for taking a medical history lies in the close connection between physical and emotional illnesses. Thyroid disease, vitamin deficiencies, coronary/cardiovascular illnesses, brain tumors, diabetes, and hypoglycemia—to name but a few—generate mood disturbances and anxiety conditions. Conversely, chronic psychological disorders can generate tissue damage, as is the case with colitis and stomach ulcers. One study found that of one hundred consecutive admissions to a psychiatric clinic, forty-six percent had an undiagnosed medical illness which either aggravated the psychiatric symptoms or completely explained them. All of these patients would have been hospitalized in a psychiatric facility otherwise. Surveys of outpatient mental health clinics have found that as many as ten percent of the clients served have medical symptoms causing the psychological symptoms (Gold and Morris, 1988). The astute clinician recommends a complete physical examination as a prelude to ongoing counseling if the client has not had a recent one.

Medical history should include any past major conditions, previous hospitalizations and surgeries, as well as treatment for current medical problems including medications. It is important to note whether medications are under a physician's care or are self-directed remedies. This pattern often represents a disguise for substance abuse problems. Counselors working in medical facilities also will note allergies to medication.

> Mr. Doe reports basically good physical health. He had his appendix removed around age eleven but has not been hospitalized for any other condition. Occasionally he is bothered by headaches for which he takes Tylenol once every two or three weeks. He reports only social use of alcohol with no history of illegal drug use. He reports no allergies to medication.

Mental Status Examination

The mental status examination is a semi-structured part of the interview which obtains a psychological instant snapshot of the client. In the same way that a camera freezes a visual moment, the mental status examination freezes psychological status at a moment in time. Besides presenting clinical data to generate hypotheses, the mental status examination provides a useful before-and-after picture to share with the client at time of discharge. A formal mental status examination typically encompasses five areas, and each one is described below. Technical terms may be looked up in the *DSM–IIIR* Appendix or in Kaplan and Sadock (1988).

General Appearance and Behavior

This section describes the client's physical characteristics: facial expression, dress, and unusual bodily characteristics. Is their motor activity normal, agitated, repetitive, or characterized by unusual posturing? Speech behavior refers to excessive or reduced amounts, slurred or stuttering patterns, and intensity. Interview behavior includes cooperative, hostile, silly, demanding, evasive, manipulative, dramatic or dependent characteristics.

> The patient is a medium height thin man who appears his stated age. He is dressed casually and correctly. Motor activity during the interview seemed somewhat slowed down and the walk to the interviewer's office was effortful. His speech

is slowed and so soft that several times he was asked to repeat his responses. Interview behavior is cooperative although there is a suggestion of dependency in seeing the interviewer as expert who would relieve client of his pain.

Mood and Affect

Mood describes the client's pervasive emotion while affect or feelings describes the current range of emotions. Mood has been described as backdrop to feeling as climate is the backdrop to weather. Mood in the mental status examination refers to such concepts as depressed, elevated, or labile (rapidly alternating feelings such as anger or sadness, joy and sorrow). Affect implies descriptions such as anxious, flat or blunted, and inappropriate.

His mood is mildly depressed during the interview and his affect is characterized by flatness and restricted range of expression, although once or twice during the interview he managed a half smile following some ironic statement.

Thought Processes

This section describes a number of client behaviors. *Productivity of speech* involves either an under- or over-production of speech. Do the words flow easily or is the interviewer prying them out? Is there too much speech so that the interviewer feels breathless in attempting to follow the client's train of thought? Flow of thought describes the client's ability to "stay on track." Does he or she never get to the point (circumstantial), fixate on a topic (perseveration), jump from one topic to another with no relationship (flight of ideas), jump from one topic to another with minimal relationship (loose association), or pause at length between sentences as if distracted or struggling to converse (blocking)? *Content of thought* includes the actual topics discussed by the client. Significant content areas include suicidal thoughts or plans, assaultive ideas or plans, suspiciousness, fears, obsessional ideas, compulsive urges and rituals, feelings of unreality, excessive religiosity and sexual preoccupation. Other serious content areas are hallucinations—false visual, auditory, gustatory (taste), olfactory (smell), or tactile perceptions—and false beliefs (delusions) relating to feeling persecuted, grandiose, controlling others (delusion of influence), having others talk about you (delusion of reference), knowing your thoughts (thought broadcasting) or about one's body (somatic delusions). Such experiences often suggest a psychotic process or a serious medical condition requiring immediate attention.

> While Mr. Doe answered all questions his pauses indicate mild to moderate blocking. He generally stays on topic but he returns frequently in a perseverative manner to the shoving incident with his wife. Content of thought indicates ideas of guilt, hopelessness and worthlessness—all to a mild degree. His frequent references to "failing the Lord" appear appropriate in the context of his religious beliefs. He admits thinking more frequently about dying but denies either suicidal ideation or impulses. He denies experiencing false perceptions (hallucinations) or false beliefs (delusions).

Sensorium

This Latinism refers to the individual's orientation. Specifically the questions of the person's awareness of the time (day, month, season), place (where the interview is held), and who the interviewer is comprise this content area. Mental health professionals often abbreviate this part of the mental status examination by writing "Mr. Smith is oriented in all three spheres." This section also comments on any memory disturbance or difficulty in concentration. For convenience, memory is split into recent or remote, and weaknesses in one or the other is sometimes diagnostic of neurological problems. A serious cognitive problem here is *confabulation* in which clients fabricate information which they are not able to remember. This may signal either a severe psychotic process or memory loss due to brain disease.

> He is oriented as to time, place and person. Memory appears sound although he acknowledges being distracted lately and feels his concentration has decreased.

Intellectual Functioning

This involves an estimate of the client's cognitive skills such as intelligence. Source books exist for structured questions tapping the meaning of proverbs, fund of information (Who wrote *Macbeth?*) or abstract reasoning (In what way is a cow and sheep alike?). Interviewers also ask the client to repeat numbers forward and backward and to subtract seven from a hundred repeatedly (serial sevens) to assess basic attention and concentration skills. Most pastoral counselors will not find formal intellectual assessment necessary and settle for global impressionistic judgments of intelligence such as average, above average, or below average. An example of one mental status examination standardly used is the Mini-Mental Status Examination which is printed at the end of this chapter. Those who need to conduct such assessments may consult source books and use them appropriately under supervision (e.g. Wicks and Parsons, 1990).

He is above average in intelligence based on his interview presentation, although formal cognitive assessment was not attempted at this time. Insight regarding the degree of his problems is adequate and he appears motivated to seek treatment.

Summary of Findings

This section formulates the counselor's preliminary assessment in narrative form. The interviewer describes all symptoms as they relate to diagnostic considerations. For example, if the client is depressed the whole cluster of symptoms are described along with their significance in terms of the client's daily life.

Mr. Doe presents with depressive symptoms including feelings of sadness, increased irritability, guilt, loss of energy, work retardation, sleep disturbance, loss of appetite, loss of satisfaction, physical worries and loss of libido. These symptoms have resulted in job dysfunction, marital problems, family problems as well as personal distress. They have been present with increasing intensity for the past six months.

Diagnosis

This states simply the formal diagnostic classification using the most recent diagnostic and statistical manual. Example: Major Depression, Single Episode.

Problem List

Many counselors customarily append a list of the client's problems, usually in a hierarchical form from most to least pressing. This helps structure the treatment intervention to focus on specific issues.
1. Clinical depression
2. Marital problems

3. Parent-child conflict
4. Occupational problems

Strengths

Some counselors also find it convenient to list the client's strengths to present a well-rounded portrait with emphasis on the positive resources which the client may marshal during the therapeutic process. This reminds the counselor of environmental resources which may facilitate therapeutic gains.

1. Supportive family
2. Excellent education background
3. Good work history
4. Reasonably good physical health
5. Motivated to seek help
6. Good self-expression

Conclusion

The chapter has presented a method for eliciting and organizing data for the initial diagnostic pastoral assessment. Assessment is an ongoing process so that the counselor will modify the original formulations as new information unfolds. The clinical use of this initial assessment is twofold: to assist the counselor in understanding the client's problems and to communicate the assessment results to the client, thereby enlisting his or her support for the therapeutic process.

The pastoral assessment requires patience, clear judgment, and weighing various options—none of which are particularly glamorous endeavors. However, assessment provides the foundation for all growth that follows.

Mini-Mental Status Examination
(Folsteen, Folsteen, and McHugh, 1975)

Let me ask you a few questions to check your concentration and your memory. Most of them will be easy.

1. What is the year? Year: _____

2. What season of the year is it? Season: _____

3. What is the date? Date: _____

4. What is the day of the week? Day: _____

5. What is the month? Month: _____

6. Can you tell me where we are right now? For instance, what state are we in? State: _____

7. What country are we in? Country: _____

8. What (city/town) are we in? City: _____

9. A. What floor of the building are we on? Floor: _____
   B. What is the address (If INSTITUTIONALIZED) or name of this place? Address/Name: _____

10. I am going to name some objects. After I have said them, I want you to repeat them. Remember what they are because I am going to ask you to name them again in a few minutes.

    "Apple"   "Table"   "Penny"

Could you repeat the 3 items for me? SCORE FIRST TRIAL.
a. Apple .... CORRECT ERROR
b. Table ....
c. Penny ....

INTERVIEWER: REPEAT OBJECTS UNTIL ALL 3 ARE
LEARNED.

11. Can you subtract 7 FROM 100, and then subtract 7 from
the answer you get and keep subtracting 7 until I tell you
to stop?

   COUNT ONLY 1 ERROR IF SUBJECT MAKES
   SUBTRACTION ERROR, BUT SUBSEQUENT ANSWERS
   ARE 7 LESS THAN THE ERROR.

		SAYS	
		CAN'T	OTHER
CORRECT	ERROR	DO	REFUSAL
	a. (93) _____		
	b. (86) _____		
	c. (79) _____		
	d. (72) _____		
	e. (65) _____		
	STOP!		

12. Now I am going to spell a word forward and I want you to
spell it backwards. The word is WORLD, W-O-R-L-D.
Spell "WORLD" backwards. *REPEAT SPELLING IF
NECESSARY.*

   NUMBER OF ERRORS   REFUSED
         1 2 3 4 5 6   _____
   ‾D ‾L ‾R ‾O ‾W

13. Now what were the 3 objects I asked you to remember?

   a. Apple: _____   _____
   b. Table: _____   _____
   c. Penny: _____   _____

14. INTERVIEWER: SHOW WRIST WATCH.

   A. What is this called?
      Watch: _____   _____

15. **INTERVIEWER: SHOW PENCIL.**

    B. What is this called?
      Pencil: _____   _____

16. I'd like you to repeat a phrase after me:
    "No if's, and's, or but's."   _____   _____

ALLOW ONLY 1 TRIAL. CODE 1 REQUIRES AN ACCURATELY ARTICULATED REPETITION.

17. Read the words on this page and then do what it says.
    Hand the person paper with printed sentence,
    "CLOSE YOUR EYES."   _____   _____

**INTERVIEWER:
HAND CARD A**
Code Correct **IF RESPONDENT
CLOSES EYES**

18. **INTERVIEWER: READ FULL STATEMENT BELOW AND THEN HAND RESPONDENT A BLANK PIECE OF PAPER.
DO NOT REPEAT INSTRUCTIONS OR COACH.**
I am going to give you a piece of paper. When I do, take the paper in your right hand, fold the paper in half with both hands, and put the paper on your lap.

	CORRECT	ERROR
a. Takes paper in right:	_____	_____
b. Folds paper in half:	_____	_____
c. Puts paper down on lap:	_____	_____

19. Write any complete sentence on that piece of paper for me. SENTENCE SHOULD HAVE A SUBJECT AND A VERB AND MAKE SENSE. SPELLING AND GRAMMAR ERRORS ARE O.K.

CARD A

CLOSE YOUR EYES

Chapter 4

Anxiety and Related Disorders

I. Signs and Symptoms
II. Panic Disorder
III. Phobias
IV. Stress Conditions
V. Obsessive Compulsive Disorder
VI. Etiology and Treatment of Anxiety
VII. Pastoral Care and Anxiety Disorders

Signs and Symptoms

Anxiety, like depression, is part of normal human experience but pathological in its extreme. Since it encompasses ordinary human experience, every reader can readily identify with anxiety as a state. Experimental psychology conveniently organizes the experience of anxiety into three distinct categories:

Overt-behavioral. Observers could measure these symptoms by focusing on external behaviors. They include trembling, shaking, pacing, being easily startled, twitching eyelids, avoidance, difficulty sleeping, stuttering and hand wringing to name a few.

Covert-subjective. These symptoms are unobservable as such and represent the person's internal, subjective experience of anxiety. They include a sense of dread, feeling tense, feeling that things seem unreal (depersonalization), fear of dying or having a seizure or acting crazy, dizziness or lightheadedness, tightness or pain in chest, feeling tense or irritable, or continual worrying.

Autonomic-physiological. These symptoms result from autonomic nervous system arousal. Some are measurable through psychophysiological instruments such as a galvonometer for skin resistance, electrocardiogram, or blood pressure equipment. The symptoms include rapid heartbeat, sweating, butterflies in stomach, nausea, shortness of breath (dyspnea), clammy hands, dry mouth, "lump in throat," difficulty swallowing, tingling in fingers or feet, hot or cold flashes and sensations of numbness.

These three categories constitute the so-called *triple response system* of anxiety and provide a convenient basis for symptom description. People are unique in their experience of anxiety: some experience symptoms in all three categories while others are restricted to one or two. Further, some may experience limited symptoms while others many.

Consider John, Bill and Mary who all fear speaking in public. When John talks in public he fidgets with his manuscript, coughs repeatedly, stammers, and his mouth twitches. Otherwise he reports feeling intellectually in command of his material. Bill gives a competent presentation and is rated excellent in his delivery by the audience. In private, however, he removes his soaking-wet underclothes and shirt, measures his pulse at 30 beats per minute higher than normal, and is so nauseous that he almost lost his lunch before giving his speech. Mary also gives an excellent presentation and even "looks cool as a cucumber." When you ask her how it went she replies, "It was awful. I thought I was going to die out there, my hands were like ice, and I was sure any minute I would pass out." John, Bill and Mary were responding anxiously in the behavioral, physiological, and subjective areas respectively.

This discussion demonstrates a curious feature about anxiety. Technically anxiety is *no thing*. Anxiety is really a summary label for a variety of experiences which we associate with fear. You will not, however, provide much comfort to anxious individuals by telling them they are experiencing "nothing." While not *one* thing, anxiety is quite real and powerfully influences behavior.

An outsider can measure the degree of anxiety in someone through one of three ways: behavioral observation, technical psychophysiological apparatus, or client self-report. Electro-recording of the autonomic nervous system measures variables such as skin conductance (moisture), heart rate and respiration rate. This arousal marks the theoretical underpinnings of the so-called lie detector test which supposedly distinguishes true statements from false ones on the basis of different levels of nervous system arousal. The American Psychological Association rejects the use of the lie detector in employment screening as well as for legal purposes due to its unreliability.

Since pastoral counselors or therapists working outside of laboratory settings are unlikely to have such devices available, they will need to rely on behavioral observation and client self-report to assess client anxiety and to evaluate changes. Behavioral observations are often straightforward. Sam is afraid of flying. Does he or does he not eventually take an airplane ride? Jane attends college but is shy. How often will she strike up a conversation with another student? Alice will not set foot in any wooded area for fear of even harmless snakes.

But because anxiety entails symptoms in more than one system the counselor must assess other experiences. Sam indeed gets on the plane but to survive the flight he considers it necessary to drink six whiskey miniatures during his cross-country journey. Obviously his subjective distress is intense. An outsider gains access to this only by questioning. "On a scale of 1 to 10, with 1 being no anxiety and 10 being sheer terror, how did you feel during your plane ride?" For those who eschew numbers, a simple "How tense were you?" may suffice.

Anxiety disorders often lend themselves to what learning theorists call a situational analysis. With the counselor's assistance the client pinpoints the number and kinds of symptoms, their frequency of occurrence, antecedent events, behavioral defenses and their positive pay-off. Jane is shy, but only around students she presumes are her intellectual superiors, and more so with men. Alice's fear of snakes extends to wooded areas but not gardens around dwellings since she senses an escape route in the second instance. Performing an accurate situational analysis lends itself to developing specific treatment goals and allows for an objective measure of progress. Both client and counselor can point to specific achievements instead of settling for vague descriptions such as "client is improved."

Keeping track of anxiety-provoking situations helps counselor and client pinpoint problem areas. Figure 4-1 provides one example of a client record. The A column describes what was happening prior to the onset of anxiety, the B column describes the experience of the anxiety itself, while the C column notes the aftermath. Keeping track of significant events between sessions increases the accuracy of the evaluation process and provides a range of situations to examine.

Panic Disorder

Diagnostic Features. Panic disorder is characterized by a sudden spell or attack when the person feels frightened, anxious or afraid yet nothing objectively harmful is present. Prominent features include a fear of losing control whether by fainting, acting crazy, having a seizure, or even dying. The person may experience one or more of the

---

Figure 4-1

Anxiety Log

A Antecedent Events (When anxiety occurs)	B Behavior Descriptor (What anxiety is like)	C Consequences (What happened afterward)
Preparing class presentation.	Tense, couldn't concentrate, worry about my performance.	Spent long time day-dreaming at my desk.
Thinking about asking Mary to join me for dinner.	Thinking—"She doesn't really like me, I'm poor company, what will we talk about?" Feeling nervous.	Put off asking her till another time.
Boss tells me my report is a day late.	Nausea, dizzy, convinced I'm losing my job.	Apologize eleven times in three minute conversation.

---

following: shortness of breath, heart pounding, feeling dizzy or light-headed, tingling in fingers or feet, tightness or pain in the chest, sensations of choking or smothering, sweating, trembling, hot or cold flashes, and a sense that events are unreal. Victims experience the symptoms initially as "coming out of the blue." The fear peaks rapidly in as little as three to ten minutes and may last up to several hours.

Psychiatrist David Sheehan calls panic disorder "one of the great impostors in medical practice" (Sheehan, 1982). Those who suffer from this disorder puzzle greatly about the causes of their symptoms. One study found that 70 percent of persons with panic disorder had sought out 10 or more physicians. This posture is logical given the symptom pattern of the syndrome.

Life Complications. Severe forms of this disorder are among the most debilitating of all mental health problems. What may start out as a rare episodic spell may eventually increase in duration, intensity and frequency. The degree of fear may be as intense as the proverbial situation of having your foot caught in the railroad track and hearing the train whistle around the bend. In the train track situation at least the person understands the source of the panic, unfortunate though it be. What debilitates panic attack victims is the absence of a clear-cut cause.

Since environmental causes appear lacking, sufferers often focus on the physical symptoms. If they experience chest tightness and difficulty in breathing, they consult cardiovascular specialists. They also seek out gastrointestinal specialists and neurologists as well. Specialist after specialist uncovers nothing. In this age of malpractice suits the cycle of repeating medical referrals continues in the hope of discovering a cause. Even when nothing definite is found, physicians will often prescribe medication, particularly antianxiety agents (e.g. Valium or Librium). While these drugs provide some symptom relief they are generally ineffective in changing the course of the disorder. Some patients will resort to alcohol or other drugs to reduce their anxiety.

If the spells escalate, the sufferer notes that the location of the attacks are usually public situations. They seldom happen at home, or if they do they feel manageable. For many a "fear of fear" ensues with the tendency to anticipate and avoid it. Often the best strategy is to restrict one's activities. If supermarkets, shopping malls, standing in lines, and driving on highways are some occasions of attacks, the person avoids them and all situations triggering them. Some will so restrict their range of activities that they become house-bound. If they feel they must leave the house, they do so only with a spouse, relative, or trusted friend. The purpose of this restriction is safety and the need to map out an escape route if an attack occurs. In extreme cases some will not venture outside their homes even with a safe partner. They manage their lives by arranging social engagements and even employment in such a way that casual acquaintances may remain unaware of their condition.

When extensive avoidance accompanies panic disorder the condition is labeled *agoraphobia*, a Greek derivative implying fear of open spaces. More technically the condition represents a fear of public places from which escape is difficult. The places need not be wide open but may include narrow areas such as elevators, trains, subway cars and buses. The essence, therefore, of the disorder is an intense apprehension that an attack may occur *and* that the person will not be able to handle it (Barlow, 1988). The actual location which the person avoids is not the relevant nor the defining feature, unlike a simple phobia (e.g. fear of flying). Rather the person dreads an unpredictable attack which he or she cannot control.

The cost of the disorder to victims and their families is immense. The condition often makes everyday tasks a monumental struggle. Dependency on friends and relatives increases as their life-space constricts and both sides may resent each other. The victims fail to complete projects, drop out of school, decline promotions, or resist any activity associated with a previous attack. Depression normally follows a chronic course of this disorder.

The National Institute of Mental Health conducted extensive research on the frequency of mental disorders in the United States. Referred to as the Epidemiological Catchment Areas study (ECA) it estimated that 1.8 percent of the population or about 1.2 million Americans suffered from panic disorders in a given six month period (Myers *et al.*, 1984). They may also represent 10–14 percent of patients consulting cardiologists. While the sex ratio is equal regarding panic disorder without agoraphobia, when agoraphobia is present twice as many women suffer from the disorder (*DSM-IIIR*). The disorder typically begins in young adulthood, generally in the mid to late twenties. This fact along with the disproportionate number of women with the condition has caused some to label panic disorder a disease of childbearing age.

An interesting aspect of this condition is that many people *without* the diagnosis of panic disorder experience panic attacks. As many as 30 percent of the general population report experiencing panic attacks occasionally. They are also associated with other anxiety disorders as well. What prevents so many from developing the full-blown condition? Psychologist David Barlow (1988) speculates that persons without the disorder find some plausible connection between their symptom attack and an environmental stressor, e.g. an argument with their spouse or tension at work. Linking the attack to a cause seems to buffer the individual from seeing the symptoms as unpredictable. Since the source is predictable, the person also would have some degree of control over the event as well.

Phobias

A phobia is a fear of situations, objects, events or experiences which present either no objective harm to the person or a threat of such low probability that most people easily ignore the potential danger. Fears may range from mild nuisance to intense and debilitating. Phobias as a psychological problem interfere in some significant way in the person's life by causing emotional upset or behavior which interferes with important activities. Some phobic individuals rarely experience emotional upset because they restrict their range of activity. Many people with a fear of flying function well in society. This fear, however, would severely restrict the options of a world-class athlete in terms of professional opportunities. An urban dweller who fears snakes survives quite well in Manhattan, but if his or her car breaks down on a rural highway that person may stay trapped inside until help arrives.

The ECA study found that 7 percent of American adults have a phobic disorder which includes slightly more than 11 million people. Of all the categories in the *Diagnostic and Statistical Manual* it represents the highest percentage of people for lifetime occurrence of a mental disorder.

While phobias are quite common, most cope successfully with them without benefit of professional counseling. Only persons with severe forms seek assistance or receive help secondarily to other problems considered more serious. Whatever their actual numbers most suffer or tolerate their condition.

Social Phobias. Social phobias refer to fear of social situations where the person worries about criticism, negative evaluation, or embarrassment. They include fear of public speaking, speaking to strangers, meeting new people, eating in front of others, using public restrooms and the like. Social phobias, like simple phobias, are limited to highly circumscribed events. A poll of research psychiatrists presenting scientific papers at professional conferences found that a considerable number admitted use of tranquilizers prior to presenting their research. Social phobias cluster with other anxiety conditions such as panic disorder. Singer Carly Simon told a television interviewer ("West 57th Street," 6/5/88) about her severe stage fright. She performed a cable television concert in the open air near her beach home with friends and neighbors as the audience to avoid the discomfort of stage lights and large crowds.

Pastoral ministers are likely to encounter social phobias in persons labeled shy. This may include students or young adults who find the singles' social scene frightening. Despite pleasant interpersonal qualities they avoid even the simplest forms of social communication. This results in poor self-esteem and avoidance of normal recreational pursuits such as dances, parties or social gatherings. Often they will gravitate toward church- or synagogue-sponsored social events because they feel secure. This may lead to seeking out a pastoral counselor for assistance with problems of general unhappiness. As will be noted below, supportive and goal-oriented counseling often benefits them.

Stress Conditions

Popular hero images to the contrary, every human being has a breaking point. Create enough environmental pressure and the strongest among us will fall apart. Stress is an elusive concept to define but generally stands for the organism's need to adapt to an environmental change. In this sense we all experience stress regularly, with stressors creating minimal to maximal adaptation. Stress plays a significant role in anxiety conditions as well as creating general physical and emotional discomfort. This section will discuss the impact of stress on ordinary daily living, its aggravation of physical conditions, and finally its maximum impact under catastrophic circumstances.

Stress and Daily Living. Scientists are attempting to unravel the mysteries of stress at many levels: 1) the biochemical triggers and route of the stress response; 2) the impact of environmental events on stress; and 3) personality contributions to stress response differences.

The impact of stress upon our body creates a situation where the body's natural coping mechanisms essentially turn on their host, causing physical breakdown. The stress response syndrome was defined by Hungarian physician Hans Selye who spent a lifetime researching its impact on the body. As a young physician Selye was impressed by the similarity of symptoms among hospital patients with different illnesses during the first few days in the hospital (Sapolsky, 1988). Later their symptoms sorted out according to their various medical problems. Selye saw these initial symptoms as a general stress response.

When the body is under stress the brain sets in motion biochemical events that result in the secretion of hormones which prepare the body to defend itself. Adrenalin flow results in elevated blood pressure via artery constriction. Glucose production in the blood flows to the large muscles to assist in flight or fight. The corollary of this hormonal production is that digestion slows as does the hormonal production for growth and reproduction. After all if we are face-to-face with a grizzly bear in the woods neither a gourmet meal nor a sexually attractive partner will capture our attention. Similarly, the body temporarily puts on hold its disease-resisting capacity during a stress crisis.

What happens when stress is chronic and hormonal activation continual? Major health problems such as ulcers, impotence, infertility, nutritional deficiencies, lack of growth and loss of immunity to disease are linked to excessive stress. Furthermore, there is a general overtaxing of the cardiovascular system.

Coronary heart disease (CHD) is one of the most extensively studied conditions of stress-associated breakdowns. Even though such physical factors as smoking, elevated serum cholesterol and high blood pressure are clear risks for CHD, biologic risk factors account for fewer than 50 percent of new cases. Contributory social conditions to CHD include occupational stress. Surveys indicate that occupational risk factors for stress-related physical illness are the degree of personal control over one's working environment and the predictability of the stressors. Occupations with high psychological demands plus little decision-making power represent the highest risk. These include waiters/waitresses, fire fighters, mail workers, cashiers, and telephone operators. Conversely occupations with low psychological demand and high decision control fare best in terms of risk for CHD. This includes occupations such as architect, dentist, skilled machinist and forester. Research on women working outside the home is instructive in this regard. Are working women developing CHD now to the same degree as their male counterparts? No. Working women in general are at no greater risk to develop CHD than homemakers. However, female clerical workers, working women with children, and women with non-supportive bosses were more likely to develop CHD.

Finally, what are the contributions of personality characteristics to stress-related breakdown? Again, CHD has been extensively studied in this regard and a reputedly coronary prone personality type identified the so-called Type A personality. The Type A behavior pattern includes a competitive style, excessive hostility, and impatience. One researcher maintains that three specific features of Type A are predictors of future coronary breakdown. These include *time urgency*—concern over brief time periods (e.g. inability to tolerate checkout lines at the supermarket or being stuck in traffic); *chronic activation*—the tendency to be keyed up or "hyper" all day; and *multiphasis*—the tendency to pursue several goals simultaneously or "to have many irons in the fire" (Wright, 1988). Additionally the *potential hostility* factor appears predictive as well. This refers to people who experience anger but who have a great deal of difficulty expressing it openly. Researchers refer to this with the quaint phrase "anger in."

Stress and Catastrophic Events. The Vietnam war made mental health workers aware of post-traumatic stress disorder (PTSD) as a diagnostic category. Traumatic stress lies in the magnitude of the event itself, not in the mind of the victim. By definition it is beyond usual experience (APA, 1987). Events which trigger such trauma include serious threat to life or physical integrity, destruction of property or threats of the same. It may involve one's own person, one's children or family members, or even witnessing others experiencing these traumas. War, famine, earthquake, fire, flood, physical and/or sexual assault and accidents represent a selection of traumatic events.

A National Institute of Mental Health publication summarizes common reactions to disasters/trauma in the following way (Lystad, 1985, p. 50).

Early reactions:
1. Numbness and shock, even some slowness in physical and mental action.
2. Uncertainty. Decisions become difficult to make.

Later reactions:
1. Emotional symptoms of anger, suspicion, touchiness and irritability, or apathy and depression.
2. Loss of appetite, difficulty sleeping, loss of concern about everyday activities.
3. Crying, worrying, burying feelings, not wanting to talk to others. Dislike for company of friends, family, and neighbors.

Ongoing reactions:
1. Physical symptoms of stress (stomach distress, headaches, etc.) sometimes progressing into sickness and physical exhaustion.
2. Children may need more parental love and physical contact and may return to bed wetting, thumb sucking, or have nightmares, and cling to parents.
3. Family discord, separation. Increase in spouse and child abuse in the community.

4. Rejection of outside help. Difficulty in accepting that the
   disaster had any impact upon one's life.

Not all stress reactions to trauma are immediate. Some defend
well against the initial stress but suffer breakdown with the passage of
time. For example, an incest victim may develop insomnia and agitation many years later when the offending parent visits after a long
absence (cf. Chapter 8 for extended discussion of the impact of child
sexual abuse). A Vietnam veteran turns to drugs to cope with the
psychic numbness which has plagued him since his return. The DSM-
IIIR refers to such cases as post-traumatic stress disorder—delayed
onset. Though removed and physically safe from the original trauma,
the victim reacts emotionally as if the trauma happened recently.

One area of delayed post-traumatic stress which is receiving a
great deal of attention is the movement for healing issues related to
growing up in an alcoholic family (McDonnell and Callahan, 1987).
These persons, popularly referred to as ACOAs (Adult Children *of
Alcoholics*), are viewed from the diagnostic perspective as exhibiting
delayed stress syndrome. In particular they manifest the psychic
numbness characteristic of persons experiencing stressors as extreme
as combat (Cermak, 1986). More will be discussed concerning the
developmental issues related to growing up in alcoholic families in
the chapter on addictions (cf. Chapter 6).

Obsessive Compulsive Disorder

Obsessive compulsive disorder (OCD) ranks among the more
challenging pastoral care situations encountered. The symptoms frequently co-mingle with religious experience. Once believed to be a
rare disorder, the ECA survey estimates that three million Americans
suffer from the disorder, or about 2 percent of the population. The
disorder consists of either distressing obsessions (recurring, unwanted ideas, images or impulses) and/or distressing compulsions (repetitive, unwanted acts). Typical obsessions include persistent ideas
such as harming or killing someone, worries about contamination, or
concern that a job was performed poorly despite excessive care. Standard compulsions involve repeating acts over and over despite the
belief that such behavior is illogical or foolish. The content of these
compulsive acts include repeated checking, e.g. stove, door locks, car
lights, stamps and addresses on mail, washing hands, making beds, or
rearranging clothing.

Rachman and Hodgson (1980) delineate five symptom areas: obsessional checking, obsessional cleaning, obsessional slowness, obsessional doubting-conscientiousness, and obsessional ruminating. *Checking and cleaning* may progress to the point that the person consumes large amounts of time going over previously completed jobs or cleaning beyond the point of antiseptic sterility. *Obsessional slowness* may paralyze the person for routine tasks such as washing, brushing teeth, hair grooming, bed making or dressing. *Doubting-conscientiousness* refers to never feeling that the person completed the task properly despite extreme care. Associated with this characteristic is an extremely strict conscience—at least in some areas. *Obsessional rumination* refers to the constant generation of intrusive, horrific ideas or images. A person may have an image of having killed someone even though it was not logically or physically possible. Other typical intrusive thoughts include sexual images or blasphemous thoughts.

While some sufferers of OCD have mild symptoms in its extreme form, OCD may result in total paralysis. The sufferer may spend untold hours sitting in a chair deciding the best way to spend the day, many hours washing and cleaning, driving very slowly to avoid an accident, repeating religious exercises, or adding up columns of numbers. In this form hospitalization may be required to break this cycle.

The central feature of this disorder, and hence its inclusion in this section, is intense anxiety. The person feels an overwhelming sense of doom if he or she fails to carry out the compulsion. A mother may fear that she will smother her newborn, so she locks up all blankets in the hope of preventing such a tragedy. A driver hits a bump on a deserted highway, yet convinces himself he has killed a pedestrian. He is compelled to double back at the next exit to retrace his route and search for the expected corpse.

Rachman and Hodgson have formulated a functional analysis of these symptoms which differs slightly from the traditional definition but which offers greater precision and clinical utility. In this formulation obsessions are *ideas, images or acts which increase anxiety,* while compulsions are *ideas, images or acts which reduce anxiety.* From the laws of reinforcement we know that people repeat reinforced behavior. When the obsessive compulsive person reduces anxiety through the compulsion, this ensures its endless repetition. Naturally this process involves magical thinking. Two puppet characters on the children's television show "Sesame Street" perform a routine which illustrates this point. Bert sees Ernie with a banana in his ear and asks him why. Ernie replies that he put it there to keep the alligators out of the city park. Bert counters by noting there are no alligators in the city park, to which Ernie responds, "See, it works." In a similar fashion the obsessive compulsive believes emotionally that the ritual behavior (compulsion) works by preventing imminent catastrophe.

Etiology and Treatment of Anxiety

Biological Theories and Treatments. Researchers have suggested various biological causes for anxiety disorders. One theory sees anxiety disorders as the excessive production of the arousal neurotransmitters in the nervous system. The body has an internal signal system to external threats which sets in motion physiological changes. This first theory sees anxiety disorders as caused by an individual's tendency to signal alarms needlessly or to have a nervous system with a hair-trigger response mechanism. While there is an intellectually satisfying elegance to this theory, no single biochemical process explains the different routes to anxiety. Furthermore, even if one accepts this theory it does not explain the precise manner in which people develop overactive nervous systems.

A second theory explains a person's state of hyperarousal through heredity. Some researchers accept the fact that anxiety runs in families and is transmitted genetically (Barlow, 1988). They contend, however, that people require environmental and psychological factors to trigger the disorder in this overactive nervous system.

Another aspect of heredity's role in the development of anxiety disorders is related to the concept of *preparedness*, i.e. humans as a species fear objects and situations which were threats from primitive times.

> Phobic fear of truly dangerous electrical outlets, for example, is rare, while fear of seldom-encountered snakes and harmless insects is common. People in our culture are more likely to receive a shock from an outlet than a bite from a snake or insect (Marks, Dept. of Health and Human Services, 1985, p. 123).

A third theory relates anxiety reactions to the enzyme lactate. As early as the 1940s researchers noticed that persons who had anxiety disorders, particularly panic attacks, often had panic reactions in response to strenuous exercise. Since lactate is a by-product muscle enzyme in response to exercise, studies were conducted in which persons with panic disorder were given either lactate injections or a saline injection. The results confirmed that the overwhelming majority of panic disorder patients experienced a panic attack when injected with sodium lactate while few receiving saline injections did.

Finally, another group of studies identified faulty breathing patterns in panic disorder patients with many tending to hyperventilate via over-breathing. These same investigators (Clark *et al.*, 1985) have altered the low resting levels of carbon dioxide in panic disorder patients through breathing retraining. Despite the promise of all these theories, no single theory, to date, has explained all aspects of anxiety disorders.

The problem with looking for one physical source is that panic disorder patients over-respond to many physical changes. Research shows that lactate, caffeine, epinephrine, mixtures of carbon dioxide and oxygen, as well as voluntary hyperventilation and exercise, all trigger panic attacks in susceptible persons. While these individuals over-respond to bodily sensations, some investigators believe that they are most sensitive to cardiac-mediated physiological changes (Barlow, 1988). This, in turn, sets off the classic "fear of fear" which characterizes the disorder.

Deficiencies in causal theories, however, have never deterred clinicians on the firing line from applying treatment approaches from any helpful source. Pharmacological interventions for anxiety disorders have existed since the emergence of the first tranquilizers. At least four types of medications are used in the treatment of anxiety disorders.

1) Anti-anxiety agents, sometimes referred to as the "minor" tranquilizers to distinguish them from the anti-psychotic "major" tranquilizers, have a long history of use in the treatment of anxiety. These include the *benzodiazepines* (e.g. Valium, Librium, Tranxene, Dalmane) or medications which are structurally similar (e.g. Xanax). The majority of physicians who prescribe Valium or Xanax are general practitioners, family practice physicians, or non-psychiatric specialists (e.g. internists or orthopedists). These medications are referred to technically as *anxiolytics*. These drugs are used for the conditions noted in this chapter. The benzodiazepines are useful for generalized anxiety or tension conditions, but are not particularly helpful for unexpected panic attacks. Xanax, however, does appear to have anti-panic effects as recent large-scale, multi-site research suggests (Klerman, 1988). Approximately 50 to 60 percent of people with panic disorder will become symptom free on Xanax.

While these substances are often helpful for many on a short-

Figure 4-2

Common Medications for Anxiety Treatment

TRADE NAME	GENERIC NAME
Ativan	lorazepam
Azene	clorazepate
Buspar	buspirone
Centrax	prazepam
Librax	chlorodiazepoxide
Libritabs	chlorodiazepoxide
Librium	chlorodiazepoxide
Paxipam	halazepam
Serax	oxazepam
Tranxene	clorazepate
Valium	diazepam
Vestran	prazepam
Xanax	alprazolam

Source: *Medications for Mental Illness*, United States Department of Health and Human Services. DHHS Publication No. (ADM) 87-1509, Alcohol, Drug Abuse, and Mental Health Administration. Printed 1987.

term basis their long-term use is not without complications. For some users these drugs are potentially addicting; some experience quite unpleasant withdrawal symptoms when the drug is stopped, and still others experience a resumption of their anxiety symptoms if the drug is withdrawn. Clinicians, however, point out that some anxious individuals stay on these medications for long periods without abusing them or developing tolerance (the need to increase the dosage to obtain the anxiety-reducing effect). Figure 4-2 lists the more common anxiolytics with their generic and trade names.

2) Antidepressant medication such as the *tricyclics* (e.g. imipramine) or the *MAO inhibitors* (e.g. phenelzine) have been found useful for panic disorder conditions and social phobia. (These drugs will be discussed in greater detail in Chapter 5.)

3) *Beta blockers* are medications generally used to regulate cardiac functioning or to treat hypertension. They also reduce rapid heart rate which led to their use for specific phobias. A physician,

who is the medical reporter for a television network morning news show, openly described his own use of the beta blocker Inderal when he travels by airplane. The beta blockers are not effective with panic disorder or generalized anxiety disorders.

4) A new anti-anxiety medication exists (buspirone, trade name Buspar), which is the first one specifically for anxiety but not related to the benzodiazapenes. This drug tends to act more like the antidepressants. It is non-addicting but also takes two to three weeks to achieve maximum therapeutic effect. Future research will determine its long-term effectiveness.

Psychodynamic Theory and Treatment. Freud viewed the source of anxiety in the ego's inability to defend against unacceptable impulses of the id. Anxiety may remain largely unattached in the unconscious and manifest itself in the so-called "free-floating" anxiety conditions of generalized anxiety disorder or panic attacks. At other times the anxiety attaches itself to symbolic objects which represent the unconscious conflict. Fear of knives or sharp objects, for example, represents unresolved castration anxiety. Fear of snakes suggests sexual conflicts. Freud illustrated this position in his famous essay on Little Hans, a child who was afraid of horses, and whose father requested a consultation with Freud. Freud interpreted the child's fear as due to worry about being bitten by the horse. In this instance the horse's teeth represented Little Hans' preoccupation with castration fears.

Standard psychoanalytic treatment for phobias and other anxiety disorders focuses on discovering the unconscious meaning that the anxiety represents. As this uncovering and interpretation occur, the expectation is that the unconscious conflict resolves and the symptoms themselves disappear. From this perspective the counselor does not directly focus on the anxiety or fear itself. Indeed, to do so is to focus on the *wrong* problem—the psychological smoke-screen as it were for the underlying conflict. Advocates of this model hold further that if the symptom is attacked directly the unconscious will simply regenerate new symptoms of a different type. This process is referred to as *symptom substitution.*

Social Learning Theory and Treatment. Learning theory maintains that people become fearful or anxious by the same process involved in all learning. Fears may be learned by direct experience with a threatening object or event (*classical conditioning*), through reinforcement of escape behavior (*operant conditioning*) or by observing others who are anxious or fearful (*modeling*).

Therapists in the learning theory tradition have developed several treatment approaches for excessive anxiety. Psychiatrist Joseph Wolpe (1978) elaborated a process of fear reduction termed *systematic desensitization*. Wolpe's and others' animal laboratory studies demonstrated that an effective way to eliminate (*extinguish*) fear is to develop a competing response strong enough to permit the animal to enter the feared situation. Typical competing drives included sex or hunger. With humans Wolpe noted that a person could not be both afraid and relaxed simultaneously.

Wolpe first taught his patients a structured form of deep muscle relaxation. While in a state of relaxation they imagine a feared situation starting with a low level anxiety scene and gradually work up to the most fearful scene. Patients repeat these sessions until little emotional arousal occurs in the frightening scenes. Between sessions the patient completes homework assignments in the feared situation so that fear reduction will transfer from the imaginary to the real situation (*generalization*).

Wolpe also introduced the concept of assertion as a competing response to inhibiting anxiety. He role-played anxiety-provoking situations with his patients until they demonstrated appropriate social skills (*behavioral rehearsal*). Afterward, he helped the patient set up a hierarchy of situations to try out these new skills. Today, therapists of many schools employ this technique under the heading of assertiveness training.

Other behavioral therapists recommend that clients face the fear directly in the environment instead of first in imagination. They expose clients to feared situations in small doses. This approach became known as *in vivo desensitization* or *graduated exposure*. Behavior therapists consider it the treatment of choice when feasible.

Others developed fear reduction strategies based on observational learning. Strongly phobic persons would approach feared situations after observing live or filmed models doing the same (Bandura, 1969). Children reduced their fear of hospitals or surgical procedures and accelerated recovery following hospitalization through viewing films of other children coping successfully with it (Melamed and Siegel, 1975).

Cognitive Theory and Treatment. Cognitive theorists emphasize the irrational self-statements or expectations which trigger excessive anxiety. If a student takes a final exam with the belief that only a perfect grade signifies personal success, then the event will generate considerable anxiety. Social situations such as meeting new people will generate anxiety for those who require the approval of every person they encounter. Albert Ellis (e.g. Ellis and Grieger, 1977) developed these concepts, and others have created variants on this theme (Beck, 1991; Meichenbaum, 1985). Cognitive approaches maintain that to reduce excessive anxiety the person must first change the maladaptive internal assumptions, the irrational expectations which generate it. The approaches to altering these "cognitions" vary from direct challenging of the irrational ideas by the therapist to self-directed *cognitive restructuring* of the maladaptive assumptions via homework assignments and in-session practice. Cognitive therapy shares with behavioral approaches an emphasis on practicing newly learned skills in the environment to ensure change.

Psychiatrist Aaron Beck (1991) emphasizes that anxiety conditions are related to misinterpreting threats. That is, the anxious person sees objectively non-threatening events as dangerous or even catastrophic. In the case of panic disorder this involves misinterpreting harmless physical sensations. In social phobia the person exaggerates the threat of the potential disapproval of others. Many therapists will combine cognitive strategies with behavioral ones in the treatment of anxiety. For example, they may suggest that clients place themselves in the fear-provoking situation (exposure) and change their automatic assumptions about its dangerousness (cognitive restructuring).

Pastoral Care and Anxiety Disorders

Pastoral care presents many opportunities for ministry to the anxious. The list of individuals who are susceptible to both situational as well as pervasive stress and anxiety is almost endless. The following groups represent a small portion of those likely to experience significant dysfunctional stress and anxiety: the bereaved, the acute and chronic physically ill, the unemployed, victims of physical and psychological abuse, rape and incest victims, victims of natural disasters, combatants and non-combatants in war areas, families of addicted persons, and crime victims.

Integration. Pastoral counselors assume that an integrated spirituality is a powerful resource for achieving emotional well-being. Since the pastoral counselor does not accept a fragmented spirit/mind/body model of human personality, he or she appreciates the importance of "right thinking" in the spiritual domain as an adjunct to reducing anxiety. Although biochemical and environmental events contribute to the development of excessive anxiety, holistic approaches emphasize the interactive effect of all human domains upon health. More and more scientists and health professionals acknowledge the influence of the person's internal universe of meaning in health recovery and illness prevention (e.g. *The Healing Brain;* Ornstein & Sobel, 1987). Pastoral counselors are well-suited and well-positioned to help anxious individuals intensify their inner world of spiritual meaning for adaptive coping.

We have accumulated evidence from at least three decades of research that supportive, caring persons without advanced degrees in mental health can provide measurable therapeutic benefits to persons experiencing anxiety and depression (Marks, 1985). In one review of patients undergoing surgery (Harvik, 1979, cited in Marks, 1985) those who received counseling prior to surgery achieved more rapid recovery than those not receiving counseling. Interestingly, 30 minute sessions were as effective as longer ones. Patients who received counseling from nurses did as well as those helped by medical doctors or psychologists. The implications of these data are clear. If hospitals are patient-centered as well as cost-efficient they would *increase* the number of ministers in health care to promote spiritual, psychological, and, therefore, physical well-being.

The difficulty with the concept of integration is that the term may have the effect of invoking a "buzzword" which provides no help to pastoral counselors in actual implementation. Integration as understood here implies a threefold process. First, the person achieves awareness of those underlying spiritual assumptions which increase rather than decrease anxiety. Is the person despairing, seeking lesser gods, making decisions based on ephemeral needs? As one's automatic spiritual assumptions are clarified, the person re-examines them to see if more nourishing ones are available. This second step involves challenging the anxiety-enhancing assumptions currently in operation. With guidance the person replaces them with spiritual assumptions more foundational to their spiritual tradition, and presumably healthier. Finally, the person monitors his or her daily anxiety experiences and consciously attempts to focus on these new spiritual assumptions as one resource in coping with stress and anxiety. A step-by-step explanation of this process is contained in L. Rebecca Propst's excellent work *Psychotherapy in a Religious Framework* (1988), a book which integrates the process of counseling, behavioral change, and spirituality.

Situational Anxiety. The most efficient approach in counseling the fearful client is to encourage gradual exposure to the feared situation. Shy, insecure people who needlessly restrict their social lives can break down social encounters into manageable chunks, gradually becoming comfortable with one level of accomplishment before moving on to the next. Church or synagogue social recreational events often provide a safe environment to rehearse new social behaviors. What maintains avoidant behavior is either an excessive regard about what others think, or perfectionism that tolerates no weakness or failure. Various spiritual traditions can speak to these rigid cognitions. The pastoral counselor may use biblical concepts such as how it is more important to trust in God than in people or how we are saved despite our sinfulness. Suggesting to clients that they approach feared situations while in the presence of God may serve as an increased motivator (Propst, 1988).

On-Going Anxiety/Stress. Individuals with continual anxiety are difficult to reassure with any degree of permanence. Unlike the situationally anxious who anticipate specific events, the chronically anxious wear themselves out with high baseline anxiety. Negative attitudes can intensify the anxiety while positive attitudes may reduce it. Certain biblical passages are relevant to this condition— particularly those dealing with the importance of faith and trust in God.

The chronically anxious may benefit from reassessing their life style, paying attention to leisure events, exercise, or plain "downtime." The pastoral counselor would review these issues and assist in planning life style changes to decrease overall stress.

When chronic anxiety or stress levels are related to past trauma, the best therapy is—as one colleague describes it—talk, talk, talk. This therapy, however, is dose-regulated by the client, i.e. at times he or she will reveal intense feelings followed by periods of avoidance and denial. The counselor remains patient, refusing to engage in a cat-and-mouse game to coax revelations. Rather, the counselor allows the client to explore the trauma at his or her own pace.

Scrupulous and Compulsive. The torments of spiritual uncertainty are among the most difficult to heal. Pastoral ministers have used various strategies to reassure those who are continually anxious about the state of their souls. The truly scrupulous (obsessive-compulsive) cannot be reassured. They persist and leave the counselor bewildered or even angry.

The problem of scrupulosity has probably existed since the dawn of religious belief. Some of the world's most revered spiritual masters have suffered from either transient or permanent scrupulosity. They have included Martin Luther, Saint Ignatius Loyola, founder of the Jesuits, and John Bunyan. This author was inundated by calls and letters after writing an article on the subject for the newsletter of the Obsessive Compulsive Foundation (Ciarrocchi, 1990). Persons from every spectrum of religious belief, including liberals, conservatives, fundamentalists, and even agnostics, revealed their agony with this "doubting disease."

John Bunyan, in *Grace Abounding* (1988), captures the torment of the scrupulous well: "And now was I both a burden and a terror to myself; nor did I ever so know, as now, what it was to be weary of my life, and yet afraid to die" (p. 84). Bunyan himself spent two and a half years in torment attempting to resolve whether or not he had committed the "unpardonable sin" (Mark 3:29). Several centuries later half of those calling from the OC Foundation were struggling with the same question.

An example from the Roman Catholic tradition provides an illustration of dealing with this disorder. Scrupulous Catholics are prone to abuse the sacrament of reconciliation (confession), using the practice ritualistically much the same way a germ phobic repeatedly washes. For centuries the church trained priests to care for the scrupulous by assuming an authoritarian stance. They ordered confession at set intervals, and penitents could have only one confessor, whom they were to obey blindly. The scrupulous were to follow moral guidance despite the overwhelming feeling that they were in sin and their need to seek absolution. This strategy is structurally identical to an effective form of behavior therapy for the obsessive compulsive called *response prevention* (Rachman and Hodgson, 1980). The pastoral counselor refuses to reinforce the obsessive compulsive person's need for reassurance. Rather, the pastoral counselor sets firm boundaries. Otherwise the act of pastoral care becomes a compulsion so that the solution is now the problem.

Severe forms of the illness require psychological or psychiatric referral, but the enlightened mental health professional does well to collaborate with the referring minister in such cases. My own strategy is to work closely with referring ministers to keep them abreast of the treatment plan so that we support each other and the client but not the disorder.

Final Comments: Pastoral Counseling and Stress Prevention. Unfortunately the science of mental illness prevention is in its infancy so that the role of personal faith in stress reduction is unclear. At this point we can only infer its significance. Nevertheless we have indirect evidence of its possible benefit. Meditation, for example, has proven anxiety-reduction effects similar to clinical techniques such as biofeedback. For some, biofeedback and relaxation exercises reduce hypertension. To what degree a regimen of meditation or daily prayer would do the same is a tantalizing question.

The time appears ripe for empirical studies to answer such questions. Even though the social sciences are gradually developing interest in such questions, we should not be surprised if pastoral counselors and those with advanced degrees in ministry must lead the way. We are the likely researchers to explore such questions since we are comfortable with religious experience, scientific methodology, and a curiosity about faith's role in emotional health.

Chapter 5

Mood Disorders

I. Introduction
II. Bipolar Disorders
III. Depressive Disorders (Unipolar Disorders)
IV. Causal Theories and Treatments
V. Pastoral Care of Depression

Introduction

Mood refers to our feeling tone. In this sense we are always "in" some sort of mood. For most people mood is generally on "automatic pilot," that is, they pay no attention to the dozens of subtle daily mood shifts. We carry out our workaday tasks without attending to our moods, or else put them on the "back burner" so that thinking about them will not intrude on essential obligations. We also know that events can trigger moods which we cannot ignore. Their intensity is such that they break through our ordinary defenses and force us to pay attention.

For millions of people, however, it is not the occasional positive or negative event which colors their mood but a continual experience of intense feeling which interferes with normal duties, destroys the quality of life, and may even result in suicide as a final desperate attempt to achieve relief. Most readers will appreciate how negative feelings interfere with life, but excessive euphoria can also devastate. The impact of intense mood swings is the focus of this chapter. We will examine first that condition which fluctuates between excessive euphoria and depression. This condition swings back and forth between the opposite poles of euphoria and depression and hence is termed *bipolar*. Research has shown that such individuals have different family histories and unique responses to medications than persons who suffer from depressive swings only. This latter group is called *unipolar* mood disorder.

69

In the typical pastoral care setting much time is spent ministering to persons with depressed moods: the bereaved, the sick, the troubled family, or the person simply having a bad day. The purpose of this chapter is to help the minister distinguish normal from abnormal moods. As any listener of country-western music can appreciate, even everyday life is hard. We will waste already rationed mental health services if we diagnose and treat every individual who experiences problems in the life of hard knocks. On the other hand, even "normal" stressors can trigger a form of sadness that is a truly clinical syndrome and which requires specialized treatment. Because mood disorders as a clinical entity are so common, pastoral counselors must discriminate sadness which is the stuff of ordinary life from that "sickness unto death" requiring appropriate referral.

Bipolar Disorders

Symptoms and Patterns

David Halberstam in his best-selling story of America's media empires, *The Powers That Be* (1979), reveals the tragic end of one of the most influential persons of his generation: Philip Graham, owner and publisher of the *Washington Post*. Graham was responsible for changing the *Post* from a small town journal into one of the top newspapers in the world. Furthermore, he was politically powerful, having once clerked in the Supreme Court, and an advisor to the Presidents. He provided counsel to John F. Kennedy and Lyndon Johnson, among other prominent leaders. Graham, however, suffered from the most debilitating form of manic-depression, as bipolar disorder was then called, causing him periodically to act in ways that brought embarrassment to himself and his family. Halberstam relates that in the grip of mania, Graham, though married to a woman of exceptional distinction, Katherine Graham, would visit European dignitaries parading his young female companion. When the mania remitted, Graham would return home, crashing into the deepest depression, sealed off in the safety of his home surrounded by family. In the depths of one depressive cycle he took his own life.

The symptoms of bipolar disorder or manic-depression range from mild and inconvenient to severe and incapacitating. In their severe form the symptoms are dramatic and easy to recognize. In its extreme form, however, the psychotic features may resemble schizophrenia. Indeed, in the United States a generation or two of mental health practitioners tended to diagnose psychotic manifestations of mood disorders as schizophrenia. This situation has changed with the advent of more rigorous diagnostic criteria such as the *Diagnostic and Statistical Manual*, 3rd edition (American Psychiatric Association, 1980, 1987).

The major symptom of mania is an intense *euphoria,* a sense of well-being not justified by any environmental cause. One may feel like the winner of a grand lottery, except there is no payoff (Tyrer and Shopsin, 1982). Typically the mood develops gradually so that friends and relatives may not notice its onset. The early-stage manic may present as someone with an infectious good nature. For many the mood will grow out of control to the point of frank delusions and hallucinations. The sufferers become *expansive,* i.e. believe they have special powers, or they may take on the identity of powerful historic personages (e.g. Napoleon). When not frankly delusional the expansiveness may look somewhat normal: they believe their cognitive powers are beyond their peers, they have developed brilliant solutions to complex problems, or that they are gifted with financial acumen.

The manic also experiences increased *energy* levels. Motor activity increases dramatically; he or she may become fidgety, unable to sit still or remain focused on one activity for long. Some channel this energy into work, pushing themselves into 14–16 hour days in an effort to exhaust themselves. If they are homemakers, every item in the household is renovated. Concomitant with this increased energy is *sleep disturbance,* often needing only a few hours nightly or none for days on end. This energy level may impel the person to take trips on the spur of the moment. One patient told me that on his way to class at the university he suddenly headed for the airport and boarded a plane bound for Pakistan. He recalled thinking at the time it was normal and adventurous.

The manic's speech is seen as *pressured,* that is, as if pushed from within into a torrent of words. They speak rapidly, jumping from topic to topic, and seem able to carry on several conversations simultaneously if in a group setting. Many have a corollary habit in the manic phase of "telephonitis": they make endless phone calls, often at odd hours, frequently long distance, and to persons they may not have contacted for some time. My patients will speak of an impulse to call an old college roommate or a cousin who lives halfway across the world. Usually the recipient of the call is bewildered, since the call is unexpected or comes in the middle of the night.

Irritability also plays a prominent role for many. While the surface veneer of manic persons demonstrates an infectious joviality, they do not brook frustration. When others stand in the way of their desires they may react angrily. A small subgroup may become violent, even dangerous. Wise clinical management avoids backing a manic person into a corner. If the minister feels personally threatened or believes that others are threatened, he or she needs to contact the police.

Poor judgment characterizes the manic episode. The manic phase may lead to spending sprees which result in financial troubles. Some make unwise investments or support risky financial enterprises. One family I worked with had a pre-arranged plan among the children when their mother put on what they called "her manic outfit." They would instantly call their father at work, and he would meet the older children at the nearest Macy's department store. When the plan worked as intended they would intercept her coming out of the store with stacks of parcels: one member would take the parcels back in the store for a refund while the husband would drive the mother directly to the hospital.

Other features include lack of attention to personal grooming, hygiene and dress. In the manic phase the individual's dress is often bizarre or garish: clothes do not match, styles or colors are not in harmony, and grooming is not attended to. In one clinic where I worked, the secretaries were adept at identifying a bipolar patient's mood swings based on dress alone. They would tip the clinician off when announcing her arrival for an appointment. Some patients have *decreased appetite.* This latter symptom is consistent with decreased sleep and increased energy level, symptoms which, taken together, resemble the behavior of persons using stimulant drugs. In the case of the bipolar person, of course, no external agent is responsible for the behavior.

Also consistent with this picture is *increased interest in sex.* Bipolar cycles sometimes trigger sexual behavior which is grossly inconsistent with the person's usual and customary value system. One woman patient who was single and president of her church council described with shame what she called her "outings." Before seeking treatment she was aware that periodically she would act in a promiscuous manner posing as a "swinging single" even though she found this behavior repugnant. Despite the pain it brought her she was able to see its irony. For example, she described picking up men in single bars, going back to their places to spend the night, and then leaving them in the morning without revealing her name.

This description of bipolar symptoms suggests why some resist treatment efforts. Not only do psychotic persons resist treatment, but those with milder forms may equate treatment with giving up the "high." If the illness is not costing social misfortune the manic euphoria feels pleasant. Some have described the feeling as "addictive." Telling such individuals that they are ill fails to persuade them.

The *patterns* for this illness are varied and complicated. The predominant feature is its *cyclic* nature. The symptoms occur and reoccur in cycles with as high as a 90 percent relapse rate (Clayton, 1983). The illness is characterized by mood swings between the euphoric, energy-laden manic cycle and the sad, listless, depressive cycle. Popular ideas about the disorder are often distorted: many believe that depressive swings follow immediately upon the manic phase. In reality many combinations and permutations occur. One pattern might include periodic manic phases followed by normal moods with an occasional depressed cycle. A second pattern might involve one continual cycle between highs and lows with little or no respite in between. Still another pattern might involve an occasional manic phase but multiple depressive cycles. Most rare is a pattern of only manic phases followed by normal mood. The most severe style involves the so-called "switchers," persons who cycle rapidly with little or no relief in between.

The counselor may *assess* mood swings in several ways. Initially, the client could provide a mood history for the past five to ten years. Figure 5-1 illustrates a mood chart for a fictional bipolar individual tracing his or her mood swings back four years. The chart depicts seasonal changes for each year as the client attempts to recall mood levels through the use of significant anchor points: e.g. birthdays, anniversaries, deaths, holidays, etc. While this may seem an impossible task, clients usually can recall their extreme mood swings. This information may assist client and counselor to predict high-risk periods. For example, the pattern in Figure 5-1 indicates that summer and fall tend to have normal moods while spring is the season for mania and winter for depression. Note, however, that some years have exceptions to this pattern and each person's chart will vary. (Figures 5-2 and 5-3 are provided for reader use and can be duplicated for charting.)

Once the annual patterns emerge, the next step is to request *daily monitoring* of mood swings. One method is to graph mood on a daily basis using a form such as Figure 5-3. This instrument was devised by psychiatrist Dr. Philip Hirsch and is useful in obtaining a concrete record of mood swings on a daily basis. The advantage of this chart is that it is "client friendly," requiring only a single mark daily

Figure 5-1

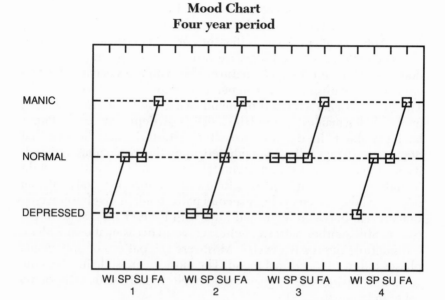

Mood Chart
Four year period

WI = WINTER
SP = SPRING
SU = SUMMER
FA = FALL

on the graph. Its simplicity facilitates client compliance and presents both counselor and client with a visual representation of mood fluctuations. Too often the client's recall of mood over the course of a week or two between meetings is vague at best or inaccurate at worst. One resourceful client keeps records for several years by superimposing on each month's chart data from the previous years. Through the use of colored pencils we can quickly determine the month's pattern over the past several years. This allows us to keep precise track of mood shifts to anticipate high-risk periods.

Epidemiology

The United States national survey cited earlier (ECA) reveals that nearly 1 percent of the population suffers from manic-depression over a lifetime. Even 1 percent prevalence has vast social impact. Prior to effective pharmacological intervention, manic depression

Figure 5-2

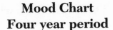

Mood Chart
Four year period

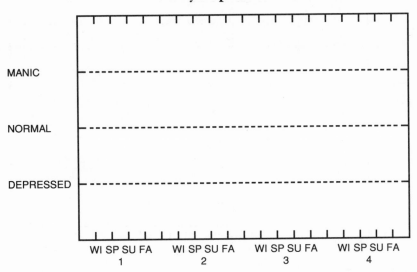

WI = WINTER
SP = SPRING
SU = SUMMER
FA = FALL

SOURCE: Joseph Ciarrocchi
Michael Ciarrocchi

cost the United States economy billions of dollars each decade in health care costs and employment loss.

The first episode of mania can strike any time but not usually after age 50. One third begin in adolescence. This highlights the importance of comprehensive evaluation for troubled teenagers. Adolescent acting-out such as rebelliousness, running away, substance abuse or school problems may disguise a manic disorder. Large group studies (e.g. Clayton, 1983) indicate that the median number of manic episodes is about 8 and they tend to occur in 6 to 9 month cycles. In individual cases, however, enormous variation exists. The sex distribution is evenly divided with a slight female majority. Exceptional creativity marks the disorder in many cases (e.g. Van Gogh) both for bipolars and their first-degree relatives.

Individuals with mood disorders often self-medicate to reduce

Figure 5-3

Daily Mood Chart

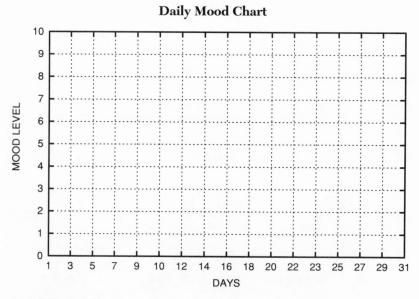

1 = WANT TO DIE
2 = SEVERELY DEPRESSED (NOT MANAGING DAILY ACTIVITIES)
3 = SEVERELY DEPRESSED BUT MANAGING DAILY ACTIVITIES
4 = BLUE, BUT NOT TERRIBLE
5 = NORMAL
6 = FEELING EXTRA GOOD MUCH OF THE DAY
7 = FEELING GOOD WITH SOME MANIC SYMPTOMS*
8 = FEELING GOOD WITH MANY MANIC SYMPTOMS*
9 = FEELING GOOD AND OUT OF CONTROL

* MANIC SYMPTOMS: POOR CONCENTRATION, FIDGETY, RACING THOUGHTS,
                  SLEEP DISTURBANCE, POOR JUDGMENT, IMPULSIVE,
                  APPETITE DISTURBANCE, GRANDIOSITY

SOURCE: PHILIP HIRSCH, M.D.

pain. Mania is no exception. Despite the euphoria, ten to fifteen percent of bipolar patients will abuse alcohol or other drugs during the manic phase. The euphoria and intense energy feels aversive to many, and they drink alcohol to quell the agitation. Psychiatric units which specialize in dual diagnosis treat a high percentage of alcoholic/drug dependent bipolar patients.

Genetics and Bipolar Disorder

Unipolar and bipolar mood disorders both run in families. The risk is substantially greater, however, for families with bipolar disorders. About 15 percent of first-degree relatives of bipolar patients develop manic-depression or unipolar depression (7 and 8 percent respectively), whereas only 8 percent of first-degree relatives of unipolar depressed patients develop manic-depression or unipolar depression (1 and 7 percent respectively) (Clayton, 1983).

Since bipolar disorder runs in families, does this mean the relationship is a genetic one? Scientists believe it is genetic but the evidence is not yet definitive. Many characteristics run in families but are not genetic, e.g. speaking French. Locating an agreed-upon genetic marker on a chromosome has alternately generated intense enthusiasm followed by disappointment. At least twice in the last decade geneticists heralded the discovery of a genetic marker for bipolar disorder only to have other scientists fail to replicate the findings. This area of research, nevertheless, holds great promise.

Twin Studies

One standard research technique in the genetics of mental disorders is research with twins. Fraternal twins (dizygotic) share the same genetic characteristics as two siblings, since they result from the fertilization of two separate ova and sperm. Identical twins (monozygotic), on the other hand, share the same genetic make-up, having split into two individuals subsequent to the fertilization of a single egg and spermatozoon.

Since twins share the same environment in the womb and similar environments after birth, differences in the rates of mental disorders between identical versus fraternal twins should shed light on the influence of heredity versus environment. Studies of monozygotic twins for which one sibling is bipolar indicate rates of *concordance* (i.e. sharing the diagnosis) ranging from 40–71 percent. Concordance rates for dizygotic twins, on the other hand, range from 0–13 percent (Clayton, 1983).

While such studies do not prove a hereditary factor they are strongly suggestive. Nevertheless, since the agreement rate is not 100 percent even for identical twins, environmental factors are also consequential. Once again this supports a *diathesis-stress* model, suggesting a constitutional vulnerability interacting with some environmental stressor. We will have recourse to twin studies throughout these chapters as they highlight genetic influences on mental disorders.

Treatment and Clinical Management

Biological Treatment

However long neuroscientists may take to establish the definitive etiology of bipolar disorders, most clinicians believe that biology makes a strong contribution to this disorder. In its extreme the disorder presents with psychotic symptoms out of proportion to co-existing environmental stressors. Furthermore, while one may not logically argue from the effectiveness of biological interventions to biological etiology (e.g. headaches are *not* an aspirin deficiency), the dramatic improvement in many manic-depressives through biological therapies feels compelling to many mental health professionals.

In 1949 a New Zealand psychiatrist first noted the tranquilizing effect of the common salt mineral, lithium, on sheep. He applied the drug to manic patients and recorded its therapeutic benefit. This application represented the first major success in the management of serious mental disorders through medication. The United States was slow to respond to the promise of lithium even though Europe and other countries introduced it a decade or more earlier. The reluctance in this country was based on at least two factors. First, lithium is a naturally occurring mineral, a salt compound listed in the periodic table of elements. As such no pharmaceutical company could claim proprietary ownership of it for patent purposes. This eliminates the economic incentive in the cost of conducting tests under the Food and Drug Administration's standards for establishing the safety of new drugs. Secondly, during World War II, when salt was in scarce supply, some fatalities occurred when lithium replaced table salt. Lithium is a toxic substance whose therapeutic dosage and toxic dosage are close. Lithium initially was administered in hospitals and not until the mid 1970s did routine outpatient administration begin. Clinicians had to wait until biochemists developed a blood test to measure the lithium level.

Lithium is effective for perhaps 60–80 percent of bipolar manic episodes. Lithium prevents both manic and depressive cycles for some; others require additional medication for control of the depressive phase. Interestingly, lithium also helps unipolar depressed persons with no manic history but who have a family history of bipolar disorder. When lithium is ineffective the anticonvulsant drugs carbamazepine (Tegretol) and valproate (Depakene) may have good results. Some may require antipsychotic medications (cf. Chapter 7) during the acute phases of mania to gain more symptom control.

Psychosocial Management

Even though bipolar disorders appear to have a strong biological component, a diathesis-stress model points to the importance of maintaining a calm environment. Psychosocial therapies such as supportive counseling are preventative by rendering the person less vulnerable to stress. Appropriate assessment, as noted above, alerts the counselor to high risk seasons or situations. For one client, job reassignment was a particularly vulnerable time. More than once this precipitated hypomanic episodes necessitating interventions such as medication adjustment. Since he often wrote angry letters to supervisors during these phases we contracted that all correspondence with authority figures went through me.

By now it should be clear that bipolar clients require close monitoring. Frequent meetings with a therapist are not always cost-effective or even necessary, yet experience proves that lengthy intervals between visits run the risk of missing a manic or depressive swing. Manic clients tend to disappear during manic phases, heading off on one mission or another. Their euphoria renders them resistant to help-seeking. When the person represents a danger to self or others, legal commitment to a psychiatric hospital is required. This places an enormous burden on family members since their interventions are viewed by the client as intrusions. Cases that do not justify legal commitment are equally burdensome to families who have to convince the manic to seek voluntary treatment. The person in a manic state usually ignores these pleadings. The pastoral counselor could support family members in obtaining treatment for their loved one. Families often need reassurance that they have acted in the best interest of the person.

Depressive Disorders (Unipolar Disorders)

Introduction

Mary H. seeks her rabbi's advice about suing her surgeon for what she terms a "botched job" on her sinus surgery. Mary is 36 years old, has a 9 year old daughter, and is employed in a middle management position for a large business firm. She is on leave from work due to her "disfigurement" and the shame of appearing in public. Her rabbi is puzzled, for he observes no obvious change in Mary's appearance. She even brings him "before" and "after" pictures which she believes document her conclusions. She seeks out a therapist and reveals that she has withdrawn from friends and extended family since she believes her appearance repels people. She has made preliminary contact with an attorney regarding a malpractice lawsuit against the surgeon. When the rabbi speaks to Mary's sisters, who are also members of the synagogue, they express their bewilderment. They, too, feel Mary's appearance is normal. Mary, however, dismisses all contrary opinions as feeble attempts to cheer her up. She is also not eating properly, has lost 30 pounds, and spends much of the day sleeping.

This vignette illustrates how clinical depression might intrude itself into a pastoral care setting without appearing like classical depression. The rabbi might interpret the situation as a greedy person engaging in a nuisance lawsuit, or remain puzzled by her uncharacteristic behavior.

In the pastoral setting excessive *guilt* is perhaps the most common symptom encountered as a manifestation of clinical depression. People seek counseling because of regrets over past misdeeds, recurring images of failures, or a pervasive sense that they have not lived the right kind of life. The discerning helper discovers that the negative feelings are out of proportion to the events. Further, the depressed person remains inconsolable despite pastoral intervention. Depression is so common that it has been called the common cold of mental illness. The intrusion of this disorder into pastoral care places an obligation on the minister to recognize its manifestations, understand its course, and be familiar with various treatment approaches.

Symptoms and Patterns

Symptoms

We all know what it means to feel depressed. Along with anxiety it is a feeling every human being can identify. Depression itself is characterized by a *distinct quality of mood,* a feeling of sadness, being "down-in-the-dumps," or feeling blue. This feeling, along with the disorder's associated features, runs on a continuum from mild/inconvenient to severe/incapacitating. What distinguishes clinical depression from normal ups and downs is the intensity, duration, and level of dysfunction associated with the condition. What follows are common features found in depression, though only the most severe cases experience all of the symptoms in a given episode.

Vegetative symptoms are often present. These represent physical symptoms which appear health-related. Sleep disturbance is common. Insomnia may present as difficulty falling asleep, waking up in the middle of the night and not resuming sleep, or waking up one to two hours early in the morning and not falling back to sleep. These patterns are referred to as *initial, middle,* and *terminal insomnia* respectively. Some experience excessive sleepiness (hypersomnia) and despite 10–14 hours of daily sleep the person never feels refreshed. Appetite disturbance may lead to loss of appetite with concomitant weight loss. Some, though, have an increased appetite and engage in binge eating. Many experience loss of interest in sex (decreased *libido*). Bodily symptoms may occur in such forms as gastrointestinal disturbance, constipation, vague muscle pain, backaches, or headaches. People may complain about a loss of energy, of feeling fatigued and tired all the time, or acting as if in slow motion (*psychomotor retardation*). The presence of physical symptoms highlights the importance of a medical referral to rule out biological sources for the mood disturbance (e.g. thyroid disease).

Depression also affects *cognitive processes.* Many persons complain of inability to concentrate or remember. They may describe difficulty reading or following a conversation. Their view of reality becomes negative and pessimistic; they experience a sense of hopelessness about themselves, the world, and their future (Beck *et al.*, 1979).

Often the depressed person thinks about *dying.* These thoughts may range from imagining that one is dead, to wishing one were dead, to planning and acting out self-destructive acts. Some may desire death but only at the hand of an external agent (e.g. a truck runs you down rather than the case of you jumping out in front of traffic). We call such thoughts *passive suicidal ideation.* Others imagine dying through their own intentional efforts, e.g. shooting oneself (*active suicidal ideation*). The counselor needs to assess suicidal feelings carefully and to take their existence seriously. About 15 percent of seriously depressed individuals ultimately commit suicide. Contrary to folklore the helper will not implant the idea of suicide in an unwary person. The suicidal person is generally relieved to talk about it.

As suggested, *guilt feelings* play a prominent role for many in depression. The pessimism which pervades this disorder often looks backward over one's life and finds it seriously wanting. The person focuses on failures or misdeeds and ruminates about them: the job I should have taken, the person I should have married, the mistakes I made with my children, or the way I mistreated my spouse. These, or similar thoughts, lock in and are not amenable to reason or reassurance. The depressed person frequently *withdraws* socially and remains isolated from family and friends. The person may describe a sense of dissatisfaction in normally pleasurable activities (*anhedonia*). Depressed persons are often irritable and cranky. Occasionally they may lose control and act violently.

In its most severe manifestation depression may generate *psychosis*—an extreme distortion of reality manifested by either false perceptions or false beliefs. False perceptions are commonly termed *hallucinations* and may include sound, sight, taste, touch, or somatic distortions. False beliefs are termed *delusions*, e.g. the belief that people on television are talking about you. In depression the hallucinations or delusions are usually *mood-congruent,* which means that the psychotic symptom has depressive features. They may take the form of hearing voices condemning them to hell for evil acts. Delusions which are mood-congruent would be similar to the case example described above for the woman who falsely believed she was disfigured. In any event psychotic symptoms may throw even trained mental health workers off the track into diagnosing schizophrenia instead of a mood disorder. Naturally the pastoral minister will seek appropriate referrals in the face of such extreme symptoms.

Patterns

While many subtypes of depression are under investigation, the literature describes three most commonly. *Exogenous* depression follows a clear precipitant in the form of some major environmental stressor: e.g. loss of a loved one, bankruptcy, natural calamity, unemployment, etc. In such cases the diagnosis of clinical depression is made only when the person fails to rebound from dysphoria after a reasonable amount of time. (If the event itself is extraordinary and the person develops severe symptoms this falls under post-traumatic stress, as noted in the previous chapter). An obvious example would be the widower still in deep mourning two to three years after the spouse's death.

Endogenous depression, on the other hand, is a condition lacking any clear precipitant and thus appears to come out of the blue. This type has several features. Often a person experiences *diurnal varia-tion* in his or her mood, with the mood significantly worse during certain periods of the day. Mornings are usually the most difficult for these individuals, with modest improvement by late afternoon and early evening. They often experience anhedonia, early morning awakening, loss of appetite and loss of libido. Many specialists believe that this variant originates in some biochemical imbalance and may entail a genetic predisposition. The major problem with this cate-gory, however, is that the symptom cluster does not reliably distin-guish depressions with or without external precipitants. The DSM terms this subtype of symptoms *melancholia*, but makes no reference to precipitating causes.

Dysthymia represents a third type which characterizes a lifetime experience of fairly regular low-grade depression that may periodi-cally worsen but seldom lessens sufficiently to have any long-lasting sense of joy or well-being.

Epidemiology

The ECA household study in the United States found the current rate of major depression to include 3 percent of the adult population with lifetime rates at 5.8 percent. Dysthymia occurred at 3.3 percent both for current and lifetime rates. Diagnosable clinical depression thus affects around 10 million Americans at any given moment.

Studies consistently find that women suffer from depression twice as often as men, with one woman in four versus one man in nine experiencing at least one severe depressive episode. Researchers agree that this represents a true difference and is not due either to sampling artifacts or to women being more likely to seek help.

Various explanations for gender differences have been offered. Since the ratios are almost exactly reversed for alcoholism, some spec-ulate that males are prone to self-medicate their mood disorder through alcohol. Currently no theory completely explains the differ-ence. In a critical review of this problem, psychologist Susan Nolen-Hoeksema (1987) concludes that *cognitive styles of men and women* may account for the different rates of depression. Women, as a group, tend to ruminate more over problems than men, whereas men appar-ently are better at distracting themselves from unpleasant cognitions. This cognitive style, therefore, may pre-dispose women to hold on to dysphoric ideas and images longer, which, in turn, generates depres-sion. If this theory is accurate, avoiding painful material via distrac-tion may be adaptive.

The age of the first episode for depression is broad, ranging from childhood and adolescence up to the end of life. The average age of onset is around 40. For those with recurrent depression, episodes tend to be longer and more severe as the person ages.

Genetics

Unipolar depression runs in families but the genetic link remains unclear. About 25 percent of clinically depressed persons have a first-degree relative with some type of depression. Alcoholism is also common in depressed families, particularly for male relatives. To date, no one has discovered a genetic marker linked to depression.

Causal Theories and Treatment

Biological Theories

Biological theories of depression have gained such prominence through the media and popular writing—e.g. Jon Franklin's Pulitzer-prize-winning *Molecules of the Mind* (1987)—that many informed persons now assume that depression results from biological dysfunction. Depressed clients referred for evaluation speak with assurance about the "chemical imbalance" which causes their mood disorder. Researchers are investigating many biological trails but the scope of this book allows mentioning only a few prominent ones.

The warmest scientific lead remains the neurotransmitter process, the electrical and chemical methods by which the nerve cells communicate with each other. As is well known, the brain is the final resting place for messages from outside the body. If I touch a hot stove, for example, pain is actually registered in the brain. Nerve cells (*neurons*) carry that message from the fingertip through a network of connecting cells to the spinal cord and eventually up to the brain. The nerve cells are organized contrary to intuition. They do not form a continuous strand to transport messages in the fashion of a telephone line; rather, each nerve cell is separated (one thousandth of a millimeter apart) from its neighbors. When a nerve cell is activated, electrical energy is created throughout the cell which, in turn, releases chemicals at its terminal. These chemicals (*neurotransmitters*) act as messengers signaling surrounding nerve cells either to fire or remain quiet. If the neurotransmitter activates a neighboring neuron, that neuron, in turn, releases its own neurotransmitters to other cells and so on. This occurs millions of times until the brain cells receive the message. The space between the nerve cells which the messengers flood is called the *synapse.* Scientists have identified dozens of neuro-transmitters but believe that hundreds more exist.

Scientists realized what potential the study of neurotransmitters had for mental illness when they were investigating the pain-killing properties of opiate drugs, a topic we shall return to in our chapter on addictions. This led to investigations of depression and other mental illness. Early clues came when scientists noted that antidepressant drugs changed the amounts of specified neurotransmitters. Also, certain medications such as reserpine, which had been in use for cardiac conditions, were known to cause depression as a side-effect. These medications tended to affect the neurotransmitters in an opposite manner from the antidepressants. Some of the neurotransmitters currently implicated in depression include *norepinephrine, dopamine, serotonin,* and *acetylcholine.*

Researchers wish to reach a point where a simple laboratory test could measure the neurotransmitter culprit in depression. Secondly, once assessed, the appropriate antidepressant could correct the chemical imbalance. The problem with this ideal scenario is that the relationship between neurotransmitter level and depression (or any disorder) is exceedingly complex. Scientists now believe that the activity of the nerve cells may have less to do with the absolute quantity of a given neurotransmitter than with the sensitivity of the *receptors* on the nerve cells which "read" the presence or absence of these messengers. The receptors may be overly sensitized causing the neuron to overreact, or they may be desensitized resulting in failure to activate to a normal stimulus. Furthermore, state-of-the-art neurotransmitter measurement does not allow assessment of these substances in the brain itself, but only measurement of their biochemical by-products (*metabolites*). Technical difficulties, therefore, do not allow clinicians to intervene with the precision that neurotransmitter theories suggest. Nevertheless, they continue to hold great promise for depression research as well as the entire mental illness field.

The *neuroendocrine* system is a second area of focus. Physicians have long known how endocrine disorders create mood swings and depressive states (e.g. thyroid disease). Endocrine disorders create measurable shifts in hormone production assessed by laboratory tests. What if, scientists reasoned, milder hormonal alterations exist? Could these also generate debilitating mood swings?

Researchers have linked two endocrine systems to depression. One regulates thyroid functioning and the second implicates the pituitary-adrenal system. Since endocrine system diseases do not cause these mild irregularities they are termed *subclinical*. Laboratory tests developed for endocrine disorders are abnormal for as many as 50–60 percent of clinically depressed patients. One test, for example, the dexamethasone suppression test (*DST*), positively identified over 60 percent of patients diagnosed with endogenous depression (Carroll, 1985). Furthermore, the DST returns to normal when depression lifts. These tests generate hope that laboratory tests might one day diagnose clinical depression. No one knows why only half of the depressed population has abnormal test results. Nor do we fully understand the significance of a positive test since the tests do not predict response to drug therapy. Nevertheless, endocrine studies remain a promising area for depression research.

Neurophysiology represents still a third attempt to locate biological influences in depression. An intriguing area of research which captured media interest revolves around the connection between light and depression. One form of depression manifests itself cyclically in the winter months and has earned the diagnostic label of *seasonal affective disorder* (SAD). One theory suggests that the production of the biological regulator melatonin is affected by light and that some individuals have a defective system for its production. This defect is associated with recurring severe depression during winter. Sufferers expose themselves during this period to a source of artificial light which relieves the depression for some.

Biological Treatments

The most common form of biological treatment today is antidepressant medication. Antidepressants probably represent the greatest number and variety of *psychotropic* medications (i.e. to improve psychiatric functioning) in use for a single disorder. As Figure 5-4 illustrates, many medications are available. The earliest antidepressants were the so-called *tricyclics*, named for attributes of their chemical structure. The more common ones include imipramine and amitriptyline and are referred to as the first generation of tricyclics (cf. Figure 5-4 for trade names).

The exact mechanism whereby they relieve depression is not known but most scientists believe they regulate the neurotransmitters. These medications do not create a feeling of euphoria or a "high" as do the anti-anxiety agents. They have low abuse potential. Their disadvantage is their slow onset. Many require two to three weeks to take complete effect. Also, some users experience unpleasant side-effects such as dry mouth, drowsiness or constipation. The fact that they are lethal in overdose renders them risky for suicidal persons. Second and third generation tricyclics have eliminated some undesirable aspects of the earlier drugs, but many believe they are less effective than the earlier ones. While each new compound has its advantages, none appears at this time to be patently superior.

The *MAO inhibitors* represent an entirely different class of anti-depressants. American psychiatrists tend to use them much less regularly than other drugs due to their dietary restrictions. The MAO inhibitors will cause a severe drop in blood pressure when taken with foods containing tyrosine (found in Chianti wine, gefilte fish, and certain cheeses). The term "MAO inhibitor" stands for an enzyme that is involved in the re-uptake of neurotransmitters. Inhibiting the re-uptake of the transmitters at the synapse results in increased circulating levels of a transmitter. The drugs' original use was for tuberculosis, but were tried in depression since they relieved depression in tubercular patients.

Other drugs commonly used for treating depression include lithium, which was discussed above under bipolar disorder, and Xanax, a Valium-like drug which has antidepressant features as well as anti-anxiety ones. The disadvantage of Xanax is that it has abuse potential similar to Valium. Lithium is sometimes used in combination with tricyclic antidepressants for bipolar patients who suffer from debilitating depression, and for unipolar depressed persons who have a family history of bipolar disorder. One complication is that the tricyclic will occasionally trigger a manic episode and therefore requires close monitoring. Less frequently used for depression are the neuroleptic drugs (cf. Chapter 7) which treat schizophrenia. Nevertheless their antipsychotic properties render them useful for depressive events involving psychotic features such as delusions or hallucinations. The tricyclics or MAO inhibitors rarely eliminate the psychotic symptoms alone, but are often used in combination with neuroleptics (e.g. Haldol, Navane).

In addition to their therapeutic delay, a major problem with the antidepressants is that there are no criteria for determining who will benefit from which type. Despite the wide array of available drugs, treatment procedes in trial and error fashion. Since a legitimate trial requires two to three weeks, experimenting with even a few may discourage the patient from seeing any benefit. Some efficiency is possible through blood tests which measure antidepressant levels. The clinician then regulates dosage to reach standard therapeutic levels, thus removing some guesswork out of prescribing.

Finally, *electroconvulsive therapy* (ECT) is a treatment for se-

---

Figure 5-4

Common Medications for Depression

TRADE NAME	GENERIC NAME
Adapin	doxepin
Amitid	amitriptyline
Amitril	amitriptyline
Asendin	amoxapine
Aventyl	nortriptyline
Desyrel	trazodone
Elavil	amitriptyline
Endep	amitriptyline
Imavate	imipramine
Janimine	imipramine
Ludiomil	maprotiline
Marplan	isocarboxazid
Nardil	phenelzine
Norpramin	desipramine
Pamelor	nortriptyline
Parnate	tranylcypromine
Pertofrane	desipramine
Presamine	imipramine
Prozac	fluoxetine
Sinequan	doxepin
Tofranil	imipramine
Vivactil	protriptyline
Wellbutrin	buproprion
Xanax	alprazolam
Zoloft	fluoxamine

SOURCE: *Medications for Mental Illness.* United States Department of Health and Human Services. DHHS Publication No. (ADM)87-1509. Alcohol, Drug Abuse, and Mental Health Administration. Printed 1987.

---

vere, intractable depression which has not responded to antidepressants, and which may represent a potential suicide risk to the individual. Despite its proven effectiveness this therapy often triggers strong negative feelings in the general public. The reader may have viewed the Academy-award-winning movie "One Flew Over the Cuckoo's Nest" which portrayed ECT as a Nazi-like punishment. The city council of Berkeley, California even outlawed its use within the city. ECT is used today in only a handful of psychiatric hospitals for less than 1 percent of all treated depressions. Patients receive ECT only when psychotherapy and standard antidepressant medications have failed. ECT itself was discovered through clinical observations of depressed epileptic patients who curiously improved following *grand mal* seizures. ECT induces a seizure experience through the administration of small amounts of electricity to one or both sides of a person's head. Modern ECT methods employ both an anesthetic to eliminate conscious trauma as well as muscle relaxant medication to prevent orthopedic damage. A typical pattern is to administer ECT two to three times a week for a course of three to five weeks. Generally only one series is given but a second series may ensue if no improvement occurs. The individual may experience mild memory loss for some events during the weeks of treatment but with no permanent neurological impairment.

Psychosocial Theories

Psychoanalytic theory developed by Freud conceptualized depression as stemming from childhood loss of an emotionally significant person (e.g. a parent). The person incorporates the love object into oneself, yet when the love object dies or leaves, rage develops. The child, however, is not able to admit consciously that he or she is enraged with the lost parent, but turns this anger inward on the self, thereby generating depression. The child may experience symbolic loss as intensely as physical loss. A symbolic loss might include long separation from or deprivation by the caretakers.

Attachment theory, developed by British psychiatrist John Bowlby and American psychologist Mary Ainsworth (1991), builds on psychoanalytic concepts but adds research insights from ethology, the study of animal behavior. Bowlby believed that early attachment of the child to his or her mother is a major influence on the child's psychological health. He saw parallels in animal research which demonstrated the importance of attachment itself. Psychologist Harry Harlow, for example, in his now classic study, showed that an infant monkey prefers clinging to a cloth surrogate monkey without milk to a wire monkey with milk. In short, attachment itself is a primary reinforcer. Studying children separated from their parents by natural events convinced Bowlby that children experienced behavioral and emotional effects identical to clinical depression: affective numbness, reduced psychomotor activity, and periodic anger outbursts to name but a few (Bowlby, 1980). These symptoms, ethologists suggested, are adaptive for the lost young animal in the wild. Remaining still and not drawing attention to its abandoned state helps the lost creature avoid predators. Attachment theory suggests that early losses affect later interpersonal relationships. Two common patterns resulting are *overanxious attachment* and *compulsive self-reliance*. Paradoxically, both interpersonal styles create problems in maintaining intimacy which, in turn, leaves the person vulnerable to depression.

Learned helplessness theory grew out of the experimental laboratory research of psychologist Martin Seligman and his colleagues (Seligman, 1975). Animals which were unable to turn off random punishment made no attempts in later experiments to avoid pain *even when they had access to escape strategies.* A typical experiment involved yoking two rats together so that each received the same amount of electric shock. One animal, however, could turn off the shock for both by a response such as pressing a lever. Both animals, therefore, had received the same amount of shock. Later, when put in a situation where all the animals could escape shock, only the "helper" rats did so, whereas the "helpless" ones simply endured the pain. Seligman then developed analogous research designs with humans which, in his opinion, corroborated the notion of learned helpless and depressed mood. The limitation of this theory, to date, is the absence of specific remedial strategies for depressed victims.

Behavioral theories of depression (Lewinsohn, 1974) emphasize the origin of the disorder in loss of reinforcers for the depressed person. The notion of loss pervades Freud's theory as well, but behaviorists do not relate the loss to remote historical events. Rather they stress the meaning of the person's current failure to place himself or herself in potentially reinforcing environments. If a person does not interact with rewarding social events, then a vicious cycle of negative mood, inertia, ongoing deprivation and continuing depression results. The source of this loss may be voluntary or due to life events such as death, unemployment, divorce, career change, etc.

Cognitive theory of depression was originated by psychiatrist Aaron Beck (Beck, 1991) and views depression as related to negative thoughts which are unrealistic and dysfunctional. Beck postulates that depression is related to the person's *negative triad:* a negative view of the self, a negative view of the world, and a negative view of the future. These dysfunctional cognitions alter emotional reality the same way that sunglasses alter visual reality. Beck lists a variety of cognitive distortions which trigger "depressogenic" thoughts. An example of one such negative assumption is over-generalization. I over-generalize, for example, if at breakfast I spill orange juice on my new outfit and say to myself, "This has ruined my whole day." This idea will likely result in feeling depressed for the rest of the day. If I keep a sense of perspective about the spill and see it as an unfortunate but discrete event, my upset will be brief.

Beck maintained that these negative thoughts have three qualities. First, they are *automatic*, in that they arise instantly in response to an event. Second, they are *involuntary*, so that they are not under the person's intentional control. Third, the negative thoughts and explanations appear *plausible* to the person, despite how exaggerated they appear to an outside observer.

In addition to cognitive distortions which are responses to single events, individuals also hold more generalized negative assumptions which Beck terms *schemas*. These schemas are pervasive maladaptive assumptions which leave the person vulnerable to depression. A schema might include the notion that to feel good about myself I require affirmation from everyone around me. Such a schema predisposes one to depression given the inevitability of displeasing some people we encounter. Readers familiar with the work of Albert Ellis and his general theory of rational-emotive therapy (RET) will notice the similarity between Beck's theory and RET.

Interpersonal theory (IPT) of depression (Klerman, Weismann, Rounsaville, and Chevron, 1984) sees depression as related to interpersonal conflicts. IPT links its theoretical heritage to the school of social psychiatry exemplified in the work of Harry Stack Sullivan (1953). Sullivan viewed emotional disorders as distorted perceptions of social relationships. The purpose of therapy is to help alter these distortions. Group therapy, for example, could facilitate correcting these distortions through the powerful process of *consensual validation*. Multiple persons share a unified perception of the person, thereby correcting the person's distorted view of self. IPT also points to empirical research which demonstrates the importance of psychosocial factors in depression. An example of this is the community survey of Brown and Harris (1978) which found that a buffer against depression for women is the presence of an intimate, confiding relationship. Women lacking this support were at a much greater risk for experiencing depression. IPT, therefore, emphasizes the importance of roles and relationships in triggering and maintaining depression.

Roles and relationships include the following: loss of a significant other, widowhood, vocational transition, marital conflict, and any significant interpersonal dispute with family, friends, or employer.

Psychosocial Treatments

In this section we consider the main non-biological therapies for depression. The criterion for discussion is that the treatments developed strategies specific for depression. For this reason generic approaches such as client-centered therapy or psychoanalysis are not discussed. Psychoanalysis, however, has a stated rationale in dealing with depression, namely uncovering the childhood loss, awareness of the self-directed rage, and acceptance of anger toward the original love object.

Cognitive therapy (CT) originally grew out of depression treatment (Beck, Rush, Shaw, and Emery, 1979) and has developed treatments for a wide range of problems, including anxiety, anger control, relationship problems, sexual dysfunctions and personality disorders, to name a few. CT has proven readily translatable to both mental health professionals as well as the general public. Psychiatrist David Burns' self-help book *Feeling Good* (1980) is based on cognitive principles and has sold millions of copies. Implementing CT involves teaching the client to become aware of his or her dysfunctional cognitions, ideas, or expectations which trigger depression. Once the person gains awareness of the distortions, the next step is to replace the dysfunctional cognition with realistic or adaptive ones. If I am prone to depression because I have excessive standards of perfection in my work, then CT would help me change my beliefs to accept good efforts. Although therapists use CT in a structured manner, enormous variation exists. Prototypical CT calls for assigning patients written homework in the form of daily self-monitoring of dysfunctional thoughts, and written exercises to reformulate dysfunctional assumptions into adaptive, realistic ones.

The structured nature of CT lends itself nicely to empirical research which indeed has validated its effectiveness in treating depression. Studies of CT have found it to be as effective as medication in some populations, and in other studies adding to the efficacy of antidepressant medication when used in combination. Below we will review the results of CT in a large study of the treatment of depression conducted by the National Institute of Mental Health.

Behavior therapy emphasizes increasing the number and intensity of positive reinforcers for depressed individuals. An example of this is the self-help book *Control Your Depression* (Lewinsohn *et al.*, 1978). In this model, depression is associated with a lack of positive reinforcers in a person's life. This deficit is assessed through the Pleasant Events Schedule. The schedule helps the individual notice deficits in pleasurable activities which may currently maintain the depression. The person then charts daily the total number of pleasant events along with a mood self-rating scale. Most persons will see a correlation between feeling depressed and the lack of positive events. They will also notice that a positive mood goes along with multiple pleasant activities. Behavior therapy then assists the person to increase pleasant events through setting priorities, scheduling, finding social supports, etc. This approach may be quite valuable for persons suffering from the "inertia factor" which characterizes many depressed persons. Some succumb to a feeling of vegetative inactivity. Yet, when coaxed by supportive family or friends to participate in social events, many depressed persons experience mood improvement, at least temporarily.

Interpersonal therapy (IPT) aims to alter the person's interpersonal conflicts, thereby ameliorating the source of depression. IPT lacks the structure of either CT or behavioral approaches but has a similar focus on here-and-now as opposed to historical events. One source of depression is the role conflict one feels after divorce or in widowhood. Rather than spend time analyzing the childhood conflicts which caused the anxious dependency, the focus of IPT would explore the woman's current ambivalence and sense of inadequacy. At the same time, uncovering personal resources and strengths would enable her to cope in her new situation. IPT does not make use of homework assignments but might utilize role-playing or behavioral rehearsal in the session to help the person view herself from another dimension.

In concluding this section a special word is in order regarding the findings of the most elaborate outcome study ever undertaken regarding the treatment of depression. The National Institute of Mental Health (NIMH) undertook a collaborative study of the treatment of depression involving multiple clinicians in different sites across the United States (Elkin *et al.*, 1989). The study investigated the effectiveness of two specific forms of psychotherapy—cognitive therapy (CT) and interpersonal therapy (ITP)—with a standard antidepressant (imipramine). The study employed only experienced therapists who were trained by experts in the different treatment modalities. To control for possible placebo effects with the use of medication, a fourth treatment group was included: a pill-placebo group in double-blind fashion (i.e. neither the patient nor the psychiatrist knew which patients were receiving medication and which were receiving a placebo). Both the imipramine and pill-placebo group included clinical management, meaning that the clinician spent considerable time (e.g. at least 20 minutes) listening to the patient's complaints and providing support. This has special bearing on interpreting the results.

Once the treatment conditions were set up, 239 non-bipolar, non-psychotic depressed outpatients were randomly assigned to one of the four treatment conditions. Patients were seen for a total of 16 weekly sessions; 32 percent of the sample dropped out of the study after starting with attrition not significantly worse for any treatment group.

The results of the study are complex, and no single statement is comprehensive. Rather, there are several outcomes:

1) Patients in all four groups improved significantly from pre-treatment to termination, including the placebo condition.

2) While the antidepressant caused more rapid positive change than either psychotherapy condition, *at termination* no significant differences existed between it and the two psychotherapies.

3) Neither psychotherapy was significantly better than the other.

4) For *severely depressed* patients the *antidepressant* and the *interpersonal therapy* were significantly better than the pill-placebo condition. Improvement here is measured by percentage of patients who recovered from their depression. With severely depressed patients not a single one recovered in the pill-placebo condition.

5) With less severely depressed patients no differences existed for any of the four conditions including the pill-placebo category.

The investigators intend to conduct follow-up at 6, 12, and 18 months following treatment to see whether the specific treatments have short-term versus long-term effects. One may speculate, for example, that teaching a coping skill such as CT or IPT would have long-term effects on depression whereas limited use of medication would not.

The NIMH study at this point suggests that for mild to moderately depressed outpatients specific cognitive, interpersonal, and supportive therapy is as effective as antidepressant medication. Severely depressed persons, however, benefit from either imipramine or a specific interpersonal brand of psychotherapy. Cognitive therapy or empathy/support alone was not effective for severely depressed persons—at least not after 16 weeks.

Pastoral Care of Depression

Biological psychiatrist Mark Gold has written an excellent popular exposition of biological theories and treatment of depression which he titled *The Good News about Depression* (Gold and Morris, 1988). The authors did not intend to catch the eye of pastoral counselors specifically with their title but, ironically, there is good news about the helpfulness of pastoral counseling in the recovery process from depression. I have outlined the complicated and divergent approaches to depression from the clinical sciences to alert pastoral ministers to the multiple avenues available to them in caring for the depressed. Throughout this book I maintain the importance of a scientist-practitioner model in psychopathology as opposed to a merely anecdotal model. In this way the pastoral recommendations are rooted in a body of research demonstrating the effectiveness of certain strategies. With this criterion in mind the following suggestions are offered for the pastoral care of the depressed.

1) *Refer the severely depressed.* Unless you are credentialed to treat this difficult group, make an appropriate referral. Severe depression would include suicidal risk, psychotic depression, and/or unremitting vegetative symptoms as noted. Optimally the professional is one who is skilled in diagnosing psychopathology, e.g. psychiatrist or clinical psychologist. More severely depressed persons should be offered the option of pharmacotherapy for symptom relief. (An excellent guide to making the referral process a therapeutic experience has been written by pastoral counselor Dr. Sharon Cheston [1991].)

2) *When you refer, stay in touch with the depressed person and the health care provider.* Whatever the effectiveness of the treatment strategy itself, the pastoral minister remains a significant person in the depressed person's environment. The minister plays an important role as a psychosocial buffer assisting the person in managing what may be an overwhelming environment. The minister may need to translate the person's condition to family, friends, or workplace, thereby reducing the stressors he or she has to handle.

3) *Help negotiate interpersonal disputes.* Research on interper-

sonal therapy reveals that effectively resolving interpersonal conflicts facilitates the recovery process. The pastoral minister is well situated to assist in resolving disputes, e.g. through marital or family counseling, encouraging assertive behavior in the work setting, and teaching problem-solving skills.

4) *Assist in role transitions.* Again, IPT research demonstrates how abrupt developmental passages affect mood: widowhood, single parenthood, death of a child, children leaving home, unemployment, entering the workforce for the first time or after a long absence, serious illness, and retirement are only a portion of transitions associated with depression. Here the minister can assist role transitions through direct counseling or through the establishment of support networks using the organizational structures of church and synagogue. Given the lack of confidence and the "inertia factor" associated with depressive withdrawal, guiding outreach ministries to these populations is recommended. The church or synagogue cannot make up for all the isolation of modern living. However, an assessment of each congregation's needs should highlight its high risk groups to buffer the many complications of these passages.

5) *Incorporate spiritual images to facilitate recovery from depression.* Cognitive therapy research demonstrates the effectiveness of correcting unrealistic beliefs and expectations with adaptive ones. On this basis psychologist Rebecca Propst (1988) found that using religious images as part of a treatment approach to altering dysfunctional self-statements led to more rapid mood recovery than the use of non-religious but rational self-statements in a matched group of depressed persons. Religious imagery may be a powerful resource to help the believer obtain perspective.

In an interesting case example of this approach, psychologist William Miller (1988) describes the treatment of a depressed seminarian whose negative mood was related to perfectionist expectations about himself. Miller found that by using the seminarian's own faith system he was able to challenge the automatic negative thoughts with such "rational" alternatives as "Even Jesus took time to rest and recharge" and "If I want to serve, I also need to take care of myself" (p. 6). As a result the person's mood improved. This illustrates how we can understand faith as "cognitions," and how a balanced spirituality may alleviate depression by challenging the person to change perspective. Readers interested in this approach should consult Propst's book on this topic for guidance so that it does not come across as mere "positive thinking."

Depression, then, need not be the devastating "sickness unto death" that it often is. Too often its devastation is due to the victim not recognizing its signs until fast in its grip. As journalist Richard Cohen (1990) has described it, "depression is like drought, which begins the first day after the last rain—but who knows it then?" (p. 11). Enlightened pastoral ministers may truly carry the good news of healing to these victims through identification, intervention and referral.

Chapter 6

Addictive Disorders

I. Impact of Alcohol and Drug Problems on Society
II. Effects of Alcohol and Other Drugs on Central Nervous System
III. Common Terms and Definitions in Addiction
IV. Etiology
V. Addiction Treatment
VI. Pathological Gambling
VII. Addiction and Pastoral Care

Impact of Alcohol and Drug Problems on Society

Alcohol Problems

The most recent *Special Report to Congress* (1990) by the U.S. Department of Health and Human Services highlights the impact of alcohol on the United States throughout this section.

Epidemiology. In the U.S. per capita consumption of alcohol for persons 14 and older amounts to 2.54 gallons of pure alcohol. This is roughly the equivalent of 50 gallons of beer, 20 gallons of wine, and 4 gallons of distilled spirits. If those who abstain are taken into account this amounts to about 4 gallons per person.

Prevalence of Drinking Problems. The Epidemiological Catchment Area survey found that about 13 percent of the American adult population experienced alcohol abuse or dependence at some time in their lives. About half of these had an additional psychiatric disorder. In one year (1987) more than 1.4 million Americans were treated for alcohol problems. Three-fourths of those in treatment were men.

Drinking Patterns. In the U.S. 32 percent abstain from alcohol, one-third are light drinkers (less than 5 standard drinks per occasion), and one-third are heavy drinkers (5 or more drinks per occasion at least once a week). Although two-thirds of adult Americans drink, 10 percent of drinkers (6.5 percent of the total population) account for

50 percent of alcohol consumed. As high as these numbers are, they represent a continued decline in drinking since a peak in 1981, and this represents the lowest amount since 1970.

Adolescent Drinking. Since the young become the future, the patterns of teenage drinking are instructive on recent trends. According to the U.S. government's annual survey of high school seniors 92 percent have tried alcohol, 62 percent were current drinkers, 38 percent had consumed 5 or more drinks in the past two weeks (presumably an intoxicating amount), and 4 percent drink daily. Again, as high as these numbers are, they, too, point to a dramatic decline in consumption over the past 6–7 years. Experts suggest that increased awareness of the harmful effects of alcohol is responsible for the decline. Despite the decrease, evidence from the same survey shows that many students remain naive or indifferent to alcohol's effects. One-third saw no problem with having 4–5 drinks daily, and one-third reported that nearly all their friends got drunk at least once a week.

Women and Alcohol. All population studies continue to report that male alcoholics outnumber females by a two to one margin. This probably represents its true prevalence in the population and not under-reporting women's problems due to greater stigmatization. Nevertheless issues related to the expansion of social opportunities for women as well as information about fetal alcohol syndrome raise important questions.

One question concerns women in the workplace, with some predicting that as women's employment patterns start to resemble men's, their alcohol intake and associated problems would also increase. This presumes increased stress for women related to multiple roles as parent and worker outside the home. This prediction so far has not come to pass. Indeed, the women who do exhibit problems associated with alcohol are those who are unmarried but living with a partner, or those with a heavy drinking partner or spouse. Researchers have concluded that drinking problems for women are associated with *role deprivation* rather than *role overload.* Thus, women in the traditional role of mother and homemaker and women employed full-time have less risk for developing alcohol problems than unmarried women living with a partner or single women working part-time.

Ethnic Groups and the Homeless. In the U.S. blacks have high rates of abstention and low rates of heavy drinking. Despite this modest consumption as a population they are at high risk for health problems in which alcohol is a factor. They are at excessive risk for cirrhosis, heart disease, and cancers of the mouth, larynx, tongue, and esophagus. Hispanics are characterized by high rates of abstinence and high rates of heavy drinking in comparison to the American population at large. Asian-Americans have the highest rates of abstention, the lowest rates of heavy drinking, and the lowest levels of drinking related problems. The American Indian and the Alaska native vary widely in their alcohol use. Overall they have high mortality rates from causes likely to be alcohol related including cirrhosis, accidents, suicide and homicide. Nevertheless, some native American groups have extremely low rates of alcohol consumption.

Adverse Social Consequences. About one-half of the 46,000 deaths annually in the U.S. due to traffic accidents are alcohol related. These accidents are the single largest cause of death for persons between the ages of 5 and 34. About 38 percent of drownings in the U.S. are alcohol related.

Alcohol use and alcoholism represent a severe risk for suicide. Fifteen percent of alcoholics commit suicide and 20–36 percent of suicide victims have a history of alcohol abuse or were drinking immediately before their death. Alcohol use is more of a factor in those suicides which appear impulsive rather than premeditated.

Family violence correlates highly with alcohol use. Alcohol dependence is more than three times more likely involved with spouse abuse than non-dependence (44 versus 14 percent). Recent studies also prove that alcoholic women are much more likely themselves to be the victims of spouse abuse than their non-alcoholic counterparts.

Interaction studies of alcoholic families indicate that drinking *increases* rates of negative verbal behavior toward their wives for male alcoholics who are episodic drinkers. However, for male alcoholics who are continual drinkers, drinking actually *decreases* rates of negative verbal behavior toward spouses. This may explain why some spouses tolerate alcoholic marriages.

Economic Costs. Comprehending the economic costs of alcohol problems challenges the intellect to about the same degree as comprehending the national debt. For 1983 alcohol problems cost the U.S. 116 billion dollars, of which 71 billion was for lost employment and 15 billion for health care costs and treatment. The projected cost for 1990 is 136 billion dollars and 150 billion for 1995. On the individual level, the annual health cost for an alcoholic is 100 percent higher than for a non-alcoholic peer, with the difference reaching 300 percent in the 12 month period before formal alcohol treatment.

The significantly higher medical costs for *non-alcoholic family members* living in an alcoholic household compared to their peers in normal households prove the high price of living with an alcoholic. Medical costs are particularly high for family members of the alcoholic in the year preceding treatment, remain high for a year after treatment, and then gradually match their counterparts in non-alcoholic households. It is, therefore, not without reason that alcoholism and other addictions are often called a "family disease."

Effects of Alcohol and Other Drugs on Central Nervous System

Current convention in the substance abuse field employs the term "alcohol and other drugs" when referring to substances of abuse. Accordingly, this text will use the abbreviation "AOD" when referring to substances of abuse as a general class.

This section will examine the basic physiological mechanisms of AOD to help the reader understand their effects as well as appreciate the power of addiction.

Clinicians and researchers divide AOD into three distinct groups according to their effects on the central nervous system (CNS), i.e. the brain and related physiological processes. These groups, while distinct, are not clear-cut, especially as newer mind-altering drugs emerge from the laboratory. Some, such as PCP or MDMA (Ecstasy), have properties of more than one class, as we shall see. The major groups include central nervous system *depressants, stimulants, and hallucinogens.*

CNS Depressants

This group's primary effect is to slow down or depress CNS functioning. Their effect is to slow down heart rate, respiration and cognitive activity. The major substances in this group are:

1) *Alcohol.* All alcoholic beverages contain the same chemical ingredient whether it is beer, whiskey, liquor or wine. All cause intoxication and none prevents alcoholism.

2) *Tranquilizers.* Sometimes called the "minor" tranquilizers, they differ from the antipsychotic medications such as Thorazine which are termed "major" tranquilizers. Unlike the minor tranquilizers the so-called major tranquilizers are non-addicting and have low abuse potential—although they may have serious side-effects. These minor tranquilizers include drugs such as Valium, Xanax, Librium, Dalmane, Halcion, and Ativan. They are prescribed appropriately for a variety of conditions such as anxiety, sleep problems, epilepsy, depression, movement disorders, and gastrointestinal problems, as well

as many other medical disorders. In the United States non-psychiatric physicians write most prescriptions for these drugs. *Iatrogenic addiction*, becoming addicted after following legitimate medical use as opposed to non-medical use, is a serious problem with this group. Some estimates suggest that as many as one person in ten who uses these substances experiences difficulty reducing usage.

3) *Sedative-Hypnotics.* As their name suggests, these drugs have as their primary effect sedating and sleep-inducing properties. Common ones include Phenobarbital, Seconal, Nembutal, and Tuenal. They are hazardous in combination with alcohol and account for more emergency room incidents than any other drug category. Alcohol and barbituates were responsible for the death of actress Marilyn Monroe. Physicians avoid prescribing them when safer drugs are available.

4) *Opiates and Synthetic Opiates.* Opiate drugs are derived from the poppy plant and include opium, heroin, morphine, and codeine. Many synthetic opiates, i.e. manufactured substances resembling either the chemical structure or effects of the opiates, now exist. These include Dilaudid, Percodan, Percocet, and Darvon. These drugs are important pain medications and are vital for treating cancer or managing surgical conditions. Increased concern over contracting AIDS from dirty needles has popularized opiates manufactured by pharmaceutical companies. These drugs also create risk for iatrogenic addiction. Several well-known entertainers and movie stars have gone public with their addiction following medical treatment.

CNS Stimulants

The general effect of CNS stimulants is to increase respiration, alertness, blood pressure, heart rate, and thinking. Their well-known ability to suppress appetite led to their use and abuse in dieting. This is no longer a valid medical use. Social drugs such as caffeine and tobacco have stimulant qualities. Neither tends to have the disruptive social impact usually associated with other substances of abuse. Excessive coffee drinking or use of over-the-counter caffeine pills may create a condition described as caffeinism. This involves jitteriness, tremulousness, and in some rare instances hallucinations. Tobacco use, of course, is a severe health hazard—but its impact is slow and cumulative. Its use has steadily declined in all age groups except for adolescent females who have increased their smoking rate. This fact is particularly troublesome since the risk of stroke increases for women who smoke and use birth control pills.

1) *Amphetamines.* These prescription drugs are used to treat hyperactive children and for sleep disorders such as narcolepsy. They include drugs such as Dexedrine and Benzedrine. Ritalin is chemically distinct from the amphetamines but has a similar effect. Ritalin has a calming effect on hyperactive children but a stimulating one on normal children. Methamphetamine, a generic amphetamine, is widely abused as a street drug. About twenty years ago these drugs had reached epidemic proportions as a health hazard causing many overdoses. Methamphetamine—termed "crystal meth"—may create a paranoid psychotic reaction when injected. Not even trained emergency room workers, without knowledge of the person's drug use, could distinguish the drug-induced psychosis from schizophrenia. One unfortunate byproduct of the legal crackdown on cocaine is that drug merchants are pushing smokeable forms of amphetamine as crack-cocaine substitutes. Called "ice" on the street, this simply creates an alternative form of cocaine.

2) *Cocaine.* The Indian tribes of South America chewed the leaves of the coca plant for centuries. The Incas considered it sacred and used it in their religious ceremonies. The Spanish conquerors found that Indian workers in the gold and silver mines worked harder and ate less if they chewed coca leaves. Even the church profited, since the land owners paid a tithe of ten percent on the value of the coca crop (McKim, 1986).

Europeans did not use the plant personally until the middle of the 19th century when a German chemist synthesized its active ingredient. Freud himself boosted the medical use of cocaine after personal use and marveled at its antidepressant effects. He wrote that cocaine cured alcoholism and morphine addiction and recommended the drug to his friends and family. Later, however, a close friend of Freud's became addicted to the drug, permanently changing Freud's opinion.

Cocaine also invaded popular culture through an Italian wine called Mariani which notable historical figures drank including Thomas Jefferson, Jules Verne, Henrik Ibsen, and even Pope Leo XIII who reportedly "always carried a flask on his belt" (McKim, 1986, p. 163). In the United States the popular soft drink Coca-Cola contained cocaine until 1906 with the passage of Pure Food and Drug Act. This led the authors of one popular textbook to comment that for many years Coca-Cola truly was the real thing (Davison and Neale, 1990).

The United States is witnessing a severe social upheaval in its urban areas related to the use and distribution of cocaine. In the early 1980s cocaine use increased among teenagers and young adults but had declined by the end of that decade. Nevertheless, enormous increases in crime rates in urban areas result from the use and distribution of cocaine, including the highest homicide rates in U.S. history.

Cocaine is a fast acting drug in comparison to alcohol or other drugs. For example, the *half-life* of cocaine (the time required for half the drug to leave the body) is about forty minutes compared to seven to fourteen hours for amphetamines. A special feature of cocaine for central nervous system functioning is its direct impact on the brain's reward circuitry. Most pleasurable experiences in life including food, sex, and alcohol appear to work on the brain's reward circuitry indirectly, i.e. through first engaging other physiological systems. The stimulants, and cocaine included, bypass these natural routes and link to the reward circuitry itself.

Laboratory studies show that animals will exhaust themselves to death working for cocaine. When experimenters use intermittent reinforcement schedules for monkeys and then stop the cocaine supply, some monkeys continue to press a lever up to six thousand times before giving up. Over a 30 day period 36 percent of laboratory animals will die if given free access to heroin, and 90 percent die within the same period if given free access to cocaine. Since the drug leaves the body quickly, humans experience a severe letdown. The psychological experience is similar to falling rapidly in an elevator from the third floor to the ground floor. In a rapidly falling elevator, passengers feel as if they are in the basement. Cocaine has a similar effect. This letdown induces repeated use to achieve the euphoria and relieve depression. Given these psychological and physiological effects, it is not difficult to imagine how an addictive pattern develops.

Three major routes of administration of cocaine exist. Snorting or sniffing cocaine powder through the nose (*intranasal use*) is the most common form. Other routes include injection or smoking. To smoke cocaine, however, the user must alter the form of the cocaine powder or else the active ingredient simply burns off. To do so the user alters the powder chemically by "freeing up its base," and hence the term "freebase." Freebasing enhances the speed with which the drug reaches the brain since it flows directly from lung to brain.

In the 1980s the drug merchants invented a "ready to smoke" form of cocaine which users call "crack." Many avoided smoking cocaine due to the inconvenience of freebasing. Some methods of freebasing require volatile ingredients which are hazardous (e.g. the serious burns acquired by comedian Richard Pryor). Crack cocaine eliminates this hazard. Furthermore, the mass production of crack cocaine along with increased harvesting of the coca plant resulted in a significant drop in the price of the drug. This price drop created a larger pool of potential customers.

3) *Stimulant Dangers.* Stimulant drugs cause several health hazards. First, stimulant overdose may result in severe psychotic reactions including hallucinations and delusions. Hallucinations may take the form of hearing voices, seeing visions, or feeling objects which do not exist. Paranoia is common in stimulant use. Many drug experts believe the homicide epidemic associated with cocaine trafficking comes from the drug's paranoid effects as much as from the profit motive. Second, stimulant overdose may also be fatal. Since stimulants generate increased sympathetic nervous system arousal, they may overtax the cardiovascular system causing stroke or cardiovascular fatalities. Cocaine overdose can also induce a continuous epileptic seizure (*status epilepticus*) which causes death. The death of University of Maryland basketball star Len Bias occurred in this manner and influenced American youth to see cocaine as a killer.

The random nature of lethal overdose makes cocaine and stimulant use even more hazardous. For example, three separate groups of laboratory animals receiving the same dose of cocaine may react by a) dying immediately, b) living several months, or c) tolerating the dosage indefinitely. These effects occur for no known scientific reason. Such effects generate a Russian roulette atmosphere for using cocaine in addition to its addiction potential.

Finally, stimulants are notorious for generating depression in their aftermath. The depression makes repeated use more likely but also increases the risk for suicidal urges and behavior. As program director of a hospital addiction unit I have seen many cocaine addicts admitted for attempting suicide after a cocaine binge.

CNS Hallucinogens

Hallucinogens create distortions in sensory-perceptual experience and/or alter belief systems to the point of losing touch with reality. Hallucinations may include disturbances in vision, hearing, taste, touch, or smell. Most mind-altering chemicals will cause hallucinations if taken in overdose. Hallucinogens create these disturbances with low or "therapeutic" dosages. The drugs discussed below represent the common varieties.

1) *Marijuana.* Marijuana comes from the cannabis or hemp plant whose intoxicating effects were known long before recorded history. Some scholars believe that God's command to Moses (Exodus 30:23) to make a holy oil included the use of cannabis as one of the chosen

ingredients (McKim, 1986, p. 213). In our culture people smoke marijuana or less often eat it (in the 1960s hippies baked marijuana in brownies). Hashish is a concentrated form of cannabis collected from the resin at the top of the female plant. Marijuana is a popular drug that approximately 60 million Americans admit using at least once. The use of marijuana has declined due to general disenchantment with illegal drugs in American society.

Marijuana does not cause dramatic depressant or stimulant effects associated with either of those classes of drugs. Most users describe a dissociative-like experience with distortions of sensory-perceptual events as well as time and space distortions.

The hazards associated with marijuana use remain somewhat controversial. Dramatically harmful effects as suggested during the 1930s clearly do not occur. Users are not driven to violence or crime simply as a function of marijuana's effect on the nervous system. Some hazards are real, e.g. the high association between serious or fatal traffic accidents and use of marijuana. These effects occur either for marijuana alone or in combination with alcohol. Chronic use is associated with irregular menstrual cycles in women and in men with decreased levels of testosterone, decreased sperm motility, and decreased sperm production. Such effects are presumed to influence fertility. Furthermore, since marijuana interferes with the production of testosterone, pregnant women who smoke marijuana may be endangering fetal development in their male children.

Perhaps marijuana's most serious complication results from how long marijuana remains in the body. According to behavioral pharmacologist William McKim (1986), 20 to 30 percent of marijuana remains 3 days after use and small amounts stay 7–10 days following use. Laboratory studies prove that marijuana interferes with human learning. These latter two facts demonstrate the hazards of marijuana use during adolescence. They suggest that a teenager needs to smoke only two to three marijuana joints a week to experience continual cognitive impairment. (We will examine its effect on social development in the section below on state-dependent learning.)

2) *Phencyclidine (PCP)*. While PCP is included among the hallucinogens, it is a drug which cuts across drug classes. The initial effect of PCP stimulates the CNS, while mild to moderate doses generate the hallucinogenic effect. Nevertheless, PCP's original development was as an anesthetic with a dissociative impact. Chemists originally hoped that PCP would be a welcome addition for anesthesiology to obliterate pain yet allow the person to remain conscious. PCP worked in this respect. But the drug caused psychotic experiences in humans

through hallucinations and delusions. Federal law now prohibits manufacturing PCP, although veterinarians used it briefly as an animal tranquilizer. The problem for law enforcement officials is that manufacturing PCP requires minimal knowledge of chemistry and relatively simple laboratory equipment.

PCP is similar to marijuana in that it remains in the body's fatty tissue (brain and gonads). This lends itself to long-time storage. Detoxification may be sporadic, with the PCP addict looking well for a day or two and suddenly acting psychotic as the body releases the chemical from storage.

PCP use carries with it multiple risks. Since it actually is a CNS depressant the danger of overdose exists. However, its dissociative qualities represent the greatest danger. Since the individual experiences no pain a psychotic PCP user may be a danger to himself or herself, or to others. The most serious risk is through drowning or falls, and documented cases exist of individuals responding violently to "command hallucinations." One newspaper account told of a mother cutting the throats of her two children, a toddler and infant, to let Satan out as God commanded when she was on PCP.

Somewhat more controversial is whether PCP causes a chronic psychiatric condition which resembles schizophrenia. A few PCP users exhibit a schizophrenic-like reaction which lasts for many months or even years following PCP use. Researchers are not sure if this condition is the result of PCP itself or the interaction of PCP use in a vulnerable individual.

In giving talks on the subject of drug abuse to general audiences, I describe PCP as "nature's revenge." Many of the documented dangers of PCP were originally attributed to LSD during the 1960s. LSD rarely causes severe side-effects. Such misinformation creates a credibility gap between health care providers and young people. This gap interferes with prevention efforts. Ironically, many of the reputed dangers of LSD actually occur with PCP, and this highlights the importance of giving accurate information to the public.

3) *LSD (d-lysergic acid diethylamide).* LSD is a synthetic hallucinogen discovered by Albert Hofmann in Switzerland in the 1930s. Dr. Timothy Leary of Harvard University popularized it in the 1960s as the "peace drug." LSD is usually taken orally and is sold on strips of blotter paper with cartoon characters or other trade marks. While LSD received bad press, the harmful effects of the drug are exaggerated. LSD itself causes rapid tolerance so that users rarely repeat its use at short intervals. Indeed, most users take the drug fewer than ten times.

4) *Psilocybin.* Psilocybin comes from a mushroom grown in the southwest United States which native Americans use in their liturgical services. The number of psilocybin users probably represents a small percentage of the drug-taking population. Among hallucinogen users it has gained popularity because it is a plant rather than a chemical. Unscrupulous drug merchants will often alter non-hallucinogenic mushrooms with LSD or PCP since these drugs are easier to get. The risk of harmful effects is probable when the user does not expect an intense experience.

5) *Mescaline.* Mescaline derives from the peyote cactus and forms the sacramental basis of the Native America church, which the U.S. Congress legalized in 1970.

6) *Morning Glory Seeds* contain a LSD-like substance which causes hallucinations. Youngsters who experiment with them are unaware that seed companies spray commercially-sold morning glory seeds with fungicides containing mercury.

Mechanism of CNS Activity

The implications for research on mind-altering drugs extend far beyond solving substance abuse as a health problem. Basic research in this area has the potential to unlock the mystery of pain, the origin of our basic emotional responses, as well as understanding the puzzle of psychotic behavior such as schizophrenia. This section will try to give a flavor of this research as it relates to substance abuse.

Despite more federal spending on alcohol research than all other drugs combined, the exact mechanism for alcohol's effect on the CNS is still unknown. Alcohol does not appear to work at the neurotransmitter level directly, and some theorists suggest that alcohol alters the flow of electrical energy in the neuron. The exact mechanism for this, however, remains unknown.

Scientific exploration of the effects of opiate drugs has led to important discoveries. For many years researchers understood that the nervous system had a special affinity for opiate drugs with their capacity to reduce pain. In the early 1970s an opiate receptor was discovered. This nerve cell structure had the capacity to "catch" the opiate molecule. This discovery led to a feverish investigation to determine whether or not the body manufactured within itself a naturally occurring opiate-like substance.

If, scientists reasoned, we are pre-programmed to receive these molecules, the body must produce its own. Otherwise, animal life evolved a nervous system with a special affinity for the molecules of a single wild plant. Simultaneously, several investigators discovered substances manufactured by the body. Gradually they located a multitude of these opiate-like substances already present in the body. One researcher labeled them *endorphins.* This word combines the terms *endo*genous and m*orphine*, meaning that endorphins are endogenous morphine-like substances in the body. This suggests that the body has its own pain control system which allows us to combat fatigue and repair injury.

Many believe that these proteins hold the key to unlocking the puzzle of drug addiction. For example, if a chemical could block the opiate receptors, then the heroin addict would be unable to get high after using. Chemists have created such a drug called naloxone (trade name Trexan). Highly motivated addicts use it as part of a recovery program.

This model may hold for other substances as well. Researchers discovered benzodiazepine receptors but no naturally occurring benzodiazepines as yet. When the benzodiazepine drugs interact with their receptors on the nerve cell, they increase the effect of GABA, a universal inhibitory neurotransmitter.

Both PCP receptors and natural PCP-like substances exist within the nervous system. PCP is an anesthetic as well as a hallucinogen, so the naturally occurring PCP substance in the body may help us dissociate. Diverting attention from painful stimuli helps us adapt in everyday life or else we would regularly find ourselves overwhelmed through constant worrying. Our endogenous PCP may be one part of an essential biological defense mechanism. Also, researchers at the National Institute of Drug Abuse have found that this endogenous PCP substance helps repair damage from strokes. It would be a fitting irony to develop a healthful medical treatment from a dangerous drug.

In the same year (1990) that science discovered that endogenous PCP benefits stroke injury, researchers at the National Institute of Drug Abuse identified marijuana receptors in the brain. This discovery may help us understand substance abuse as well as the nervous system. The next step, quite naturally, will be to search for any endogenous marijuana-like substances in the body. Marijuana is an effective treatment for glaucoma, and future research might uncover the nervous system's own preventive mechanism for this condition as well as suggest alternative treatments.

The mechanism of action for the stimulants does not appear to exist as endogenous substances. Rather, the stimulants appear to operate at the reward circuitry system within the brain. Cocaine, as well as other stimulants, blocks the re-uptake of dopamine. Since the presence of dopamine excites other neurons, blocking its uptake has the net effect of prolonging the excitation.

Common Terms and Definitions in Addiction

This section briefly defines some of the more common terms in the substance abuse field.

Tolerance. Repeated use of alcohol and other drugs results in the diminished effect of the substance. Users need to take more and more to maintain the same effect. Some drugs have a rather narrow band of tolerance. Alcohol, for example, has a narrow band of tolerance between initial use and amounts used in the alcohol dependent state. Heroin and the benzodiazepines, by contrast, require proportionately greater amounts than alcohol before lethal doses will occur in dependent individuals. Many misunderstand tolerance, since folk wisdom suggests that those who "hold their liquor" are immune to serious alcohol problems. In reality, persons who have developed tolerance are exhibiting one classic characteristic of dependency.

A related phenomenon is *reverse tolerance.* Alcoholics who are experiencing major organ damage will notice a dramatic drop in their tolerance. Formerly they may have consumed up to a fifth of alcohol daily; now one to three drinks may cause intoxication. Reverse tolerance frequently happens with the aging alcoholic and often signals life-threatening physical problems.

Dependence. Chemical dependency specialists distinguish *physical* dependence from *psychological* dependence. Physical dependence exists when stopping a drug results in physical withdrawal symptoms. Psychological dependence refers to an intense felt need for alcohol or other drugs. No one-to-one correlation exists between psychological and physical dependence. An individual may become physically dependent on a pain medication yet never develop a drug problem because psychological dependence does not occur. This person simply stops using the drug after the physical illness ceases. On the other hand some drugs do not create physical dependence yet generate psychological dependence. Marijuana and the other hallucinogens are examples of this.

Cross-Tolerance. For some drugs, particularly those in the CNS depressant group, tolerance develops not only to the person's drug of choice but to similarly acting drugs. This happens even if the person has never used those drugs. An individual tolerant to one form of pain medication will be tolerant to other varieties as well. We advise recovering alcoholics who are preparing for medical or surgical procedures to inform their physicians of their alcoholic histories. This permits physicians to adjust pain medications in light of increased tolerance. Otherwise they may not receive enough medication for pain relief. This represents an added burden to the alcoholic who must consider the dangers of relapse through a different mind-altering substance.

Cross-Dependence. A person physically dependent on alcohol or other drugs can substitute another drug in its same group to prevent physical withdrawal. Physicians use this principle to achieve detoxification from alcohol or other drugs. The use of Valium or Librium to detoxify an alcoholic applies the principle of cross-dependence to prevent serious withdrawal problems. Logically one could detoxify with alcohol as happened in earlier times, but the benzodiazepines are safer and more efficient. Alcoholics and drug addicts use this principle to manage their own addiction. If a heroin addict runs out of money for heroin, alcohol represents an inexpensive if not satisfying alternative. Similarly, an alcoholic who drinks heavily after work may discover that Valium or Xanax will take the edge off early morning withdrawal. This allows the person to function normally until evening when drinking resumes. Some addiction patterns—and this is common with women—represent a "mix and match" form of chemical dependency. Here the individual uses different drugs regularly rather than extensive use of one favorite substance. Such a pattern might involve Valium during the day but alcohol at meals and in the evening. This picture may become more complicated when pain medications for "legitimate" medical conditions are also present.

Addiction. Addiction is probably more loosely defined than any other in our mental health vocabulary. During an average day a person may hear the word addiction refer to every condition from heroin use to excessive intake of Hershey Kisses. Some professionals argue that addiction should refer only to conditions generated by alcohol or drugs. Others use the word to refer to a general tendency to engage compulsively in dysfunctional behavior. (This chapter takes the position that alcoholism, drug abuse, and pathological gambling at least qualify for this term.)

For many years the substance abuse field maintained that addiction referred to individuals who experience both tolerance and physical dependence. Evidence grew that marijuana, cocaine and other drugs might not create physical dependence, yet severe impairment resulted from their repeated use. Therefore, the modern concept of addiction refers to the repeated use of a substance which results in significant problems in *any* of the following areas: physical or psychological health, occupational functioning, social or interpersonal relationships, family life, legal or financial issues. While this definition may look excessively broad, it combines both repeated use and adverse consequences. Furthermore, the definition avoids the potential for denial that other definitions foster. For example, the definition does not comment on whether an individual needs to use alcohol or drugs daily. Nor does it require physical dependence as essential, although the broader definition would include it. In short, this modern definition of addiction cuts into much of the rationalizing which occurs among substance abusers.

Cross-Addiction. Cross-addiction refers to a pattern in which addicted individuals acquire an addiction to drugs outside of their favorite group. For example, high rates of alcoholism among heroin addicts illustrate the principle of cross-dependence since alcohol is in the CNS depressant group. But if a heroin addict acquires cocaine addiction, this exemplifies cross-addiction, or switching to drugs in another group (CNS stimulants).

Cross-addiction is common among drug abusers. Adolescents, in particular, begin their drug careers by sampling a variety of substances with different CNS effects. As a result these youngsters get hooked on altering their mood rather than to a favorite drug. Gradually, with increased financial resources and lengthier experimentation, they will focus on a single substance. However, the current pattern is for users to sample a variety of drugs and alcohol. As a result most rehabilitation programs have become "ecumenical" about the individual's drug of choice. Separate programs for alcohol or drug abuse have almost disappeared, since polysubstance addiction is the norm today rather than the exception.

State-Dependent Learning. This principle from experimental psychology plays an important role in understanding the challenges facing the recovering person. Briefly, this principle shows that learning takes place in a specific context and we exhibit learned skills best in situations which resemble the original learning environment. Some learning skills (e.g. reading) occur in many aspects of life and generalize across many situations. Behavior learned in an intoxicated state does not generalize to a sober state. Recovering alcoholics tell humorous stories about losing items such as their wallets during alcoholic blackouts. One patient told me he lost his car in an alcoholic blackout and only found it when he got drunk again.

The impact of this principle hits adolescents and young people who face developmental tasks daily. To take but a single example, we noted that marijuana is stored in brain tissue, thereby impairing memory and learning. If the youngster smokes only three marijuana joints a week, academic dysfunction is likely, since the substance takes several days to leave the brain. Furthermore, since adolescence is a critical period for learning developmental tasks such as social communication and interpersonal skills, the marijuana user might feel inadequate when trying these behaviors while *not* under the influence of the drug. This suggests that those starting their alcohol and drug use in adolescence will have fewer tools available in the recovery phase than those who develop their addictions at a later developmental stage.

Etiology

Psychologists William Miller and Reid Hester (1989) list eleven distinct addiction models. Obviously an in-depth exploration of all eleven models is far beyond the scope of this chapter. Nevertheless, some familiarity with the more important models will show the diversity of opinions prevalent. While some models are contradictory, the treatment field itself is quite eclectic. Treatment providers often use strategies from distinct systems despite their own theoretical orientation. For example a counselor might use the Comprehensive Drinker Profile to obtain a situational analysis of the client's drinking behavior with an alcoholic who is also attending AA. This use ignores the fact that the drinker's profile derives from a learning theory analysis of alcoholism while Alcoholics Anonymous represents the disease model. In the addiction field most counselors are shamelessly pragmatic and lose little sleep over using techniques which may have evolved from contradictory theories. However, only the most grandiose counselor would try to integrate all eleven models.

Moral Model. A moral model maintains that excessive alcohol use is the result of a weakness of will power or a loss of personal responsibility, or, in a religious context, the result of sin. Moral models held sway for most of human history and are now enjoying some resurgence (e.g. Peele, 1989).

The advantage of this model is that it highlights personal responsibility in the decision to use alcohol or drugs. Peele justly points out that too often people use their addiction to exonerate immoral behavior. The disadvantage to the model is that focusing on will power alone often creates a mental obsession. This obsession then generates a high tension level itself which often leads to drinking or using drugs.

American Disease Model. From this perspective, addiction is a chronic, progressive illness which, untreated, leads to death or serious physical or psychological illness. In this model addicts are different because they respond differently to alcohol or drugs than do non-addicts. This implies a constitutionally abnormal relationship to alcohol or drugs, much the way a diabetic responds abnormally to sugar.

Treatment in this model involves following the philosophy of a Twelve-Step program through self-help groups such as Alcoholics Anonymous and Narcotics Anonymous. The advantage of this model is that it provides a coherent framework for understanding self-defeating and compulsive behaviors over which the addict experiences little control. Paradoxically, many discover that when they surrender the notion that they *should* have control over their drinking, they then begin to exercise limited control. A further advantage is a worldwide fellowship of participants who reinforce this view and who are available to other struggling members. The disadvantage is that dropout rates are high and many are uncomfortable with the avowedly spiritual emphasis in the program even though AA is non-sectarian.

Characterological Model. This model, represented by psychoanalytic approaches, points to the underlying personality in explaining the cause of the person's addiction. Traditional psychodynamic approaches view alcoholics as exhibiting excessive oral dependency traits, with therapy helping to work through this conflict. Other approaches might simply state that excessive alcohol or drug use is a coping device to work through painful experiences such as lack of assertiveness, fear, depression, poor self-esteem, or parental conflict.

The advantage of this model is that it looks at long-term developmental issues which, if not addressed, could potentially trigger relapse. The disadvantage is that this model may downplay the significance of the addiction itself, viewing it as symptom rather than cause of the addict's difficulty. An extreme example of this was a patient who told me he was in psychoanalysis for eight years and often spoke of his alcoholism but his drinking was never discussed directly by this therapist. Several years later he met his therapist in a social situation and told him that he had joined AA and was now sober. The therapist patted him on the back and said he was really glad the patient finally came to that decision!

Learning Theory Model. According to this model a person learns excessive substance use through the same laws of learning as other behavior. Learning theory points to a variety of influences leading to excessive use: tension reduction, the biological reinforcement of the chemical itself, the enhanced sense of control provided, or watching role models use alcohol as their predominant coping device. Implicit for many learning theorists is the controversial notion that some addicted individuals can control their drinking or drug use (Miller and Hester, 1989).

The advantage of learning theory is its emphasis on empirical methods such as a rigorous assessment. Taking time to perform a comprehensive analysis of an addict's strengths and weaknesses yields considerable rewards and leads to practical strategies for treatment. The disadvantage of learning theory today is mostly political. Many mainstream treatment professionals dismiss learning theory out of hand because it aligned itself with controlled drinking advocates. Learning theory evolved from experimental psychology, and psychologists as a group are under-represented as addiction treatment providers. Psychology as a discipline, however, continues to make significant research contributions to the substance abuse field.

Biomedical Model. This model is the scientific arm of the disease model—working toward locating its etiology in specific physiological sources.

Hereditary theories remain prominent for alcoholism. Sons of alcoholics are three to four times more likely to become alcoholics than sons of non-alcoholics. About one-third of all alcoholics will have an alcoholic parent and about 25 percent of male alcoholics will have an alcoholic father. Clearly alcoholism runs in families. Nevertheless, as research psychiatrist Donald Goodwin, himself an investigator of heredity in alcoholics, likes to point out: speaking French runs in families but is not hereditary.

Goodwin's (1981) own studies of adopted children reveals that even when adopted male children of alcoholics are raised by non-alcoholic parents their rates of alcoholism far exceed rates in the general community. Adopted daughters of alcoholics raised in non-alcoholic homes have no higher incidence of alcoholism. However, when adopted girls are raised by alcoholic parents they have much higher rates of depression whether or not their biological parents are alcoholic.

Sons of alcoholic parents, therefore, are more prone to alcoholism whether they are raised by alcoholic or non-alcoholic parents. Daughters of alcoholics raised in alcoholic families are more prone to depression but not alcoholism.

Cloninger (1987) has recently delineated two types of inherited male alcoholism. Type I or *milieu-limited alcoholism* begins after age

25 and is associated with low novelty-seeking and high harm avoidance and reward dependence. Type II, *male-limited alcoholism*, starts before age 25 and is associated with personality traits high in novelty-seeking but low in harm avoidance and reward dependence. Type II alcoholics are sensation seekers who frequently are antisocial personalities, impulsive, with poor interpersonal relationships. Type I represents individuals who begin drinking much later in life with passive dependent personalities. This research may lead to early identification of young people at high risk for alcoholism. A disadvantage is needless concern over specific alcoholic offspring, since most children of alcoholics do *not* grow up to be alcoholic.

Sociocultural Model. A sociocultural model highlights the importance of social attitudes toward using alcohol or drugs. For example, changes in teenagers' perceptions of the risks of alcohol and drugs is related to decreased substance use. This model also emphasizes the role of supply on people's drug use. A strong relationship exists between higher alcohol beverage taxes, decreased use, and declining cases of cirrhosis.

Other examples of this model include studies of alcohol use among ethnic groups. Cultural values strongly influence consumption. Low rates of alcoholism exist among Jews and Italians while high rates exist in the Irish and Northern Europeans. Some might see an argument for a genetic influence in these facts. However, when these groups emigrate their rates of alcoholism *change to resemble the rates in their new country.* Rates of alcoholism for the Irish in the United States are less than in Ireland while rates for Italians in the United States increase.

This model points to the importance of social influence on health-related behavior. It suggests that cultural attitudes in the media, schools, and religion can play a strong role in influencing members in appropriate alcohol use. It also points to the power that government has in moderating consumption through taxes or other means of regulation.

Summary. The above theories represent a modest portion of available models for understanding addiction. The reader may sense a situation similar to the poem of the ten blind men describing an elephant each from his own perspective. Each is partially accurate but altogether false.

Some have proposed a *public health model* to incorporate multiple dimensions (Miller and Hester, 1989). In this model a health problem is seen as the interaction of the *host* (person), the *setting* (environment), and the *agent* (alcohol/drugs). No one variable fully explains the illness in this model. A public health model in addictions would acknowledge many factors, including: 1) (*host factors*) genetic predisposition, personal expectancies about substance use, individual personality variables, coping skills for dealing with stress, and fetal alcohol syndrome; 2) (*setting factors*) family history of addiction as role models, environmental deprivation such as poverty or lack of opportunity, social or cultural bias; and 3) (*agent factors*) intoxicating property of alcohol/drugs, and specific central nervous system effects. Whatever approach one takes, only a comprehensive model allows a holistic appreciation of this devastating biopsychosocial disorder.

Addiction Treatment

Each model has developed treatment methods consistent with its theoretical framework. Miller and Hester (1989), in an extensive review of the empirical data, conclude that "there is no single superior approach to treatment for all individuals" (p. 11). These authors further state that some treatments have shown promising results in research studies but the field has no clear-cut criteria for matching type of clients to specific treatments. Discussion of treatment of addictions could easily fill volumes. We will divide treatment approaches according to treatment setting and to intervention type.

Treatment Setting. Several settings are available, with outpatient treatment providing the most extensive service. Both private and public outpatient facilities are available, but waiting lists are common for public facilities.

The advantages of outpatient treatment include cost effectiveness and minimal disruption to the client's occupation and family life. Outpatient treatment permits observation of the client's reaction to the "real" world as tensions occur naturally. A disadvantage is that the client remains in the environment associated with the addiction. Some may not have adequate skills to remain abstinent. Furthermore, clients may deceive their counselors about their drinking or drug use to avoid consequences from external sources (e.g. court-mandated treatment as a substitute for criminal charges). Random urinalysis for drug and alcohol use is often necessary to prevent deception and may increase the cost of treatment. Nevertheless, outpatient treatment is the treatment of choice initially, especially in the absence of acute medical or psychiatric risks (e.g. severe withdrawal or violent behavior directed toward self or others).

If one or two weekly sessions are not enough to support absti-nence, intensive *day or evening programs* provide closer supervision and yet keep the client in the community. When child care programs are adjunctive to these settings, parents can maintain employment during treatment. Such programs operate as either step-up facilities when outpatient treatment fails or step-down facilities when residen-tial treatment ends. Few such programs existed until recently, but cost management efforts by health insurance companies provide an incentive to develop them as alternatives to expensive inpatient treatment. Since this trend is continuing, many communities are de-veloping day or evening programs.

Residential programs grew rapidly during the 1970s and 1980s, particularly in the private sector. Based on treatment formulas pio-neered in Minnesota, the so-called "Minnesota Model" provides a standard 28–30 day structure. The model follows the disease con-cept for addiction or "chemical dependency." The treatment mix combines detoxification, education about chemical dependency through lectures and audiovisual aids, daily group therapy, individual counseling, family therapy, and participation in Twelve-Step self-help groups. The treatment setting is a general hospital or a "free-standing" (i.e. not hospital-aligned) residence with as few as twenty or as many as several hundred residents.

More comprehensive are "dual diagnosis" programs in psychiat-ric hospitals for addicts with co-existing psychiatric problems. Since the Minnesota Model views addiction as a medical disorder, residen-tial programs are staffed with general medical personnel as well as addiction counselors. Dual diagnosis programs, on the other hand, exist for addicts with severe psychiatric disorders as well. The staff includes psychiatrists, psychologists, and social workers, as well as addiction counselors. Patients may receive psychotropic medication such as antidepressants or antipsychotics. Psychological testing and psychotherapy are also available. These programs additionally pro-vide many aspects of standard residential treatment, including educa-tion, group therapy, family therapy, and Twelve-Step meetings.

About 10–15 percent of chemically dependent persons seeking treatment will require *medical detoxification.* Alcohol withdrawal may be life-threatening for those experiencing severe withdrawal (*Delirium Tremens* or DTs), including disorientation, hallucinations, or delusions. About 10 percent of those experiencing *delirium tre-mens* will die even in the finest medical facility. Medical detoxifica-tion usually occurs in a hospital setting and takes from two to ten days depending on the drug. Occasionally complications arise from seizures (with the central nervous system depressants) or violent behavior (PCP). Xanax has a complicated withdrawal pattern which triggers seizures if withdrawal occurs abruptly. Most chemically dependent persons do not require medical intervention for withdrawal, but medical evaluation and monitoring is customary even with social detoxification.

Deciding which treatment setting is best for a client requires careful assessment. The lack of criteria regarding effectiveness of treatment type complicates the process. When no medical complications exist, most would suggest outpatient treatment first. Residential or dual diagnosis programs follow failure of outpatient treatment. Medical problems or risks of physical injury to self or others usually require an inpatient setting. Repeated failure of outpatient treatment is often enough reason to attempt more intensive treatment. Even residential treatment may fail if a dual diagnosis is a contributory factor. In these cases comprehensive psychological evaluation will assist arranging appropriate placement.

Abstinence Treatment Intervention. Two general intervention strategies dominate the treatment field. One group focuses on abstinence control strategies with its immediate aim to get control of drinking/drug use. The second group focuses on the broader range of problems which contribute to addiction and whose resolution will reduce relapse. In the first category we will consider pharmacological treatment and behavioral therapies.

1) *Pharmacological Intervention.* The most widespread pharmacological treatment in the addiction field is disulfiram (*Antabuse*) for alcoholism. The alcohol enzyme breaks down in two steps. The first step breaks alcohol into acetaldehyde and thence into harmless carbon dioxide. Acetaldehyde is highly toxic to the system but breaks down so rapidly that it causes no harm. Disulfiram prevents the change from acetaldehyde to carbon dioxide, thereby causing the system to poison itself. If a person drinks with Antabuse in the system a toxic reaction occurs causing severe nausea and vomiting.

The alcoholic takes disulfiram to prevent drinking. As clinicians will tell the alcoholic, "You need to make only one decision a day—to take your medication. Otherwise you have to make a hundred decisions a day not to drink." Disulfiram's advantage is that it helps break the compulsive drinking pattern by giving the alcoholic breathing room to develop coping skills without the distraction of continual relapse. Its disadvantage relates to depending on the pill alone rather than working on the problem areas likely to trigger drinking. Nevertheless, disulfiram has helped many alcoholics as one part of a comprehensive treatment plan.

Pharmacological treatment exists for opiate dependency (heroin, Dilaudid, codeine, etc.). Two distinct types of treatment exist. The first strategy substitutes one addicting drug for another. These *agonist* drugs reduce the craving for the addicting substance and enable the person to maintain employment and family life. The addict obtains the substitute drug in clinics which monitor its use. Methadone, a synthetic drug similar to heroin, is distributed to heroin addicts in methadone maintenance programs. Legal dispensation of methadone eliminates the need to seek illegal sources of the drug and allows the addict to remain employed and maintain family life. Research documents remarkable decreases in criminal behavior for heroin addicts on methadone maintenance.

Another pharmacological treatment for opiate dependence includes *antagonists* which block the euphoria or "high." One such drug is naltrexone (trade name Trexan). Naltrexone occupies the opiate receptors which have an affinity for pain reducing substances. A pain reducing substance works on the receptor site as a key turns in a lock to open a door. Naltrexone occupies the receptor space much as wax might fill in a keyhole. The heroin is not able to occupy the same receptor space so it cannot "turn the key" to open the door to euphoria. The addict will not get high on even massive amounts of heroin.

Scientists expect to develop treatments for all addicting substances which work at receptor sites. Although antagonist treatment is available only for the opiates, treatment for PCP, the benzodiazapenes, and marijuana may follow. Even pharmacological treatments, however, require motivation. Indeed the major drawback of naltrexone therapy is that fewer than 10 percent of all heroin addicts agree to it.

Chemical aversion therapy for alcoholics straddles pharmacological and behavioral treatment. In a controlled hospital setting, physicians inject the alcoholic with a drug (Emetine). The patient then looks, smells, and tastes the preferred alcoholic beverage. A severe drug reaction immediately follows, resulting in nausea and vomiting. Several trials are repeated over the course of hospitalization which generates a conditioned aversive reaction to drinking. The description of this treatment process sounds unappealing to the consumer, yet outcome data shows considerable effectiveness.

2) *Behavioral Interventions.* Abstinence control behavioral strat-

egies include covert sensitization and stimulus control. Covert sensitization creates an unpleasant reaction to the idea of drinking/using drugs by having the client imagine a repulsive image associated with drinking or drug using (Rimmele *et al.*, 1989).

Stimulus control procedures base their strategies on thorough assessment of the person's drinking or drug use, calling particular attention to the antecedents and consequences. When client and counselor identify these patterns they develop strategies together to narrow the circumstances surrounding use. Similar ideas are used in weight reduction programs as well. To overcome a late night potato chip binge habit, the first stimulus control strategy is keep them out of the home. Members of Alcoholics Anonymous coined their own version of stimulus control with the slogan, "If you don't want to slip, stay out of slippery places."

Broad-Focused Treatments. All treatment seeks to eliminate problem drinking or drug use. Some focus on broader issues beyond the immediate urge to use. They focus on specific potential conflicts (e.g. family issues) or attempt to outline a program for living (self-help groups).

1) *Self-Help Groups.* The oldest and most well known self-help group is Alcoholics Anonymous (AA) which is over fifty years old and the source of the Twelve-Step approach. Many other self-help groups have copied the AA model (e.g. Narcotics Anonymous, Gamblers Anonymous, Overeaters Anonymous, etc.). No doubt most readers are acquainted with AA, so we will not belabor its influence or methods. For those interested in the spiritual foundation of AA, a riveting historical account is E. Kurtz's *Not God* (1979) which the author condensed and updated as *AA: The Story* (Kurtz, 1988).

Self-help groups try to provide both a fellowship and a program for living. The Twelve Steps are a means to overcome the "character defects" associated with addiction. Regular group meetings encourage immediate abstinence control, and members select a "sponsor" who mentors the member through initial abstinence. The disadvantages of Twelve-Step programs are high dropout rates and the initial discomfort many feel with the program's spiritual language. (Most pastoral ministers would view this spiritual dimension as a strength.) Although AA staunchly maintains a non-sectarian philosophy, some have difficulty seeing AA's distinction between spirituality versus religion. Indeed, in the United States several recent court cases have ruled that federal or state governments may not compel alcoholics to attend AA, on the grounds that such coercion violates constitutional rights for freedom of religion.

2) *Marital/Family Therapy.* Ever since Jackson (1954) described seven stages of adjustment to alcoholism in the family, clinicians acknowledge the importance of family treatment for both the addicted person and significant others. These stages include: 1) attempts to deny the problem by keeping up a front; 2) attempts to eliminate the problem by organizing family to control the addiction and fool outsiders; 3) disorganization—a period when family members are overwhelmed and begin to question their own normality; 4) attempts to reorganize despite problems—the non-addicted partner takes control and isolates the addicted person from assuming family responsibility; 5) efforts to escape problems—the spouse may separate along with the children or the marriage may end altogether; 6) reorganization on the part of the family—the non-addicted partner and children reconstitute themselves as a family; and 7) recovery and reorganization of the whole family—if the addict achieves recovery and partners renegotiate roles and duties within the families.

Most readers are familiar with the destructive impact of addiction on families. The self-help sections of bookstores burst with titles on topics related to adult children of alcoholics, codependency, or recovery from dysfunctional families. These ideas grew out of family work with alcoholics. Two major themes emerged from this work: a) certain attitudes and behavioral responses toward the alcoholic by family members tended to make matters worse, and b) growing up in an alcoholic family scarred many children.

From the first theme the concept of "enabler" emerged (Kellerman, 1973). An enabler is an individual who unwittingly allows the alcoholic's denial to continue through silence or covering up the alcoholic's misdeeds. At first the term coalcoholic described this behavior but gave way to the term codependent. This refers to the alcoholic-like behaviors engendered in significant others who interact closely with the addict. In this sense addiction becomes a "family disease." The popular literature on this subject has moved away from changing codependent behavior for the sake of the alcoholic to overcoming codependent behavior for the personal growth of the family members.

The second theme triggered a distinct but eventually converging movement on behalf of adult children of alcoholics (ACOA). Early clinical writers on this subject (Black, 1982; Wotitze, 1983) identified distinct personality patterns resulting from growing up in an alcoholic family. This movement ranks as the fastest growing self-help organization in history, gathering thousands of participants within less than a decade.

The movement, however, is not without controversy. While some alcoholic families are clearly dysfunctional, the popular literature does not nuance its conclusions in accord with empirical research. Research shows that not all ACOAs exhibit the symptom patterns. As few as one ACOA in four runs the risk of developing alcoholism. Research shows further that alcoholic families which maintain family rituals such as meals, celebrations, family events, etc. are not different from normal families. Controlled studies (Jacob *et al.*, 1991) illustrate that although alcoholic families have disturbed communication patterns, the type of disturbance is identical to other distressed family units (e.g. families with a depressed parent). A study of Roman Catholic nuns, for example, found that those who were children of alcoholics had no more health-related symptoms than nuns who grew up in non-alcoholic families. Nuns who reported physical, emotional or sexual abuse, however, reported significantly more health problems than non-abused nuns whether raised by alcoholic parents or not (Toole, 1991).

In summary, the family literature suggests that the acute stages of addiction are especially painful and confusing for families. Marital/family therapy is useful both for aiding the addicted person and for relieving the family's stress. No sweeping generalizations apply, however, to all alcoholic families, nor is every child raised in this environment emotionally crippled.

Pathological Gambling

About one to three persons in one hundred in the United States have a gambling problem according to population surveys (Volberg and Steadman, 1989). To put this figure in perspective, it is as common as schizophrenia or manic depression.

Most indicators suggest that the problem will only increase as gambling achieves greater public acceptance as a form of recreation. Some form of gambling is now legal in forty-eight out of fifty states in America. One trade publication estimates that in 1988 Americans wagered 210 billion dollars legally (Christiansen, 1989). In 1974, 61 percent of the U.S. adult population gambled. More than 80 percent of the population gambles legally today, with the total amount increasing more than 1,000 percent in the past 15 years (Lesieur and Rosenthal, 1991). Gambling is legal in 90 countries. We can get some sense of its social cost by noting that the average indebtedness for a gambler seeking treatment is $92,000 (Politzer, Morrow, and Leavey, 1985).

Numbers alone can never fully reveal the human dimensions of the disorder. A gambler's wife whom I interviewed on the CBS News show "60 Minutes" described sitting on the kitchen floor cradling her 2 year old while movers repossessed her refrigerator and remaining household furniture. She and her husband were both college graduates with professional jobs, and their only possession was a small kitchen table. She described sitting on the floor blankly wondering what to do with her last dollar bill—purchase peanut butter to feed her son or toilet paper.

While alcohol and other drugs create equally horrible stories, the challenging feature of gambling is that it represents a *purely psychological addiction.* No external agent enters the body, nor is there an overwhelming physiological experience (e.g. sex). The activity alone can generate the compulsive behavior.

Assessment. The following criteria for pathological gambling represent those proposed for the next revision of the *Diagnostic and Statistical Manual* of the American Psychiatric Association. The guidelines propose that individuals exhibiting at least four of the nine indicators receive a diagnosis of pathological gambler. They include the following:

1) *Mental preoccupation with gambling.* The person spends a great deal of time thinking about gambling, ways of betting, how to improve one's chances and efforts to get money to gamble.

2) *Increasing the amount wagered to achieve the desired excitement.* The gambler needs to wager more and more to achieve the euphoria associated with gambling. The amounts wagered are relative and limited by the person's access to money.

3) *Irritability and agitation when not able to gamble.* As the previous criterion is similar to tolerance, this criterion is similar to withdrawal. The gambler may exhibit restlessness, jitteriness, racing thoughts, easily triggered anger, as well as the physical and psychological symptoms of anxiety.

4) *Gambling as a form of relief from negative feelings or problems.* This parallels "relief drinking" in alcoholism. In this sense gambling provides relief from stressful emotional states. This effect often characterizes women compulsive gamblers. Pathological gambling in women resembles women's alcoholism patterns. That is, it typically begins later in life than men's and often serves to cope with some developmental crisis, e.g. bereavement, retirement, or role conflict (career versus family).

5) *"Chasing" losses.* The activity of "chasing" distinguishes

most pathological gamblers from social or recreational gamblers (Lesieur, 1984). Chasing is a gambling pattern which "doubles up" or "throws good money after bad" to try to recoup one's losses. A gambler down five hundred dollars on a football game bets a thousand on the next to get even. Few gamblers can sustain long periods of chasing without incurring serious social problems.

6) *Deceiving others regarding the extent of gambling.* Gamblers lie to explain away questionable activities and to conceal the degree of gambling involved.

7) *Gambling causing significant problems in important relationships, marriage, educational endeavors, occupation, or resulting in the loss of any of these.* Simply put, nothing matters more than the gambling behavior.

8) *Engaging in illegal behavior to procure money for gambling.* Theft, forgery, embezzlement, fraud, and misappropriation of funds are common. In a Gamblers Anonymous survey 20 percent (out of 150 members) had a history of criminal arrest, while in a survey of 250 gamblers treated at Taylor Manor Hospital nearly 40 percent had criminal arrest records (Ciarrocchi and Richardson, 1989).

Some gamblers meet criteria for an antisocial personality disorder (ASP) (cf. Chapter 9). Most gamblers, however, seeking help on their own or through family members are not antisocial. The urgency to gamble results in many illegal acts to get money to gamble. The presence or absence of ASP is important in that ASP has a poor prognosis with no known treatment. Pathological gambling, on the other hand, has a recovery rate similar to chemical dependency, if not slightly better.

9) *Requiring one or more persons to give money to remedy a financial crisis caused by gambling.* In the gambling treatment field this indicator is termed a "bailout." Since families or loved ones are often a soft touch for the gambler's financial needs, comprehensive family treatment is essential.

Stages in Pathological Gambling. The late Dr. Robert Custer, a Veterans Administration psychiatrist who founded the first gambling treatment program, identified several phases in the development of pathological gambling (Custer and Milt, 1985).

1) *Winning Phase.* The so-called "big win" characterizes this phase. Early in their careers many gamblers win a large amount equivalent to about half a year's income. This reinforces gambling as the royal road to an easy fortune.

2) *Losing Phase.* Eventually the law of averages catches up with

the gambler and he or she starts to lose regularly. Social gamblers tend to "cut their losses" while the pathological gambler persists despite mounting losses.

3) *Desperation Phase.* Chasing and irrational betting character-ize this stage. The gambler's behavior in this stage is frantic and may appear manic without an authentic manic-depressive disorder. This stage, in addition to massive financial losses, usually leads to severe social dysfunction and even illegal behavior.

Not all gamblers go through these stages in an orderly fashion. Some shift back and forth between stages, and at times the outsider may not easily discern the shift. Labeling a particular stage is less important than assessing the negative results of the gambling itself.

Treating Pathological Gambling. The early stages of treating pathological gambling closely resemble a crisis intervention model (Callahan, 1991). Several immediate tasks emerge (for a lengthier discussion of steps to take in pastoral counseling with pathological gamblers, cf. Ciarrocchi, 1993):

1) *Abstinence Control.* Obviously, stopping gambling is the first goal. An immediate referral to Gamblers Anonymous (GA) is the first order of business. GA involvement supports counseling goals and en-hances the prognosis for many clients. The next step is a situational analysis of the gambling behavior. Gambler and counselor identify the determinants of the gambling behavior—the who, what, where, when, how, why, how often, and what-does-it-feel-like dimensions of the gambling behavior. This analysis provides ideas for prevention, e.g. situations to avoid, necessary support systems, persons, places, or activities which will act as deterrents to gambling.

Important abstinence control procedures include direct deposit of paychecks to a responsible family member/financial manager, tak-ing away all credit cards, stopping access to bank teller machines, setting up bank accounts not in the gambler's name, asking an em-ployer to hold paychecks so that responsible family members may get them, closing out lines of credit, securing tight access to retirement accounts, children's investments, savings bonds, stocks, or other se-curities. In short, if there is a way for compulsive gamblers to get money they will find it.

2) *Resolving Financial Crises.* Positive steps include immediate budget planning for the next 30 to 60 days. Planning involves making immediate contact with creditors to enlist agreement to reduce mini-mum payments. The gambler or supporters from GA inform betting creditors that no more gambling is possible and they will receive payment at a reduced schedule.

3) *Legal Crisis.* Gamblers seeking treatment will frequently need an attorney as much as a therapist. Illegal activities include writing bad checks and obtaining loans fraudulently. Others steal from employers by misappropriating funds or illegal bookkeeping. Attorneys, accountants, or bankers "borrow" clients' funds to gamble. For self-employed gamblers, tax problems are usually present. Committing violent crimes for money is not common.

4) *Assessment of Immediate Risk.* Various studies indicate that nearly 1 gambler in 5 seeking treatment reports a previous suicide attempt (Ciarrocchi and Richardson, 1989; Custer and Custer, 1978). Although the depression may be situational, suicide may represent a reasonable solution. Assessment of suicidal potential must occur during the initial evaluation of all pathological gamblers. Co-addictions occur regularly with this disorder, and assessment of alcohol and drug use should be routine.

5) *Marital/Family Crisis.* Research on gamblers treated in a psychiatric hospital revealed that spouses measured as high on psychological tests of anxiety, depression and emotional upset as the hospitalized gamblers themselves (Ahrons, 1989). Thus, *the spouse's emotional distress is as severe as the hospitalized partner's.* The level of support, therefore, needed by family members parallels the gambler's need. GamAnon, a Twelve-Step support group for families and friends of compulsive gamblers, provides emotional support from those who have lived with similar problems. The popular concept of codependence fits families of gamblers as well. Since many spouses of compulsive gamblers are also adult children of alcoholics, they may benefit from COA support groups.

Resentment frequently grows in families as they realize the permanent change in their standard of living. Vacations are cancelled or down-scaled, dreams of sending children away to college die, and plans for a new car are postponed. If an alcoholic sustains liver damage, the tissue may regenerate; a failed bank account never does. This highlights the utility of support groups for long term recovery.

Addiction and Pastoral Care

Ministers, theologians, and pastoral counselors have contributed to the addiction field through theory building, spiritual help, and direct counseling. They have contributed to the field earlier and in greater numbers than mainstream mental health professionals (cf. Clinebell, 1978; Kurtz, 1979; Royce, 1989). AA's description of alcoholism as a threefold disease—physical, psychological, and spiritual —certainly encouraged this participation. The sources noted above provide the history and guidelines for pastoral ministry in addiction counseling. In this section we will focus on two aspects of addictions ministry: countertransference issues and working through shame and guilt.

Countertransference Issues. Countertransference refers to feelings, perceptions, or reactions in counseling which the counselor projects onto the client as a result of prior experience. Some use the term in a broad sense to include any emotional/cognitive reaction toward a client. We will use the term in that sense here.

Working with the addicted person generates feelings and expectations which often complicate the pastoral relationship (Ciarrocchi, 1987). *Negative* reactions may occur as a result of prior experience with alcoholism or drug addiction in one's own family or relationships. A past history of victimization via physical, sexual, or psychological abuse from an addicted person may generate negative feelings toward addicted persons. Some counselors or pastoral ministers do not anticipate their negative reactions until they are in the midst of an encounter.

Even without prior negative experiences the pastoral counselor may absorb the cultural bias toward addicted persons. Such biases would see the addict as immoral, lacking will power, or simply irresponsible. These attitudes impede the counseling relationship since chemically dependent persons are sensitive to judgmental feelings. Bias may also intrude if the pastoral counselor overidentifies with the suffering family and prematurely recommends physical separation or divorce. Here the counselor directs the family rather than allowing it to work through the developmental process outlined above. The decision to break up the family unit requires discernment.

Ironically a previous history of familial alcoholism may generate a *positive* countertransference. Some have seen loved ones die or deteriorate from addiction. They may have seen insensitive or poorly trained health care providers fail to help the addicted person. Now, in turn, they may tend to nurture the person excessively or fail to emphasize taking personal responsibility for recovery. Such workers prevent recovery by failing to set the necessary limits required for the healing process.

A final note pertains to those special instances when the counselor himself or herself is a recovering person. If health care workers often deny addictions, recovering persons may see it everywhere.

This may result in misdiagnosis or power struggles with those who are not ready to face their issues. A useful self-reminder for the counselor is to "take your own inventory" rather than someone else's. A nurse colleague, who is a recovering alcoholic, once modeled this when we evaluated a client who protested the label of alcoholic. Despite tons of evidence to the contrary, my colleague simply remarked, "Only you can make that diagnosis for yourself."

The Healing of Shame and Guilt. Ernest Kurtz (1981), using early psychoanalytic concepts, presents a profound analysis of the recovery process. Guilt results from a failure of *doing* which leaves us with a sense of wrong-doing. Shame results from a failure of *being* and leaves us feeling inadequate and worthless. Using a football field analogy, Kurtz compares guilt to going out of bounds on the sidelines—trying to circumvent the rules. Shame, on the other hand, results from falling short of the goal. Readers may recall the seeds of this notion from Chapter 2 in Freud's distinction between conscience (guilt) and ego-ideal (shame).

Both emotions profoundly influence the recovery process, but failing to differentiate them impedes recovery. For many addicts guilt abounds through behaviors such as infidelity, lying, stealing, fraud, use of substances during pregnancy, driving under the influence, etc. Shame issues are often prevalent but perhaps subtler: believing that one has not lived up to potential, feeling a sense of failure or worthlessness.

Distinguishing the two emotions is useful since the healing strategies are distinct. Forgiveness and repentance heal guilt while self-acceptance and recommitment are proper for healing shame. The pastoral counselor helps the client to distinguish the two emotions and is present as the client heals each. The delicateness of this process highlights the importance of working through the countertransference issues noted above. Only a non-judgmental stance by the pastoral counselor allows the client to engage in the self-confrontation necessary for healing shame and guilt.

Pathological Gambling and Pastoral Focus. The public is more likely to view pathological gambling as loss of will power rather than as a health problem. As recovery unfolds, the gambler acknowledges many behaviors which are dissonant to his or her value system. The pastoral counselor creates an accepting relationship which allows the gambler to: a) examine this behavior in the context of the addiction, b) seek forgiveness from those offended, c) re-evaluate his or her personal standard of conduct to derive further motivation to remain abstinent, and d) understand past conduct through developing a relationship with God or a higher power. This last point may evolve into a religious ritual of forgiveness-seeking as practiced by a faith tradition.

A second area of pastoral focus revolves around the meaning of money. Compulsive gamblers are not materialistic by nature. Nevertheless, they often give that appearance. The active gambler will purchase conspicuous items for gifts or personal use such as jewelry, clothes, or expensive cars. These items keep up a winning front so that bookies or colleagues will bankroll the gambler. This public image dies hard even in recovery. Often an emotional attachment remains to the meaning of money. For some gamblers money was the only symbol of affection they received in an impoverished childhood. In such cases money heals psychic wounds.

The counselor's task is to assess non-judgmentally the emotional meaning attached to money, to reflect to the person his or her view, to question its negative impact, and to explore alternative meanings.

Pastoral counselors have played prominent roles in the addiction field. Renowned clergy and pastoral ministers involved themselves early in the AA movement and made significant contributions. The field of pathological gambling treatment holds the same promise for pastoral ministry. Indeed the founder and first president of The National Council of Compulsive Gambling was Monsignor Joseph Dunn, long active in the addictions field in New York City. These historical examples highlight the multiple avenues available to the pastoral counselor in the recovery process for pathological gambling. They include pre-intervention, family support, coordination of available community resources, addressing the issues of moral lapses during the addictive cycle, and helping the recovering person to clarify values about money.

Chapter 7

Schizophrenia

I. Impact of Schizophrenia
II. Symptoms and Diagnosis
III. Etiology: Diathesis-Stress
IV. Specific Biological Theories
V. Psychosocial Factors
VI. Treatment
VII. Pastoral Implications

Impact of Schizophrenia

Schizophrenia ranks among the most costly health problems in the world for financial loss, personal suffering, and treatment intensity. In the United States schizophrenics occupy 40 percent of all inpatient mental health beds. The estimated number of schizophrenics in the United States ranges between 1.5–2 million adults. About 1 percent of our population is at risk for having the disorder. While exact costs are difficult to quantify, we can glean some idea of its impact through an Iowa study which followed up more than 500 state hospitalized schizophrenics (Tsuang, 1982). The study indicated that 67 percent never married, 66 percent were in an institutional setting (hospital or nursing home), and 58 percent could not hold a salaried job.

The tragedy of the illness is that it strikes in the prime of youth—late adolescence through the early twenties—robbing victims of a chance to establish themselves socially or occupationally. This stolen developmental period contributes in no small measure to the chronic social dysfunction which highlights the disorder. Many lack basic social competencies even after acute symptoms cease. One patient living independently following many years of hospitalization required regular feedback about table manners and personal hygiene. His colleagues arranged for cleaning personnel to arrange his laundry according to day of the week to guarantee that he would change regu-

larly. This was essential despite his having a superior IQ and a graduate degree. The flip side of these gloomy statistics is that about one-
third of treated schizophrenics maintain employment and normal
relationships.

Symptoms and Diagnosis

The actual symptoms and even the definition of this devastating
disorder remain imprecise. Even though the United States government spends millions annually on treatment and research, a comprehensive definition of schizophrenia remains elusive. Agreement exists for a narrow list of symptoms: beyond that, confusion reigns. Is
schizophrenia one disorder with various expressions? Is it one label
for many distinct conditions? Is it a label for a single genetic disorder
which varies in its expression due to the intensity of environmental
stressors? Are there one set of symptoms for the acute phase, another
for the chronic? Or do these apparently different symptom sets represent two separate disorders? We are not likely to have answers to
these questions soon despite ongoing research programs. The hallmark of schizophrenia is that cluster of symptoms we term *psychotic.*
Psychotic behavior characterizes the most severe manifestations of
mental illness. The American Psychiatric Association's official code-
book of mental disorders (APA, 1987) defines psychosis as gross impairment in reality testing. When psychotic the person creates a new
reality. Psychotic behavior includes false perceptions (*hallucinations*), false beliefs (*delusions*), and severely disorganized behavior
which indicates impairment in reality testing. Psychotic reality represents severe distortion, e.g. believing you are Babe Ruth versus believing you are a good ballplayer.

Following the DSM-IIIR (APA, 1987) we will describe schizophrenia's eight behavioral characteristics.

1) *Content of Thought.* Major disturbances in thinking characterize schizophrenia. Delusional thinking involves false beliefs which
take multiple forms. *Delusions of reference* involve giving people,
objects, or events unusual significance. The term "reference" implies
that these outside experiences in some way "refer" to the schizophrenic. They may believe that the TV anchor is talking about them
when discussing a gruesome crime. They may believe that others
control their thoughts, feelings, or behavior. Conversely, they may
believe that they have the power to influence others' thoughts, feelings, or behaviors. One schizophrenic told me, "I have a plastic film

which I can lay on young people and tell them what's right." In an interview with another schizophrenic patient I dropped my appointment book while scheduling our next session. The patient said, "I'm sorry I did that to you," though he was a good six feet away.

Other delusions include *thought broadcasting*—a belief that one's mind is a cipher from which even innermost thoughts leak out in full view. *Thought insertion* is the power to place ideas in someone else's mind. *Thought withdrawal* means that others have the power to remove thoughts from my mind.

2) *Form of Thought.* Schizophrenic language may confuse or startle the listener with its oddity—a trait that some term *cognitive slippage.* The person moves from topic to topic with little apparent connection among the ideas (*loosening of associations*) and the speech may become incomprehensible. The listener experiences confusion in trying to comprehend what appears to be a sincere attempt to communicate but is nonsensical. Some examples of loose associations from interviews I have conducted are as follows:

Clinician: "Define breakfast."
Patient: "Early time to eat before awakening."

Clinician: "Define cloth."
Patient: "Most tents are made from 100 percent cotton and material dyes."

Clinician: "How are a novel and a statue alike?"
Patient: "I like Longfellow and Hawthorne: their statue (sic) is their character, they're able to attract people."

Clinician: "Define cavern."
Patient: "A cocktail lounge I visited."

More extreme examples of *formal thought disorder* include: *neologism* (making up words), *perseveration* (coming back to a single idea repeatedly), *clanging* (rhyming speech), and *blocking* (failing to complete a statement due to losing train of thought.)

3) *Perceptual Disturbances.* False perceptions (*hallucinations*) are common in schizophrenia, with auditory hallucinations accounting for the majority. The person hears sounds or voices when no one is about. The voice may speak intelligently or nonsensically. Some voices are disparaging: a patient reported a voice frequently calling her "bitch." Some hear obscenities and accordingly may have diffi-

culty sharing the content with their counselors. *Command hallucinations* order the person to do something. Sometimes the orders are to harm oneself (e.g. "kill yourself") or others ("kill them"). Naturally these frighten the sufferer.

Some describe hearing voices as terrifying, particularly when requesting violent behavior. Others accommodate in startling ways. One patient heard voices three to four times daily when she was not taking her medication. She stated that they seldom bothered her and that "sometimes we have fun together." However, she also said that when she starts taking her antipsychotic medications, "they tend to get downright nasty, because they don't like anybody else being in control."

Less common hallucinations are visual, tactile, taste and smell. A serene hallucination involved one patient's daily Bible reading next to the river during lunchtime. He stated that the angel Gabriel would appear to him "in a white flowing robe" and interpret passages "particularly the hard parts."

4) *Affect.* The term *anhedonia*, noted in our discussion on depression (cf. Chapter 5), refers to a lack of pleasure in normally enjoyable events. This experience also characterizes schizophrenia. The lack of reactivity for both positive and negative events results in little responsivity in facial appearance (*blunted affect*) or in an unresponsive facial response (*flat affect*). Sometimes *inappropriate affect* predominates. This involves emotional responses which are either exaggerated or at variance with the social context. An individual may laugh or giggle when reporting finding as a child his or her mother dead from a heart attack.

5) *Sense of Self.* Persons with schizophrenia describe loss of a sense of self. Some note loss of boundaries as if they were outside themselves looking in (*depersonalization*). One described this experience in the following words: "Sometimes I can see myself changing (i.e. physically)." Others feel a kind of blending in or merging with objects or people. In the middle of an interview a patient asked, "Am I still here?" Whether this loss results from disturbances in thinking or developmental failure in ego identity remains unknown.

6) *Volition.* For many years researchers have speculated that schizophrenia is "frontal lobe" disease since this area of the brain appears most responsible for goal-directed behavior. Schizophrenics often cannot carry out intentions, and their behavior will appear devoid of purpose, direction, or self interest. They are unable to "execute" behavior plans, and neuropsychologists describe this as an "executive deficit." From a practical standpoint this leads to severe

motivational problems when trying to influence them to help themselves or engage in treatment. This very "loss of will" (*avolition*) discourages the patient and treatment provider alike.

7) *Impaired Interpersonal Relationships.* Poor skills in interpersonal relationships often accompany the disorder. They will appear oblivious to social cues or sensitivity to others. This apparent callousness results from a preoccupation with their own inner world and is termed *autism.* They get lost in their own world, speaking a language intelligible only to themselves. The following represents a response to my question as to why the patient was seeking help at this time: "At age sixteen after an irrational sex act with a girl something happened to my eyes and people starting calling me 'boy.' "

The person may be insensitive to personal space and will move so close that others are uncomfortable. This *asociality* creates discomfort in other ways as well. They may be indifferent to personal hygiene or table manners. Feedback alone does not remedy interpersonal deficits due to these avolitional traits.

8) *Psychomotor Behavior.* Pharmacological treatment reduces the more dramatic motor disturbances of schizophrenia. Various forms of motor disturbance include complete immobility and loss of awareness of one's environment (*catatonic stupor*), remaining fixated in one posture for immensely long periods (*catatonic rigidity*), as well as odd mannerisms and facial expressions. Some mannerisms called *stereotypy* are repeated endlessly such as a ritualistic shuffle or peculiar hand or arm movements.

DSM-IIIR Classification. The DSM-IIIR recognizes 5 distinct types. *Paranoid type* involves either auditory hallucinations or organized delusions which usually have a coherent theme (e.g. all delusions consistent with the belief that the CIA is after them). In *Catatonic type* the psychomotor disturbances are prominent. The *Disorganized type* involves severe cognitive slippage such as loose associations, incoherence, or chaotic behavior. Hallucinations and delusions may be present but as a hodgepodge without a unifying theme (e.g. the CIA, the Pope, and the Health Department are all after him). *Residual type* characterizes the disorder after the acute phases when the more dramatic or florid symptoms disappear. Nevertheless asociality, illogical thinking, and affect disturbances remain. Finally, the *Undifferentiated type* represents a waste basket category when no other diagnosis fits.

Recent Diagnostic Developments. In the past 10 years researchers have advocated another typology for the disorder which may have greater *heuristic* benefits (i.e. leading to scientific advances). This typology considers the symptom clusters as either *positive* or *negative* symptoms. One expert describes it thus:

> One idea that is currently widely discussed is the distinction between positive or florid symptoms versus negative or defect symptoms. *Positive symptoms* include those that represent a distortion of some normal function such as hallucination (abnormal perception), delusions (abnormal inferencial thinking), disorganized speech and disorganized behavior. *Negative symptoms* refer to symptoms that seem to represent a loss of normal function as opposed to an excess or distortion. Typical negative symptoms include alogia (poverty of speech and of content of speech), blunting of emotional responsiveness (affective blunting), loss of will, energy, and drive (avolition), and loss of the ability to experience pleasure normally and relate to others (anhedonia-asociality) (Andreasen, 1987, p. 3—italics mine).

The possible utility of this positive-negative distinction may relate to distinct causes, distinct pathophysiology, and perhaps distinct treatment along with prevention. Another possibility is that positive symptoms occur early in the disorder while negative symptoms represent residual effects. This requires confirmation. We will discuss these implications in the biological section.

Etiology: Diathesis-Stress

The general consensus in psychopathology is that biological/physiological causes are paramount if not exclusive in the genesis of schizophrenia. Readers are now familiar with the diathesis (vulnerability)-risk model of mental illness, and schizophrenia may best exemplify the utility of this model. Of all disorders represented in this book none may be more relevant to a biopsychosocial model. Carl Rogers, a fierce opponent of diagnostic labeling, observed after extensive research on the effectiveness of client-centered therapy with schizophrenics, "These people have something wrong with their brains" (Meehl, 1989, p. 936). The unanswered question is: "Exactly what?"

Genetics. Family studies show an increased risk for the disorder in families of schizophrenics. As stated above, the risk of schizophrenia in the general population is around 1 percent. The risk for blood relationships is as follows: 13 percent for children of schizophrenics,

9 percent for siblings, 6 percent for parents of schizophrenics, and 3 percent for grandchildren, aunts, uncles, nephews, nieces, half-brothers and sisters (Gottesman and Bertelsen, 1989; Tsuang, 1982). If both parents are schizophrenic, the risk is 40 times that of the general population.

While this may sound definitive for proving a genetic basis, the logic of research design leaves open environmental explanations as well. After all, being raised with a schizophrenic may cause enough stress to cause a breakdown. To solve this problem in interpretation, researchers employ twin studies. Geneticists study identical (monozygotic) and fraternal (dizygotic) twins in which one or both co-twins are schizophrenic. Identical twins share the same genes, but fraternal twins are no more similar genetically than non-twin siblings. The presence or absence of schizophrenia in twins should provide clues about the relative importance of genes versus environment. If genes are the major cause of the disorder, identical twins will share the disorder (*concordant*) while fraternal twins will not (*discordant*). On the other hand, if environment is the major influence, then concordance rates for both identical and fraternal twins will be similar.

Studies to date show a concordance rate of approximately 50 percent for identical twins and 17 percent for fraternal twins (Tsuang, 1982). This suggests a greater influence of heredity. Further confirmation of a hereditary influence comes from studies of the offspring of schizophrenic twins. The risk of schizophrenia in the children of schizophrenic identical twins *and* their normal co-twins *is around 17 percent for both*. So, a normal identical twin with a schizophrenic co-twin is just as likely to have a schizophrenic child as his or her sibling. Further, the schizophrenic fraternal twin has a 17 percent risk of having a schizophrenic child, but his or her normal co-twin runs only a 2 percent risk (Gottesman and Bertelsen, 1989).

All of these studies taken together suggest a general vulnerability model demonstrating an increased hereditary risk when family history is positive for schizophrenia. However, since the rate of concordance for schizophrenia is not 100 percent, environment must play an important role as well. Once again this evidence promotes a diathesis-stress model.

Specific Biological Theories

Assuming that genetic factors are paramount in its etiology, schizophrenia requires a further biological mechanism to express the illness. One may have the *genotype* for schizophrenia (the genetic vulnerability) yet never express the *phenotype* (its outward signs and symptoms). The biological trail from genotype to phenotype remains unknown although theories abound. We will look at several theories but caution the reader that none is definitive.

Brain Structure Abnormality. Typical autopsy procedures for brain study never produced any reliable differences for brains of schizophrenics from normal brains. Furthermore, as one expert notes, "there is abundant evidence that most parts of the schizophrenic brain are entirely normal" (Meltzer, 1987, p. 8). To borrow a maxim from neurological assessment, however, "the absence of evidence is not evidence of absence," meaning that gross negative findings do not eliminate the possibility of a pathological condition.

Advances in radiology including computerized scanning (CT Scan) and magnetic resonance imaging (MRI) have demonstrated that 30–40 percent of schizophrenics have enlarged ventricles and brain wasting around the cortex and ventricles (Meltzer, 1987). Some studies point to a correlation between brain structure abnormalities and negative symptoms (blunted affect, avolition, social withdrawal, etc.). Furthermore, schizophrenics with brain abnormalities frequently have poor social adjustment *before* their first major schizophrenic episode. This usually predicts poor response to medication.

In a study of persons at high risk to develop schizophrenia, researchers found two separate types of brain abnormalities (Cannon *et al.*, 1989). The first involved multi-site damage in brain areas undergoing rapid development during the second trimester of pregnancy. The second type involved damage to the ventricle area (periventricular) and is associated with birth and delivery complications. As previous researchers concluded, such damage would suggest schizophrenia expressed mainly as negative symptoms.

While brain studies of schizophrenics have promise, complete trust in this hypothesis is not yet warranted. One problem is that the studies involve quite small samples. Second, when control subjects are included (e.g. mood disorder brains), similar percentages of patients show these brain changes. The evidence at this point suggests that brain abnormalities may account for schizophrenic symptoms in a subset of patients but not all.

It appears likely that evidence for structural brain damage will eventually be found for some patients diagnosed as schizophrenic, but as evidence for the reversibility of psychopathology in many schizophrenic patients continues to emerge, the possibility that no major structural changes are present in the brains of many schizophrenics becomes increasingly likely (Meltzer, 1987, p. 9).

Neurotransmitter Theory. As the extreme vegetative symptoms in depression led many to postulate a biochemical source, so too the attentional, cognitive, and executive deficits in schizophrenia also led researchers to consider biochemical sources. In discussing anxiety, depression, and substance abuse we highlighted the centrality of neurotransmitters in explaining many nervous system problems. Since potentially hundreds of transmitters exist, identifying any single culprit or combination is a monumental task. The transmitter receiving the bulk of scientific attention in schizophrenia is *dopamine.* Clinicians have appreciated for several decades that amphetamine overdose is indistinguishable from florid schizophrenia. Research with volunteers discovered excessive dopamine in their system after using amphetamines.

A second line of research resulted from investigating drugs used to treat schizophrenia—the *neuroleptics.* The neuroleptics block dopamine receptors in the brain, thereby reducing the amounts of dopamine present in schizophrenia or similar disorders. Third, the neuroleptics have side-effects which mimic the neurological disease known as Parkinson's. The drug L-Dopa converts to dopamine and treats Parkinson's disease. Thus, the side-effects of the medications used for treating schizophrenia are due to a dopamine deficiency. Finally, some post-mortem studies of schizophrenic brains found increased numbers of dopamine receptors in schizophrenic brains.

These factors led one psychiatric researcher (Crow, as cited in Meltzer, 1987) to postulate two schizophrenic syndromes:

(1) a *Type I Syndrome* characterized by reversible delusions, hallucinations, and thought disorder with good response to neuroleptic treatment and possibly due to increased numbers . . . of [dopamine] receptors; and

(2) a *Type II Syndrome* characterized by frequently unremitting negative symptoms (flat affect, social withdrawal, poverty of thought content), poor response to neuroleptics, and a presumptive etiology of cell loss structural brain damage possibly due to a viral infection (Meltzer, 1987, p. 98—italics added).

This theory has stimulated research although no final consensus exists on its merits. Indeed, the biochemical complexities grow as science discovers different types of dopamine receptors (D_1 and D_2) and puzzle over their relationships to one another. Early research indicated that D_2 was the primary culprit for positive symptoms, a finding which is less clear now. The original neuroleptics seem to influence D_2 but not D_1, while some promising new drugs appear to target D_1. The only safe conclusion at this point is how rapidly the field will develop.

Pathophysiology. Experimental psychologists have investigated many types of neuropsychological deficits. They have studied reasoning abilities, logic and planning, general intelligence, and attentional deficits with the hope of finding a specific marker for schizophrenia. A marker, in turn, might reveal information about its cause.

In the past fifteen years researchers have identified an *eye movement* abnormality among schizophrenics. When we track moving objects visually our eyes combine both smooth and rapid movements. Our nervous system balances both movements in harmony to cause smooth eye movement. Schizophrenics' eyes follow objects in a jagged rather than smooth fashion. Studies confirm this abnormality for about 80 percent of schizophrenics versus 10 percent of normal subjects (Holzman, 1987). Neuroscientists believe that this deficit results from a failed inhibitory mechanism in the nervous system related perhaps to the frontal or parietal brain area. While this abnormality is found in some neurological diseases (e.g. Parkinson's), the intriguing finding is that 45 percent of family members of schizophrenics also manifest it. Only 10 percent of the relatives of nonschizophrenic psychiatric patients manifest the condition. Scientists believe that this may represent a marker which may ultimately shed light on the abnormal physiological processes underlying schizophrenia.

Psychosocial Factors

A diathesis-stress model is multi-causal and as such recognizes the importance of environmental as well as biological influences on the development of schizophrenia. Since the concordance rate (rate of co-existing disease) in identical twins when one co-twin has schizophrenia is less than 100 percent, environment must play some role in the etiology of the disease. We will discuss several possible psychosocial influences on the development of schizophrenia.

Children of Schizophrenics. About 10–16 percent of children of schizophrenics develop the disease themselves. Ongoing studies of these high risk children hope to identify those likely to become schizophrenic. Research so far is only marginally useful. Studies in infancy show that no single deviant behavior pattern relates to later schizophrenia but a general pattern of deviance exists. In middle to late childhood (10–13) some attentional and information processing deficits relate to eventual psychiatric symptoms, while those with normal processing did not develop symptoms (Goldstein, 1987).

Stressful Life Events and Schizophrenia. If schizophrenia is not entirely biological in origin, stressful life events might play a role in triggering the disorder. From the 1950s clinicians have implicated family life stressors as important in the etiology of schizophrenia. One prominent example was the so-called *double bind theory* which linked disordered communications with schizophrenia. In this theory parents communicate regularly by messages which are contradictory at the verbal and emotional level. The classic example in the literature describes a young schizophrenic patient meeting his mother on visiting day at the hospital. He approaches her eagerly but she stiffens as he tries to embrace her. When he backs off she criticizes, "Aren't you happy to see your mother" (Bateson, as quoted in Davison and Neale, 1990). Double bind theory as well as other early family theories has two major problems. First:

> . . . the data on which theories were based did not justify such sweeping conclusions and the family therapy models that emerged from them did not appear effective in curing schizophrenia (Goldstein, 1987, p. 176).

A second problem was that such theories "had the unfortunate side-effects of alienating the relatives of the schizophrenic patient and increasing their sense of guilt about the disorder" (Goldstein, 1987, p. 176). Part of the reason for this alienation is that theorists stated that these disordered communication patterns predated the onset of schizophrenia. This view oversimplifies what current developmental psychologists maintain:

> It is now recognized that children have unique biologically based individuality that has a powerful impact on the type of parenting behavior elicited by the child as well as determining the impact of variations in parent behavior on the child at various stages of development (Goldstein, 1987, p. 176).

Family communication patterns, therefore, are bi-directional. Disordered communication patterns are as likely to *result* from interacting with a seriously disturbed family member as they are to *cause* the disturbance.

With this caution in mind, newer studies focus on two types of stressful family processes. One is disordered communication and the other is negative affective climate. The negative affective climate is termed high expressed emotion (EE). It includes both a hostile and intrusive interactive style on the part of family members toward the schizophrenic. Studies suggest both EE and disordered communications relate to first episodes of schizophrenia. Right now the evidence is correlational, which means we cannot be sure of the cause of the relationship. Does A cause B, B cause A, or an unknown X cause both A and B? More promising, however, is the practical aspect of this research—mainly changing communication patterns in high EE families. As discussed below under treatment, changing family environments from high EE to low EE significantly reduces relapse rates for schizophrenics.

Treatment

In this section we will discuss two general interventions: medication and psychosocial treatments.

Pharmacotherapy. The class of drugs used to treat schizophrenia and other acute psychosis is the neuroleptics. The most used antipsychotic drugs in the United States are thioridazine (Mellaril), haloperidol (Haldol), chlorpromazine (Thorazine), trifluoperazine (Stelazine), thiothixene (Navane), and fluphenazine (Prolixin) in that order, and they account for more than 90 percent of all prescribed anti-psychotics (Wysowski and Baun, 1989). Controlled research as well as clinical practice confirms the benefits of these drugs for treating schizophrenia. Relapse rates without medication run as high as 80 percent for schizophrenia, whereas relapse with medication ranges from 8–40 percent—a significant improvement (Tsuang, 1982).

A major difficulty with neuroleptics is their side-effects. Parkinsonian-like symptoms include stiffness in facial muscles, tongue, arms, and legs, and general restlessness which may prevent the person from sitting still. Impotence in males and upward fixation of eyes are also possible. To reduce these symptoms, physicians prescribe anti-Parkinsonian drugs (e.g. Artane and Cogentin) along with the neuroleptics. Neuroleptics may cause a serious neurological syndrome *tardive dyskinesia*. This is an unremitting condition involving lip smacking, tongue protrusion, grimacing, and side-to-side chin movements. No cure for this condition exists, so it represents a major concern for those using neuroleptics continuously.

Neuroleptics are effective in reducing the positive symptoms of schizophrenia—including the acute psychotic signs such as hallucinations and delusions. They are less effective in remediating negative symptoms such as avolition or social withdrawal. A new drug, Clozapine (Clozaril), reportedly is more successful in targeting negative symptoms as well as positive ones. The drug is controversial since its manufacturer has sought to reduce liability through strict control over its dispensation and monitoring. One side-effect is blood dyscrasia which is potentially fatal and the company requires regular blood monitoring by its own representatives. This results in an expensive package to the consumer (approaching $10,000 annually) and therefore remains a barrier to widespread use. For example, one would expect such a drug to benefit the typical chronic state-hospitalized schizophrenic, yet few states could afford to treat more than a handful at this cost.

The problem of unpleasant side-effects from neuroleptics leads to non-compliance by many patients. One solution for non-compliance is the invention of long-acting injectible forms of the neuroleptics (*depot neuroleptic*). For example, instead of taking multiple pills daily a patient receives a single injection every 2–4 weeks at a doctor's office or clinic. This relieves pressure on family members who often have to oversee medication compliance.

Psychosocial Treatment. To date, most research indicates that verbal psychotherapy alone is not effective in the treatment of schizophrenia. Insight-oriented and client-centered therapies, in particular, do not prevent relapse when used alone. In fact, intensive therapy appears to have a toxic effect in stimulating relapse (Tsuang, 1982). Two interventions prevent relapse. The first is social skills training which teaches the person practical strategies for interpersonal functioning: e.g. conversation skills, conducting a job interview, assertion skills, refusing unreasonable demands, paying compliments, etc.

The second target is family intervention. As noted, high expressed emotion in families correlates with increased relapse rates. While not blaming family members, research indicates that psycho-educational interventions, which reduce the amounts of criticalness and over-involvement by family members, also reduce relapse. Indeed, one study found that by combining family management, social skills training and drug therapy, no relapse resulted in their study group in one year (Hogarty *et al.*, 1986).

Pastoral Implications

Dealing with schizophrenia as the foregoing suggests can overwhelm the most idealistic and enthusiastic helper. Until a cure is found, we all have severe limits on our effectiveness in helping its victims. Nevertheless, we can assist schizophrenics and their families in several ways.

1. *Maintain Balance.* Schizophrenics do poorly with either overstimulation or understimulation. Overstimulation results in feeling overwhelmed and may trigger an acute relapse. Understimulation results in the triumph of the negative symptoms resulting in total loss of motivation and complete social withdrawal. Effective care involves walking a thin line between constant nagging versus ignoring them. Avoid controversy whether in the political or theological arena. They are not the audience for trying out new biblical or theological interpretations. Nor should one challenge their own religious positions even if heterodox. Rather, an action-oriented ministry serves their needs best—one that relates via prayer and ritual. The message should be that the God of your understanding loves and supports you in your pain and confusion. The religious symbols will have more healing power than creeds or intellectual disputations no matter how much the schizophrenic desires such pursuits.

2. *Be Practical.* Complex psychological strategies are unnecessary. Rather support the basics of life—a quiet place to pray, to recreate, to work. If congregational resources exist, create non-stressful part-time employment or volunteer work. If the individual acts inappropriately, private verbal feedback is helpful. Role playing helps if he or she lacks skills to solve problems. Praise and positive acknowledgment in social interactions will help when not overdone. If the person has no family, developing a volunteer program to assist with daily needs would be especially supportive. Be willing to be a liaison with treatment providers and give feedback to the providers when appropriate.

3. *Support Families.* Families with any chronic illness undergo considerable stress, and this is no less true for families of schizophrenics. Often family members, particularly parents, blame themselves for the patient's illness. They may have the proverbial "little

knowledge" which leads to dangerous guilt—perhaps believing they caused the disorder through bad parenting or bad genes.

Family members will often neglect themselves while caring for the ill member. They restrict their own social relationships and outside interests, which leads to burnout and depression. The pastoral minister may wish to point out how counterproductive this is for both patient and family. What helps the schizophrenic is balanced involvement—some attention and some time alone. Family members are usually good at the former but poor at the latter. The pastoral counselor may need to support family members when the disorder requires hospitalization or even civil commitment. These are painful decisions for families and they often look for encouragement that they are "doing the right thing" and do not wish to act punitively. Pastoral support can reassure families that they must provide stewardship when the person can no longer care for himself or herself.

4. *Advocacy.* Issues of social justice arise in advocacy for this population since as a group it lacks the means to speak effectively on its own behalf. Groups of family members, patients and concerned citizens have formed advocacy groups (e.g. National Alliance for the Mentally Ill) to promote a variety of causes on behalf of the seriously mentally ill. They lobby state and federal legislators for treatment, research, and prevention services. They also lobby for community resources to improve the quality of life for these victims. Pastoral ministers and counselors have the resources to support such endeavors through personal commitment as well as the technical and material support available through their congregations.

Chapter 8

Sexual Problems

Religion and Sexual Problems

No more sensitive area in pastoral care exists than sexual behavior. Since the dawn of recorded religion each one has outlined a code of sexual behavior. Some have argued that religion ought not to exert this control. They see religion as a force for sexual repression and eventual emotional disturbance.

Evidence for this viewpoint comes from literature, medicine and law. Countless works of art have as their theme the destructive impact of sexual guilt on religious people (e.g. Hawthorne's *The Scarlet Letter*, the plays of Tennessee Williams). In sexual medicine we have the detailed outlines from Masters and Johnson (1970) for their treatment program for sexually dysfunctional couples. They found that religious orthodoxy accounted for more treatment failure than any other variable. The criminal justice arena tells us that child sexual abusers (pedophiles) frequently are religiously conservative, and a surprising number of clergy have been arrested and convicted for this crime.

One complication in discussing this topic requires distinguishing sexual pathology from sexual morality. Sexual practices condemned by religious moral codes do not automatically meet criteria for an official psychiatric disorder. Presumably all religions condemn pedo-

146

philia which psychiatry also sees as a disorder. On the other hand, some religious groups forbid homosexual acts and masturbation which are not psychiatric disorders. In this chapter we discuss disorders coded officially by the American Psychiatric Association. We also discuss homosexuality due to its prevalence as a pastoral care issue.

The religiously committed person may feel defensive about religion's negative impact on sexuality. My own position is that evidence for a direct causal link between religion and sexual disorders does not exist at this time. The Masters and Johnson data establish only a relationship (*correlation*) between religious orthodoxy and failure of sexual treatment. As any student of introductory statistics appreciates, correlation is not causation. For example, a high correlation exists between number of churches and high crime rates. Just as a third variable is the likely explanation (population density), so too variables other than religion may explain treatment failure rate. Perhaps the cause is a rigid personality style which tends to latch on to a belief system in a closed manner. Such a person would not likely be open to the techniques of sex therapy. Also, to demonstrate the negative effect of religion on sexual functioning, logic requires studying a *nonpatient* population to see whether a greater proportion of believers develop serious sexual problems than non-believers.

Indeed, a recent study employing a national probability sample in the United States (Greeley, 1991) indicates that religion may play an important role in sexual satisfaction in marriage. Contrary to popular myths a majority of married couples in the United States rate their marriages as highly satisfying. One of the variables most closely associated with a satisfying sexual relationship is that the couple prays together. In fact praying together was strongly associated with sexual play and adventurousness within the marriage. This study highlights the hazards of drawing sweeping conclusions from treatment groups. Further, it highlights a main theme of this book—that religion's potential for positive mental health remains untapped. Imagine the impact if all pulpits preached that praying together could improve a couple's sex life.

This chapter discusses sexual problems and issues in light of scientific and clinical concepts. At the conclusion we will return again to the relationship between religion and pastoral care to offer specific guidelines for pastoral counseling.

Paraphilia: Description

The Concept of Paraphilia. Paraphilia is sexual behavior outside the ordinary or "normal" patterns within society. The word derives from the Greek *para* meaning altered or outside of, and *philia* meaning love. Psychiatry had used the words perversion and deviant to describe this class of disorders. The terms changed to avoid the pejorative connotations in the original labels. In a paraphilia the sexual behavior or arousal occurs in response to three content areas: a) children or non-consenting adults, b) non-human objects, and c) sexual acts which cause suffering or humiliation in others or oneself (APA, 1987, p. 279). The essence of a paraphilia is that the person sexually acts out the impulse or is distressed by the sexual urges.

Social values obviously enter into the definition of a paraphilia. For many years mental health professionals considered homosexuality a psychiatric disorder, but officially changed that notion in 1973 when the American Psychiatric Association removed it from the diagnostic nomenclature of mental illnesses. Nor does the APA's diagnostic manual name literally all paraphilias described in the literature. Moral judgment may also influence a counselor's opinion as to what is paraphiliac or non-paraphiliac. behavior. Some sexual behavior termed kinky in the vernacular may actually be normative statistically (e.g. oral sex), while other behavior is neither normative nor frequent (e.g. bestiality).

Psychologist John Money (1986) coined a word to describe the driving force in paraphilia as well as other sexual interests. Money uses the word *lovemap* to define the characteristic sexual response pattern for a person at both a behavioral and fantasy level. The statistically normative lovemap in the predominant culture today is a heterosexual one with infinite variations on this theme (e.g. hair color, eye color, body build, etc.). Lovemaps develop as a result of the interaction of biological, psychological and social forces. Money's point, and one we shall return to frequently, is that humans have no single determining force in their lovemap development. We presume that biological forces play an important role in sexual attraction. Natural selection decrees that heterosexual responsiveness ensures survival of the species. Unlike lower animals, however, which are "hormonic robots" and biologically programmed regarding sexual responsiveness, experience shapes sexual interest for humans into myriad patterns.

Money, as well as many other experts, believes that these lovemaps are essentially immutable by adulthood. He would maintain that lovemaps operate like our native language. Our brains do not determine us to speak English versus Spanish. However, our brain *is* programmed to develop *a* language. Once learned, a native language is forever unless brain injury occurs. The development of paraphiliac lovemaps also occurs outside the person's willful intentions. The forces of biology and social learning will shape that development into normative or paraphiliac modes. We will now describe the specific paraphilia listed in the APA's diagnostic manual.

Exhibitionism. The exhibitionist achieves sexual arousal through public display of his genitals to strangers. Most of our knowledge about the disorder comes from the criminal justice system. The official crime is public indecency and the perpetrators are called "flashers" in the vernacular. Only men receive this diagnosis, as is true for many paraphilias. According to Tollison and Adams (1979) most begin exhibiting in their adolescence. Less than one-third are married, and 20 percent have a record of other sexual offenses. The portrait, therefore, emerges of a lonely, isolated young male who may have other troublesome sexual predilections. Its appearance in adolescence should alert youth workers not to accept flashing episodes as youthful pranks that boys outgrow.

Exhibitionists seek a strong emotional reaction from their victims such as shock, surprise or disgust. Some simply display their genitals while others will engage in public masturbation. The degree of the victims' emotional reaction apparently enhances their sexual feelings. The act may occur in circumstances where no physical harm to the victim is likely, e.g. on a busy street corner in a large city. But often the act occurs when the victim is alone or vulnerable and will trigger intense fear. Since 20 percent have committed other sexual offenses, no one can predict the ultimate intention of the exhibitionist. Further contributing to its noxiousness is the fact that 20–25 percent of their victims are children.

Voyeurism. Voyeurs achieve sexual arousal by secretly watching others in a state of undress or sexual activity. The vernacular term for a voyeur is Peeping Tom. Tom was the townsman who stared at Lady Godiva in the medieval legend. Lady Godiva rode naked on a horse through town as payment to the evil baron for release of her imprisoned husband. The townspeople all agreed to avert their eyes but Tom violated the agreement, and hence the term.

Voyeurs may masturbate at the time they observe or later in private. Generally they are only interested in gazing, but reports exist of peeping associated with rape and even murder. Again, nearly all reported cases involve men. Most voyeurs who are arrested are young men in their mid-20s. About 25 percent are married, and many report minimal sexual arousal through marital sex (Tollison and Adams, 1979). The male-limited feature of this disorder may relate to the central role of visual sexual erotic stimuli for men. This behavior is also a crime. Controversy exists over the relationship between the incidence of voyeurism and availability of explicit pornography in a culture. Denmark reported significant decreases in arrests for voyeurism immediately after pornography became legal in that country.

Pedophilia. This disorder represents recurrent and intense sexual urges toward prepubescent children. The disorder exists if the person acts out his or her urges or experiences marked distress about them. Pedophilia is a criminal act in most cultures. Also criminal in the United States is sexual activity with a pubescent minor although not technically pedophilia. Some clinicians use the term ephebophilia to designate persons attracted to pubescent adolescents.

Probably few human behaviors generate as much personal revulsion as pedophilia. Even fellow prisoners mark out the pedophile as an object of physical and psychological retribution (Tollison and Adams, 1979). Highly publicized accounts in the media of child kidnaping and rape, child pornography, child sexual abuse in families and day care centers, sexual abuse by clergy, and even pedophilic murders have sensitized the public to the disorder's prevalence.

In most cases (85 percent) the child knows the pedophile as a relative or acquaintance. In about one-third of the cases the perpetrator uses physical coercion. Intense physical violence occurs in about 2 percent of the cases. Violence, of course, is a relative term, and coerced sexual contact even without violence may generate significant fear.

Three age groups represent most offenders. These include a puberty group, a mid-to-late 30s group, and mid-to-late 50s group. The DSM sets the minimum age of a pedophile arbitrarily at 16 and further arbitrarily states that there has to be at least a 5 year difference between the pedophile and the victim.

Pastoral counselors need to know the local child abuse laws since the legal definition of child abuse and the psychiatric diagnosis of pedophilia may differ. Most jurisdictions require reporting of child abuse to child protective agencies, and the legal definition usually includes a broader range of acts than the psychiatric definition. Unlike most other acts of sharing confidences with a clergyperson, child abuse admits of no privileged communication in some jurisdictions.

Heterosexual pedophile acts outnumber homosexual ones by a margin of two to one. Most offenders are married, and even a large number of homosexual offenders were married. Older pedophiles prefer prepubescent children while younger ones prefer adolescent girls. Despite our culture's legitimate concern about child sexual abuse, most acts of pedophilia are of an incidental nature. For a small group pedophilia is pervasive, frequent and chronic.

Studies describe three personality types among the offenders. The *personally immature* offender is the most common and represents someone unable to establish close relationships. The *regressed* offender has had a more or less stable development but commits a sexual act with a child during a period of unusual stress. Some alcoholics will report incidental pedophilia during active drinking phases. In recovery they may experience no interest whatsoever in this behavior. The third type is the *aggressive* offender who combines both sexual and aggressive motives. This type parallels the motivation of those who rape women. Contrary to myth, pedophiles are not older men—only about 17 percent are over 50. The age of the average offender is 35.

The social characteristics of pedophilia have useful implications for pastoral care. The pedophile is not an immoral libertine or social profligate in most areas of life. Indeed the majority are politically and religiously conservative and tend to have strict consciences regarding moral questions. Newspaper accounts of many pedophiles are striking in the contrast between their antisocial sexual proclivities alongside their social conservatism and rigid intolerance. Religious institutions typically value tradition and are conservative forces within a culture. We should not be too surprised, therefore, that some members of our own congregations with this disorder, including ministerial leaders, are drawn to organized religion for its extrinsic appeal. The broader implications of this phenomenon for pastoral care will be discussed below.

A survey of the sexual abuse literature reveals both the negative effect of the abuse as well as the resiliency of some victims (Browne and Finkelhor, 1986). The initial effects of the abuse (within 2 years) differ from long term effects. The initial impact depends on a child's age. The highest rate of emotional distress (40 percent) occurred for children in the 7–13 year range. The next highest was 4–6 years (17 percent), with few adolescents reporting immediate negative effects. The most common immediate emotional reaction is fear (40–83 percent), followed by anger and hostility (13–55 percent) with middle childhood children expressing the most upset. About 25 percent report shame, guilt and depression. Some children, particularly very young ones, act inappropriately sexually.

Long term effects measured in adulthood indicate greater depression in abused adults compared to non-abused ones by a margin of 2–1 (17 percent versus 9 percent). They also are more likely to engage in self-destructive behavior, have poor self-esteem, feel anxious and isolated, have higher rates of substance abuse, avoid sexual activity, have more sexual dysfunction, and tend toward revictimization. This last feature means that some victims manifest a learned helplessness during interpersonal relationships which prevents them from exiting subsequent abusive relationships.

Current research concludes, therefore, that 20–40 percent of child victims demonstrate significant pathology for two years after the abuse. As adults, child sexual abuse victims have greater impairment than those not abused, but less than 20 percent manifest serious psychopathology.

Some pervasive myths about child sexual abuse foster a traumatizing impact on its victims. The first myth is that the children make up stories of abuse. In fact 10–20 percent of children have experienced sexual abuse (Kaplan and Sadock, 1988). Kinsey's original report of interviews with 1,200 women revealed an astonishingly high rate of abuse. Twenty-eight percent of the women interviewed reported that they had some sexual experience with an adult before age 13. Even if we keep in mind the many criticisms of Kinsey's sampling methods, one may sadly conclude that in too many instances there has existed a sexual open season on little girls. Lower class girls reported more intimate sexual contacts than middle class ones. As is also typical, few victims reported the abuse to legal authorities.

The second myth is that children provoke the sexual contact or are responsible for its continuation. Some pedophiles do create a warm, nurturing relationship with their victims so that children may respond with intense ambivalence toward the sexual abuse. At one level fear and anger may result, yet the pedophile may represent a nurturing caretaker in an emotionally deprived environment. This ambivalence often prevents the child from revealing the abuse. This may also interfere with recovery since it involves coming to terms with pleasant aspects of the abusive relationship. A self-help movement has emerged for victims of child sexual abuse including group support (Survivors of Incest Anonymous) and bibliotherapy. Many survivors report great benefit from reading *The Courage To Heal* (Bass and Davis, 1988) or listening to the companion audiotapes.

Fetishism. This disorder involves recurrent, intense sexual urges toward objects which are usually related to the human body. The disorder occurs almost exclusively in males, and common fetishes are women's apparel such as undergarments, shoes, boots, pantyhose, stockings and the like. The person may use these objects as part of a masturbation ritual or need his partner to wear the object during intercourse. For some the fetish is the exclusive means to sexual arousal so that impotency occurs unless it is present. A fetishist may seek treatment if he is distressed by these urges or they interfere with his relationships. Occasionally the person develops a fetish toward objects which he must steal (e.g. women's shoes) and thus enters the criminal justice system. The incidence of this disorder is unknown because the fetishist rarely comes into conflict with the legal system and the person usually can satisfy his desires privately and/or with a tolerant partner.

Transvestic Fetishism. Transvestism was an earlier term for this disorder but has been dropped since it refers to cross-dressing. Since cross-dressing may occur as an act rather than a psychiatric syndrome (e.g. costume parties, theater, police disguises) the DSM now uses a more exclusive term. Transvestic fetishism applies exclusively to men and describes someone who achieves sexual arousal or orgasm while fantasizing or actually dressed in women's clothes. The degree of cross-dressing may be partial (e.g. wearing ladies' undergarments beneath male clothing), episodic (only during periods of explicit sexual activity), or total (cross-dressing exclusively and living in a transvestic subculture).

Clinicians distinguish this syndrome from transsexualism which is a gender identity disorder. When a transvestic fetishist is heterosexual he usually has a strong male identity. Since cross-dressing is illegal (for males only) he may come into conflict with the legal system if he cross-dresses in a flamboyant or public manner. More often such persons present themselves for treatment due to impairment in a relationship. Some spouses may not tolerate engaging in sexual activity with a cross-dressed partner. Or the man may choose only solitary sexual activity in accord with his fantasies. Many spouses accommodate to their partners' interests, however, and such relationships do not come to the attention of counselors.

Some specialists see the syndrome affecting men who have split off their masculine/feminine qualities. The condition may develop because the man has exaggerated stereotypes of masculine and feminine. Masculine may mean hard driving, ambitious, and risk-taking; feminine may mean nurturing, caring and affectionate. The fetish allows the person to incorporate these conflicting parts within himself through a sexual-dramatic performance (Money, 1988). The developmental histories of some men with this disorder reveal parental punishment through humiliating them by dressing them up in a girl's clothes ("petticoat punishment").

Frotteurism. This disorder involves a male obtaining sexual gratification through rubbing his genitals against fully-clothed women—usually in public places such as crowded buses, trains, or subways. To escape detection the offender flees the scene as rapidly as possible after the act. These men are extremely limited in heterosocial skills and feel inadequate around women. They resort to this behavior as one means of achieving sexual arousal without the threat of social interaction with a woman.

Sexual Sadism and Masochism. The sexual sadist experiences sexual excitement from the physical or psychological suffering of his or her victim. The person may act out these urges or feel marked distress by the fantasies. The word derives from the 18th century French novelist, Marquis de Sade, whose novels reflect sadistic sexual acts, and who himself was arrested and convicted for violence toward women.

The victim may be a consenting partner (see sexual masochism below) or a non-consenting partner. Cases of non-consent may include rape, although rape usually demonstrates a primary aggressive disorder with sexual gratification secondary or unimportant. Sadistic acts include restraint (tying, handcuffing, blindfolding), humiliation (treating the person like a slave, making the victim crawl or perform degrading acts), or torture (whipping, cutting, strangulation, spanking, mutilation). Some sadists will kill their victims in acts termed lust murder. Lust murderers who repeat this behavior become known as serial killers. Sadists may be either homosexual or heterosexual as the histories of serial killers demonstrate.

The authors of the DSM-III revised edition proposed rapism as a disorder but dropped it over the objections of those who saw the diagnosis as a way for rapists to avoid legal responsibility by pleading insanity. Some rapes, however, are probably paraphilic in their origin and intention, particularly those involving lust murder.

The sexual masochist is the complement to the sadist. Such people derive sexual excitement from suffering physically or psychologically. Sexual satisfaction occurs when they or their partners inflict injury on themselves through hitting, spanking, binding, cutting, choking or similar violence. Some prefer psychological suffering through self-debasement or self-humiliation. The term itself comes from the name of a 19th century Austrian novelist Leopold von Sacher-Masoch whose novels portrayed males who sought out such treatment from women (Kaplan and Sadock, 1988).

One potentially lethal form of this disorder kills 1 to 2 young men per million in the population annually. These men, the majority of whom are adolescents, accidentally self-strangulate during masturbation. The DSM calls the disorder *hypoxyphilia*. The person attempts to achieve a more intense orgasm through oxygen deprivation. He may achieve this through drugs (e.g. nitrous oxide—"poppers") or through self-strangulation. The person attempts to induce orgasm close to but not reaching loss of consciousness. Unfortunately some fail in the split-second timing and choke to death.

Counselors need to distinguish sexual sadism and sexual masochism as paraphilias from the non-distressing fantasies or *simulated* acts between consenting adults in which no real physical or psychological suffering occurs. Such behavior is common between sexual partners and does not constitute a paraphilia.

Other Paraphilias. The DSM lists seven other paraphilias which do not fit into any of the preceding groups. *Zoophilia* involves sexual contact with animals but is rare as an exclusive preference. The person often lives in an environment deprived of potential human sexual partners or is extremely lacking in social skills necessary to obtain a desirable partner. A number of teenagers in New England were executed during the Salem witch-trial era for engaging in this behavior. *Telephone scatologia* involves making obscene phone calls. Unsolicited obscene calls are illegal as well as a social nuisance. U.S. law permits obscene telephone conversations between consenting adults. Callers who are willing to pay a fee may engage an operator with such a "service company" in lewd conversation. No information exists to determine if these legal services have reduced illegal calls. Family-oriented public interest groups have supported laws to make such phone calls by minors illegal.

Coprophilia and *urophilia* involves experiencing sexual pleasure associated with the act or products of human waste elimination. Persons urinate or defecate on a partner or undergo the same. Somewhat related is desiring sexual excitement through receiving enemas (*klismaphilia*).

Partialism is the exclusive focus on a single non-genital body part so that customary penile-vaginal contact is not satisfactory. Least common of all the paraphilias in this section is *necrophilia* which is preference for sexual contact with corpses.

Paraphilia: Etiology and Treatment

Psychoanalytic Theory. In psychoanalytic theory paraphilia results from failing to resolve the oedipal stage. This stage occurs around ages three to five and requires the boy to solve his castration anxiety and maternal separation fear. In normal development children identify with their same-sex parent. Other paths for coping with this anxiety result in paraphilic behavior.

Homosexuality, transsexualism and transvestic fetishism involve the boy identifying with mother instead of father. One person may choose to cross-dress while another may have a reversed gender identity. An exhibitionist also fails to identify with his father and as a result of feeling castrated must exhibit his genitals to females whose shocked expression affirms a masculine identity. Voyeurs alleviate a similar anxiety but their method is to focus on observing women's genitals and thus gain reassurance about their own masculinity.

The sexual sadist uses the defense mechanism of identification with the aggressor to defend against castration fears. He relies on the principle of doing first to others what they would do to you. He derives satisfaction, according to psychoanalytic theory, in his role as aggressor. The sexual masochist, on the other hand, copes with castration fear and loss of control through facing pain and humiliation stoically. By suffering intense harm and degradation he demonstrates his indifference to both.

Finally, psychoanalytic theory sees the fetishistic disorder as representing unconscious castration fears. Most fetish objects are phallic symbols to which the person attaches libidinal energy. The fetish displaces the man's fear of castration by redirecting sexual energy toward substitute objects.

Psychoanalytic treatment of paraphilia requires resolution of the oedipal conflict via intensive psychoanalysis. Such treatment would characteristically require many sessions given the long-standing nature of the disorder.

Biological Treatment. Biological treatment of paraphilia as well as other criminal sexual misconduct (e.g. rape) now exists through administering an injectable antiandrogen hormone to the paraphiliac. The treatment is used in conjunction with traditional counseling as well as support groups. The drug's trade name is Depo-Provera and is a synthetic progestin. Its effect is to reduce the production of testosterone so that the man's sex drive is markedly reduced. The man has fewer erections and ejaculations. The drug reportedly reduces the blood level of testosterone to that of a prepubertal boy (Money, 1988).

Patients are encouraged to remain on the drug long enough for counseling to help the person find acceptable alternative relationships. While some patients choose to remain on the drug indefinitely, many cease after 2–3 years. Long term follow-up contact is recommended to allow for treatment resumption in the case of anticipated relapse. Within two weeks following cessation of treatment, sexual drive and erectile capacity return—although return of fertility may take 3–6 months.

Learning Theory and Behavioral Treatment. Learning theory in the Pavlovian or Skinnerian tradition (cf. Chapter 2) views sexual problems as learned through inappropriate associations or reward systems. If a mother calms her male child by putting him to bed every night in her slip, the child may eventually develop a fetish for female undergarments or perhaps engage in cross-dressing. Sexual sadism may develop if a boy undergoes brutal whipping while naked, since there is inadvertent sexual arousal associated with the panic reaction to such pain. A young woman who experienced sexual abuse as a child and physical abuse by a spouse may lose all ability to respond sexually to men. She may turn initially to women for emotional comfort which eventually triggers sexual feelings and behavior.

Behavioral treatments based on learning theory are multidimensional. If sexual aversion is related to social inhibition, assertiveness or social skills training can teach the client the necessary skills for establishing intimacy. In the case of paraphilia, aversive conditioning or punishment strategies have had some limited success. Aversive conditioning involves simultaneous presentation of the inappropriate imagery (e.g. via slides, pictures, fantasy) with aversive stimuli (e.g. electric shock, noxious odor) or nauseating verbal descriptions. For example, psychologist B. Maletsky successfully treated exhibitionists by having them imagine typical scenes which triggered the misconduct while smelling a noxious chemical (O'Leary and Wilson, 1987).

Another routinely used treatment to alter inappropriate sexual imagery involves associating masturbation with appropriate stimuli. Under the somewhat Clockwork-Orange title of *orgasmic reconditioning* the treatment involves having the person switch the paraphilic stimuli in imagery to an appropriate one during masturbation. For example, a pedophile might begin masturbating to a child image but introduce appropriate adult imagery near the moment of orgasm. Gradually the person introduces appropriate imagery earlier and earlier during masturbation. Some religious traditions find this an acceptable therapeutic strategy in light of the serious nature of pedophilia and other paraphilic behavior. Others, however, would object to any use of masturbation as a therapeutic strategy no matter what the goal.

Biopsychosocial Approaches. John Money (1988) proposes an alternative model for understanding the etiology of paraphilia. Money challenges the tendency in psychology to look for the cause of behavior in either nature (biology) or nurture (social learning). Human sexual behavior, rather, involves three dimensions: biology, critical event, and social learning. As an example, a pregnant mother's ingesting barbiturates during a fixed critical period in male fetal development alters the sexual hormonal programming in the fetal brain. While this alone creates demasculinizing influences, if parents rear the child as a boy and also permit medical treatment, the youngster will likely possess male gender identity/role. Money's theory reinforces again the diathesis-stress model so often discussed in this text. It suggests that biological and social events are both necessary in the development of paraphilia.

Money also uses his "lovemap" model for the etiology of paraphilia. In this model each person's lovemap represents the idealized lover and how the person behaves in a romantic and erotic relationship. The lovemap first develops in fantasy and perhaps finds expression with a partner. Money maintains that when no complications arise a lovemap develops as heterosexual.

Several factors may interfere with normal lovemap development. These include deprivation, neglect, prohibition or abuse. For example, child sexual abuse may traumatize the victim for all sexual activity. A woman brutalized as a child may find that she can have sex with her husband only if she is under the influence of alcohol or drugs. Money describes this alteration of normative sexual development as vandalization of the person's lovemap. This vandalization results in splitting off love from lust (an idea similar to Freud's notion of seeing women as Virgin or Prostitute). Lust becomes something dirty, forbidden, and sexual, while love is pure, romantic, and non-genital. Lust then saves itself through deviancy. A paraphilia develops for the expression of lust, but remains separate and distinct from love. Since sexual drive is powerful and reinforcing, the person tends to repeat the behavior—first in imagery and perhaps later in deed. The strength of the drive usually leads the person to experience the paraphilia as compulsive or "addictive." The following case illustrates this viewpoint.

> Paul was a 24 year old seminarian seen in counseling for pedophilic sexual imagery which dominated his sexual fantasies. He had one or two episodic encounters with adolescent boys since reaching his twenties, but was worried that as a newly ordained minister his superiors would likely assign him to youth services. He had just recently "fallen in love" with a 14 year old boy. The patient worried constantly that he might act out his sexual feelings toward the youngster. Initial history-taking revealed the paradox of heterosexual adult sexual orientation but sexual orientation to pubescent adolescent boys. The patient reported that he attended a religiously affiliated high school whose religious teachings were severely prohibitive regarding sexual behavior. Repeated warnings that sex with girls would result in pregnancy left him paralyzed in heterosocial relationships. Though handsome and socially skilled he never dated in high school. In the seminary he had one brief sexual affair with a male seminarian but did not find this experience satisfying. He had discovered that he could "express his true feelings" to adolescent boys, but eventually sexual feelings arose and bothered him. Nevertheless, he found adult women sexually attractive.

In this case strong prohibitions against heterosexual contact, as perceived by the patient, generated anxiety sufficient to prevent normal heterosocial contact. This led, in turn, to few opportunities to interact with girls. The personal lovemap here is a strong adult heterosexual interest in fantasy but homosexual fantasy and behavior with minors.

Gender Identity Disorders

Much confusion reigns about gender identity disorders. Many people believe that someone who cross-dresses (transvestic fetishism) is homosexual. Heterosexuality is actually the norm. Others believe that homosexuals are uncomfortable in their gender identity and desire to change it. To clarify such misconceptions psychologist John

Money described his now universally accepted concept of gender identity/gender role (Money, 1988).

Gender identity is the person's internal perception of his or her maleness, femaleness or androgyny. It refers to the persistence, pervasiveness and unity of the person's experience of his or her gender. It is a private world of meaning. No one has access to my gender identity unless I choose to reveal it. *Gender role* is the flip side of gender identity. It represents the public expression of maleness or femaleness through speech, dress and behavior.

Related to these concepts but much narrower is *sexual identity*, i.e. one's chromosomal sex type as XX (female) or XY (male). These sex types usually include male or female genital-reproductive characteristics. Gender identity/role is more inclusive than sexual identity since it involves wide-ranging psychosocial characteristics which influence the person's behavior and place in society.

In the course of normal development, sexual identity, gender identity, and gender role are congruent. That is, a sex assigned male (XY) will have penis, testes and scrotum, will experience himself as a male, and will behave publicly so that others will respond to him as male. Anomalies of development, however, may result with someone having an assigned sex at birth (e.g. male) but later chromosome testing proves to be female (i.e. XX). If this occurs late in development (e.g. around eight years old) and the child has been reared as male, a discrepancy will exist between sexual identity and gender identity/role.

A second anomaly without known biological source is *gender identity disturbance* in childhood/adolescence or *transsexualism* in adulthood. In these disorders a disparity exists between gender identity/role. For example, the person's gender role is male but his gender identity is female. He will use language to describe this predicament as "being a woman trapped in a man's body." To outsiders he appears male but his inner experience is female. Transsexualism in adults represents a continuum of variations. Some accept this disparity and alter their gender roles only minimally, e.g. cross-dressing in private on a limited basis. Others will seek hormonal treatments to alter their physical appearance—e.g. to lower their voice or develop breasts. They may endure electrolysis to remove body hair. Still others will seek sex reassignment surgery to alter even their genitals to conform to their gender identity. For males this involves removal of penis and testicles and construction of a vagina. For females it involves tissue grafting and surgical construction of a replica penis.

Responsible medical clinics which perform sex reassignment surgery usually screen transsexuals to rule out psychosis or other mental disorders. Additionally they require the person to undergo a lengthy real-life test (1–2 years), where the person attempts to live completely as a member of the opposite sex socially and economically. Since surgery is irreversible the clinicians want the transsexual to experience first-hand the problems in adjusting to an opposite gender role. They perform surgery only if the person demonstrates social and psychological adjustment.

Gender identity disturbance in childhood occurs early, with the child (usually male) preferring opposite-sex dress and play activities even by age four. The disorder differs from transsexualism since one-third to one-half of these children identify as homosexual by adolescence yet return to a masculine gender identity. Whether this represents a stage for a subgroup of homosexuals is unknown. Behavior modification treatment of the problem effectively changes the child's gender role behavior if parents seek treatment when the child is young. Gay rights' groups have questioned the ethics of clinical intervention for this condition.

Homosexuality

Condition Versus Illness. The American Psychiatric Association removed homosexuality from its official list of mental disorders in 1973. Member protests led to a referendum the following year which sustained the decision by a 58 percent vote (Kaplan and Sadock, 1988). This changed homosexuality from a disease to a condition.

In the first edition of the DSM-III (APA, 1980) a disorder remained called *ego-dystonic homosexuality* which described homosexuals who are distressed by their sexual orientation and wish to change. The revised edition (APA, 1987) removed this disorder since the task force believed it discriminated against homosexuals and ignored the sociocultural forces working against them. Homosexual distress more often results from feeling devastated by the culture at large rather than from the condition itself. Also, the diagnosis characterized as a disease a developmental phase that most homosexuals go through in coming to terms with their own identity. This would be similar to making a disease entity out of "vocational confusion" in adolescence or young adulthood. The accepted convention now is to assign any ego-dystonic sexual orientation condition to the category of Sexual Disorder Not Otherwise Specified.

Despite its removal from the DSM, homosexuality remains controversial. As is true for most sexual behavior discussed in this chapter, it intersects moral, religious, political and legal domains. The Supreme Court of the United States in 1986 upheld the Georgia sodomy law, thus allowing any state the right to criminalize sexual acts performed by homosexuals (and even married heterosexuals!). Many religious denominations and groups characterize homosexual behavior in any circumstance as immoral. The issue of ordaining to ministry homosexuals living with a partner has generated intense divisions within and between denominations. Some question the wisdom of ordaining even celibate homosexuals.

Gay rights activists have successfully challenged a number of discriminatory regulations and have gained considerable political power in select areas. Despite some political gains the AIDS crisis has renewed widespread expression of prejudice toward homosexuals along with an increasing incidence of violent hate crimes directed toward homosexuals. All of these reasons point to the necessity of including a discussion of homosexuality in a volume directed toward pastoral ministry. Even though not considered mentally ill, homosexuals do and will continue to turn to pastoral counselors for guidance, acceptance and support in their process of self-exploration.

Classification. One difficulty with discussions about homosexuality starts with classifying it. So much variation exists that generalizations are impossible. The transvestic drag queen homosexual no more resembles his athletic Pentagon-worker counterpart than a black New York City Democrat resembles a white Mississippian Democrat. The biologist Alfred Kinsey helped solved this difficulty through a classification scheme called the *Kinsey Scale* (Kinsey *et al.*, 1948). Seven points ranging from 0–6 identify a person in terms of the number and degree of physical/psychological/sexual responses to same-sex or opposite-sex persons. Zero, for instance, represents exclusive heterosexual responsiveness representing no physical contact with or no psychic responses to same-sex persons. Six represents the exclusive homosexual counterpart. Persons who are rated 1 or 5 have only incidental physical contact or psychic response to a same (1) or opposite sex (5) partners. Those rated 2 or 4 have more than incidental contact but the preponderance of physical contact or psychic reactions is with an opposite sex (2) or same sex (4) partner. Finally, those rated as 3 respond equally to heterosexual or homosexual stimuli and have no strong preference for either.

The scale is useful in several ways. First, it illustrates how only a small percentage of people fall at the extremes as exclusively either heterosexual or homosexual. Kinsey found that only 4 percent of males were exclusively gay as adults. About 13 percent were predominantly gay for a 3 year duration after puberty. Interestingly, 37 percent, or more than one male in three, had a sexual contact leading to orgasm with another man after puberty. For women the incidence of homosexual behavior is about one-third that of men's; 2–6 percent of single women and less than 1 percent of married women were exclusively gay. About 28 percent had some gay experience while 13 percent of all women admitted having a sexual experience with another woman leading to orgasm. Many have faulted Kinsey's sampling methods. Nevertheless, the data point to the wide prevalence of such behavior in American culture and suggest that it will be a common problem in pastoral care.

The scale also raises interesting questions to reflect on with concerned clients. At which point are persons homosexual? If they are a 6, or anywhere from 3–6? Who is bisexual? Only a 3 or anyone between 1 and 5? The scale illustrates the hazard of premature labeling. Most people think of their sexual orientation and behavior as a binary system, that is, an either/or condition. Reality suggests it is infinitely more complicated. Should we seriously label 37 percent of all men and 13 percent of women as homosexual since they have had an intimate sexual contact with a same-sex partner?

The scale may also serve a practical purpose in the counseling relationship. Asking clients to rate themselves on the scale may lead to greater self-awareness and self-acceptance for those asking developmental questions about their sexual orientation. Many obtain relief in finding their own position on the scale and using this as a springboard for further counseling.

Etiology. Theories abound to explain the origins of homosexuality. The sensible conclusion at this time is that the jury is still out on a definite cause. As John Money notes, we know as little about the development of heterosexual orientation as we do about homosexual development.

Freud suggested that an intimate binding mother with an absent or uninvolved father created the environment leading to homosexual development in males. For females he postulated unresolved penis envy during the oedipal phase (cf. Chapter 2). Some clinical case reports validated Freud's viewpoint for male homosexuals. Those reports, however, cannot prove a probable etiology since they represent men seen in treatment which is a biased sample. If we generalized about heterosexual development from only interviewing mentally ill heterosexuals we would find considerable family pathology as well. Also, studies of lesbians have found close father-daughter relationships which contradicts Freud's position (Kaplan and Sadock, 1988).

Intuitively, many have explored biological sources in the development of homosexuality, particularly examining the role of hormone levels. While an occasional study indicates differences between homosexual and heterosexual men, no consistent findings have emerged. Researchers argue that the absolute levels of hormones do not contribute to homosexual development.

While further research may discover consistent biological influences we are currently limited in investigational techniques. Perhaps the most crucial developmental phase regarding sexual development occurs *in utero*. The developing fetus responds to its inner genetic programming regarding hormonal release in timing and degree. Tissue sensitivity and even environmental stressors to the fetus can alter effective hormonal programming. The *in utero* programming does not just determine the development of a fetus' reproductive system. During this period it also lays down the structures in the brain necessary for the sexual chemical messenger system which activates in adolescence and thereafter throughout adulthood. Ethical constraints naturally prevent experimentation on developing fetal brains. However, animal research and human "experiments of nature" indicate that *in utero* influences create physiological anomalies (e.g. external male genitalia but internal female reproductive system). These same *in utero* biological influences may lead to measurable gender role influences, e.g. tomboyishness in girls.

What we also learn from these experiments of nature is that biological sources alone do not seem to determine sexual orientation outcome. Girls whose mothers received steroids during pregnancy which released excessive male hormones in the developing fetus required corrective surgery at birth to eliminate male physical features. Reared as girls they were tomboys as children. All eleven girls studied with this condition were only heterosexual by adulthood in terms of behavior, interests and fantasies (Money, 1988). Other studies illustrate the importance of social learning influences in addition to biological ones.

Even more dramatic cases exist such as chromosomally female children (XX) who obtained excessive androgen (masculinizing) hormones during pregnancy from mothers with endocrine system tumors. These children have internal female reproductive organs but male external ones. Three cases exist of these children reared as boys (Money, 1988) who received hormonal treatments at puberty to prevent feminization. They grew up as men, assumed heterosocial roles, and in two cases married and adopted children. As Money notes, no one, including their spouses, considered them lesbian or bisexual.

These studies highlight the immense plasticity of human sexual development and the important role that both biology and social learning play. Lower animals are sexual robots whose hormonal programming determines sexual response. Humans and even higher animals are more sensitive to critical developmental periods as well as learning factors.

Research and clinical data now tend to converge on the notion that sexual orientation of whatever variety—homosexual, heterosexual, or bisexual—occurs early in life. Once established, it is irreversible. Some studies exist (e.g. Masters and Johnson, 1979) which report reorienting homosexual men toward heterosexual lifestyles. Most agree that these reoriented individuals had strong bisexual tendencies and were highly motivated for this treatment. Generally treatment strategies to change homosexuals fail. Those cases which report change have included up to 350 hours of therapy or, as in the case of the work of Masters and Johnson, involve a cooperative heterosexual partner in the treatment. Many will find such strategies economically or ethically constraining, particularly if surrogate partners (i.e. men or women paid for participation) are involved.

Treatment. Counseling the homosexual may require attention to some common themes. Developmentally the "coming out" phase or awareness stage in homosexual discovery may require counseling. Often the person must cope with feelings of depression or anxiety as he or she introjects the negative social stereotypes about homosexuals. Loss of self-esteem, shame, and guilt are common, as well as anger directed toward society, parents and God. A second major theme is how to evolve a moral framework for personal sexual behavior including discussion of options. Finally, since our culture does not have a structurally supportive environment for homosexual social development, the homosexual generally experiences this at a much later age than heterosexuals, often as young adults. Many will begin to deal with these issues as late as their 50s and 60s. Some experience a confusing period of trial and error. They experiment with various roles as they pursue an integrated identity. In this age of AIDS certain forms of experimentation can be lethal, so the counselor needs to challenge the individual on the importance of self-care.

Homosexuals are susceptible to the same mental health issues as heterosexuals, but their isolated status in society may contribute to higher rates of anxiety or depression. Also, much homosexual social life revolves around gay bars, and alcohol use often develops into a problem. Most clinicians agree that homosexuals have greater rates of alcoholism than heterosexuals. Counseling chemically dependent homosexuals requires attention to their special needs (cf. Ciarrocchi, 1991), and referral to gay AA meetings often facilitates recovery.

Sexual Dysfunction: Description

In helping students distinguish sexual dysfunctions from paraphilia I refer somewhat crudely to paraphilia as object choice problems and sexual dysfunctions as equipment problems. Although the distinction is imprecise it gets the point across. Sexual dysfunction, as we shall note, has a wide range of causes: physical, psychological, or combinations of each.

Researchers William Masters and Virginia Johnson (1966) are responsible for delineating the human sexual response cycle in a scientific manner. Many criticized their methods when they published their findings. They relied on direct observation and physiological recordings of individuals and couples engaging in sexual activity in a laboratory setting. Despite objections to their methodology, their data base has stood the test of time, and most specialists today work from the foundation that Masters and Johnson built. Among the opinions they disproved was Freud's view that for women a vaginal orgasm indicated greater sexual maturity than a clitoral one. As a result of Freud's authority many therapists and sex educators transmitted this position to women students and clients. According to Masters and Johnson, however, all female orgasms whether clitoral or vaginal are physiologically identical.

The DSM-III revision (1987) lists four distinct phases of sexual arousal. Phase one (*appetitive*) involves the person's interest level in sexual activity. The frequency and degree of such interest is manifested by the intensity, duration and frequency of sexual fantasies. No specific physiological changes characterize this phase, but rather it reflects what is popularly termed a person's sex drive.

Phase two (*excitement*) consists of both physiological and psychological changes. For the male it involves penile erection along with physical changes accompanying this, including testicular elevation, mucoid secretion from Cowper's gland, hyperventilation and tachycardia. For females the excitement phase involves vaginal lubrication as well as withdrawal of the clitoris, mucoid secretions from Bartholin's gland, hyperventilation and tachycardia.

Phase three (*orgasm*) for males consists of pelvic contraction with resultant ejaculation of semen. Females also experience contraction of pelvic muscles. Men and women experience orgasm as the peak of sexual enjoyment and a release from sexual tension.

Phase four (*resolution*) includes a general sense of well-being and state of relaxation following orgasm. Males have a *refractory* period in this phase during which they are incapable of achieving orgasm again. The length of the refractory period differs for individual men and also increases with age. The refractory period may range from 10–30 minutes in youth to days in the elderly. Women do not experience a refractory period and are physically capable of repeated orgasms.

Sexual Desire Disorders. These disorders relate to the appetitive phase of the sexual response cycle. The DSM describes two types of sexual desire disorder—hypoactive sexual desire disorder and sexual aversion disorder.

Hypoactive sexual desire disorder involves a low sex drive so that the person engages in few sexual fantasies and does not seek out sexual activity through masturbation or with a partner. If a relationship results in genital stimulation the person may respond physiologically but with little sense of personal satisfaction. Sex therapist Helen Singer Kaplan describes this as similar to eating a meal when you have no appetite (Kaplan, 1979). When teaching pastoral counselors I call low sexual desire the biggest bedroom secret in America. Contrary to sexual myths portrayed on television and in the movies, a significant number of married and single people have infrequent sexual activity due to lack of interest. One study of stable married couples found that 8 percent reported having intercourse less than once a month. Another study found that one-third abstained from sexual relations for periods up to eight weeks (Kaplan and Sadock, 1988, p. 364). The DSM III-Revised (1987, p. 292) claims that 20 percent of the total population has this condition.

The disorder of hypoactive sexual desire is arbitrary regarding the exact amount of sexual interest. The diagnosis requires the clinician to take the person's age, sex, and social circumstances into consideration. Also, loss of interest may not result from another serious mental disorder, e.g. depression. Often one makes the diagnosis when the condition creates distress for the partner even though the level of sexual activity is acceptable for the identified client.

Related to this condition is *sexual aversion disorder* which involves an intense aversion to all genital sexual contact with a partner. Not only is there loss of interest but distinct repulsion regarding sexual activity. Again, the diagnosis is independent of other major mental disorders. Both sexual desire disorders are more common in women.

Sexual Arousal Disorders. These disorders relate to the excitement phase of the sexual response cycle. For males the condition is *male erectile disorder.* It involves 1) partial or complete failure to maintain an erection long enough to complete sexual activity, or 2) no sense of excitement or pleasure during sexual activity. Male erectile disorder includes *primary impotence* if the male has never sustained an erection sufficient to achieve penetration. This condition is rare. *Secondary impotence,* however, occurs in 10 to 20 percent of all men and involves inability to maintain an erection currently although he has achieved this in the past. *Selective impotence* means that a man can maintain an erection only under select circumstances, e.g. with a mistress but not with his wife.

Female sexual arousal disorder is either a partial or permanent inability to achieve the lubrication-swelling response of sexual excitement long enough to complete the sexual act. The disorder's occurrence in the general female population is unknown, although one study found that 33 percent reported difficulty maintaining sexual excitement (Kaplan and Sadock, 1988, p. 365).

Orgasmic Disorders. These conditions represent disorders of the orgasm phase of the sexual response cycle. *Inhibited female orgasm (anorgasmia)* represents an inability to achieve orgasm despite an adequate amount of sexual activity during the excitement phase. The disorder may be primary—meaning she has never experienced orgasm, or secondary—meaning she has experienced orgasm at least once. Kinsey found that only 5 percent of his female sample over 35 had never experienced orgasm. The DSM-III estimates that 30 percent of the female population has inhibited orgasm.

Inhibited male orgasm (or retarded ejaculation) means that a man either never ejaculates during coitus (primary type) or he once experienced orgasm during coitus but now cannot (secondary). It also refers to those men who achieve orgasm during coitus only with great difficulty. These men usually achieve orgasm outside coitus through masturbation. Approximately 5 percent of the general male population has this condition.

A second male orgasm disorder is *premature ejaculation.* A man with this syndrome either ejaculates prior to coitus or sooner than he desires after penetration. The diagnosis is subjective and requires assessment of circumstances such as the man's age and the partner's wishes. There is no equivalent female disorder. The DSM claims that

30 percent of men have this condition, but other sources (e.g. Kaplan and Sadock, 1988, p. 369) put the figure at 35 to 40 percent of men treated for sexual dysfunction.

Sexual Pain Disorders. Both men and women may experience physical pain before, during, or after intercourse, but the incidence is far greater in women. No pain disorder diagnosis is made if the discomfort is due to lack of lubrication, which is either a sexual arousal disorder or an attempt at intercourse without sufficient preparation.

Two sexual pain disorders exist. The first is *dyspareunia* which is persistent genital pain associated with intercourse. The second type is *vaginismus,* an involuntary muscle spasm of the outer vagina which prevents intercourse. The condition may also prevent gynecological examination as well. It is less common than inhibited orgasm and tends to occur more among the well-educated and those with strict religious upbringing (Kaplan and Sadock, 1988, p. 370).

Sexual Dysfunction: Etiology and Treatment

Physiological Causes

Many organic conditions influence sexual dysfunction. The study of sexual dysfunction has changed the former viewpoint that most sexual dysfunctions are psychological in origin. For example, even recent literature attributed 90 percent of male impotency to psychological causes (O'Leary and Wilson, 1987). Some experts now suggest that perhaps 50 to 60 percent is caused by organic factors (Renshaw, 1990).

Organic factors include pharmacological agents and diseases. Alcohol, drugs, and prescription medicines may affect sexual desire and performance. Acute or chronic alcohol use leads to loss of desire or inability to achieve arousal for both women and men. Chronic cocaine use as well as ingestion of most illegal substances lowers sexual performance (cf. Chapter 6). Many prescription drugs also interfere with sexual arousal or impair ejaculation. Drugs used to treat mental illness may cause impotency as a side-effect. They include antidepressants and some neuroleptics used to treat schizophrenia or psychosis. Additionally, some drugs in general medicine, particularly those used to treat hypertension, may impair ejaculation or retard arousal for both men and women.

Many diseases also interfere with sexual functioning. The list is endless and the reader may consult comprehensive discussions (e.g.

Sadock, Kaplan, and Freedman, 1976). Briefly, they include such common illnesses as cardiovascular disorders, diabetes, endocrine disorders (e.g. thyroid problems), nutritional disorders, respiratory problems, kidney disease and gynecological disorders such as endometriosis. Almost any impairing physical condition will affect sexual interest. Consider, for instance, the effect of intestinal flu on sexual interest. Furthermore, certain medical treatments or procedures may impair sexual performance. Radiation therapy, chemotherapy, surgery such as colon resection and prostate operations—all may reduce interest and impede performance. Scar tissue from episiotomy and gynecological surgery will also influence comfort level during sexual activity.

The foregoing highlights the importance of comprehensive medical evaluation to rule out the presence of any contributory medical condition to the sexual problem. If organic factors are maintaining the problem, psychological intervention alone will fail. At the same time, even if physical problems caused the original dysfunction, medical treatment alone may not reverse the condition since it may have affected the person's beliefs and self-esteem. The person may need psychotherapy to resolve psychological concerns in conjunction with medical treatment.

Biological Assessment and Treatment

Methods to distinguish organic from psychological sexual dysfunctions are not always conclusive. The standard assessment for male erectile disorder is recording nocturnal penile tumescence (NPT). NPT occurs in healthy males during REM sleep with some decline with age. This assessment assumes that an erection achieved during sleep rules out organic causes. A strain gauge records penile circumference while the man spends 2 or 3 nights in a sleep laboratory.

This technology is not 100 percent accurate since some men without organic problems have NPT deficits while others achieve an erection but insufficient for coitus (Mohr and Beutler, 1990). Penile blood pressure recording through ultrasound represents one method to assess vascular problems. Physicians do not recommend extensive (and expensive) workups if evidence exists that sexual arousal occurs in situations other than attempts at intercourse. Examples of this would include the ability to masturbate to orgasm for men and women or an early morning erection for men. Sleep studies for women measure vaginal lubrication. As is the case for men, their active sexual response tends to occur most often during the REM sleep phase.

Direct biological treatments for sexual dysfunction are lacking except for male erectile disorders. When physicians locate some biological cause of any sexual dysfunction, the first strategy is to treat the primary medical symptom (e.g. diabetes). If this does not relieve the sexual problem, counseling strategies (cf. below) may improve adjustment. Biological solutions for male erectile problems include penile implants, surgical revascularization, testosterone administration, stimulant injections, and mechanical vacuum assistance.

Penile surgical implants include either a rigid rod or an inflatable device. Decisions to obtain an implant should involve the sexual partner since studies indicate that partner cooperation is related to success following surgery (Mohr and Beutler, 1990). In cases of vascular disease, arterial bypass surgery in the penis may restore erections. Testosterone administration is more likely to increase sexual interest than to ameliorate erectile difficulty. Physicians, however, will sometimes experiment with its use in male erectile disorder. A more invasive intervention is self-injection of the vasodilator papaverine into the penis. Patients learn to self-inject the drug and an erection occurs in about a half hour lasting about 20 minutes or more. Problems may occur if the erection continues too long as gangrene may set in (Renshaw, 1990). A non-invasive Vacuum Erection Device is a new product which uses a cylinder to create an airtight seal over the penis. The vacuum effect creates an erection for up to 30 minutes (Mohr and Beutler, 1990).

Psychosocial Theories

We will describe two psychosocial theories of sexual dysfunction. The first derives from Freudian theory, and the second evolved from clinical sex therapy and emphasizes social learning events.

Freudian theory views sexual dysfunction as caused by unresolved developmental conflicts. For example, low sexual desire is the result of unresolved oedipal conflict (cf. Chapter 2). Freud described one fixation from this stage in men as *vagina dentata*, an unconscious fear that the vagina had teeth and hence would castrate them. As a result, the man avoids heterosexual intercourse. Freud also saw some male disorders as resulting from an inability to reconcile sexual feelings with affectionate feelings toward the same woman. The male psyche then splits off woman into types representing either the Madonna or the Prostitute. (We could speculate about Freud's amusement over the popular singer Madonna who capitalizes on this unresolved unconscious material by playing out both images theatrically in concert and music videos.) Once split in such fashion, the man can no longer function sexually with the woman representing the Virgin or Madonna—usually his spouse. He may need to turn to a lover or prostitute or engage in a comparable fantasy to achieve sexual satisfaction. Female disorders may result from a variety of internal perceptions about the sexual experience. These include intense guilt feelings about sex, fear of pregnancy, viewing orgasm as a loss of control, or viewing the sex act itself as a form of aggression directed toward her.

Masters and Johnson conceptualize sexual dysfunctions in their second landmark book *Human Sexual Inadequacy* (1970). They begin by emphasizing the involuntary nature of the sexual response. Their basic research in *Human Sexual Response* (1966) taught that sexual arousal occurs when the person attends to erotic stimuli. No one can will an orgasm; rather it occurs as a result of letting go and becoming absorbed in the sexual experience. The main culprit in sexual dysfunction, therefore, is *performance anxiety*. The individual begins to worry about how he or she is doing. As a result one falls into the "spectator role." Rather than being absorbed in the sexual experience, the person is a "third party" in the room observing and grading the performance. As soon as the person takes the spectator role, he or she loses contact with the immediate experience of the erotic stimuli. This concern over performance, then, sabotages performance. Once failure occurs, it tends to create a vicious cycle. Now the person enters new sexual experiences with worry about repeating the past— a process which distracts the person further. The atmosphere is now ripe for a self-fulfilling prophecy.

Masters and Johnson saw many factors contributing to a negative emotional set toward sex which also results in distraction and inattention during sexual activity. Women and men develop sexual problems from religious prohibition, negative family attitudes, financial problems, repulsion at the partner's physical appearance, jealousy from attention directed toward rivals, and, of course, past traumatic coercive sexual experiences (O'Leary and Wilson, 1987).

Treatment Format of Masters and Johnson

Modern sex therapy owes its heritage largely to Masters and Johnson who treated 790 patients in their original study, which included 5 year follow-up data on 313 of their original group. The initial outcome after their 2 week program indicated an 81 percent success rate with 75 percent success rate at five year follow-up. Men and women did not differ in their success rates. Behavior therapists Joseph Wolpe and Arnold Lazarus had reported using similar techniques earlier (1966). Nevertheless, the sheer size of the Masters and Johnson sample, the length of follow-up, and implementation by two scientists whose earlier research in sexuality had revolutionized the field all resulted in their treatment strategies having enormous impact. A powerful influence was their high success rate in treating what most clinicians regarded as intractable conditions.

We will discuss their techniques for specific disorders but first consider the components of their overall format. They conducted treatment in an intensive 2 week format using dual therapist teams of men and women professionals. All couples received extensive medical and psychosocial assessment with portions conducted by their same-sex therapist to encourage openness. Masters and Johnson approached each partner non-judgmentally no matter what the dysfunction. To minimize pressure on either partner they made explicit the notion that "the relationship is the patient."

As stated above, they viewed performance anxiety and cognitive distractions as the major culprits in sexual dysfunction, so their format attempted to minimize this influence. They gave couples direct instructions. First, they forbade couples to engage in sexual intercourse. They wanted to minimize the demand features of therapy to reduce performance worries. The couple's first task was to engage in a series of exercises directed toward *non-demand pleasuring*. Each partner took turns physically pleasuring the other through touch, massage and caressing as directed by the receiving partner. No direct genital or female breast stimulation was permitted at this stage. This process teaches the couple generic communication skills about what they do or do not enjoy physically, yet at the same time avoids the anxiety associated with sexual performance. Masters and Johnson termed these exercises *sensate focus* to illustrate that their function is to achieve sensual pleasure from a wide range of body contact, not just sexual stimulation.

In the next phase, sensate focus moved to direct stimulation of genital areas but, again, with the recipient guiding the partner as to what was enjoyable. The ban on sexual intercourse remained in effect during this phase as well. When the couple became thoroughly comfortable with sensate focus, the therapists introduced strategies for specific dysfunctions. At this stage the couple was able to maintain adequate levels of sexual arousal but without intercourse.

These strategies represent an obvious application of systematic desensitization which is a staple of behavioral treatment of anxiety disorders (cf. Chapter 4). Since Masters and Johnson construe fear as the source of most sexual dysfunction, they developed a logical application of desensitization to their program. A behavior therapist would label their method as *in vivo* desensitization because it occurs "live" rather than in imagination.

In the years since the pioneering work of Masters and Johnson, clinicians and researchers have validated the usefulness of this treatment approach. Clinical practice and research discovered, however, that some components of the original program are not essential for success. A single therapist can achieve similar results to a dual therapist team. Therapy can also take place in an outpatient setting over an extended period rather than concentrated into 2 weeks. These changes are more cost-effective and practical, given customary mental health resources. We will now discuss specific treatments for men and women which Masters and Johnson originated but to which later therapists contributed.

Treatment for Women

The negative cultural attitudes toward women enjoying sex plays a large role in the etiology of fears associated with sexual dysfunction. Sensate focus treatment helps the woman feel comfortable about experiencing sexual feelings. She learns which body parts enjoy stimulation and the manner of the stimulation. She learns to communicate directly with her partner about these feelings and even to request sexual stimulation. This leads her to view sexual responsiveness as a legitimate right instead of something dirty, shameful or "unladylike."

Education in the anatomy and physiology of the sexual response teaches the woman and her partner information relevant to the timing of sexual phases. Men are capable of achieving orgasm on average within 3 minutes of direct sexual arousal. For women 13 minutes is the average (Renshaw, 1990). In addition, most women feel considerable discomfort if breasts or genital areas are stimulated before they have achieved a certain level of arousal. Sensate focus exercises teach the couple this timing discrepancy. For a mutually satisfying response the man appreciates the importance of accommodation to his partner's needs. The woman learns to feel more comfortable directing the timing of different forms of direct stimulation as well as communicating readiness for actual intercourse. Therapists also instruct in different sexual positions so that, through trial and error, couples may discover which ones are conducive to prolonging the experience and which minimize any discomfort.

In addition to sensate focus for couples, directed masturbation strategies for women will enhance sexual responsiveness. Women who have inhibited orgasm, vaginismus, or dyspareunia can learn to achieve and maintain sexual arousal leading to orgasm through masturbation. Such a program might include instruction from a female therapist, then masturbation in the presence of the woman's partner for his instruction and potential assistance, followed by the partner directly stimulating the woman to orgasm. Studies show the benefits of such a program in improving female responsiveness (Heiman, Lo-Piccolo, and LoPiccolo, 1976).

Treatment for Men

Sensate focus exercises provide the groundwork for treatment of male problems as well. Both men and women benefit from the communication aspect of the exercises. Women, as a group, benefit from overcoming sexual inhibitions. Men, as a group, benefit from redirecting their focus from a narrow sex-as-intercourse view. They learn other relationship goals such as generic sensual pleasure, loving dialogue, and psychological satisfaction from mutual giving-and-receiving. This shifting of focus reduces concern over performance and allows the man to appreciate that many goals are possible in an intimate encounter.

Masters and Johnson described techniques for specific dysfunction. In the case of premature ejaculation the partner stimulates the man to full arousal. The woman then squeezes the penis with her thumb and first two fingers around the corona of the penis. This eliminates the need to ejaculate. The couple repeat this procedure and eventually the man sustains erections for longer periods. When he is able to do so the couple unite sexually with the woman on top. The couple remain still so that no urge to ejaculate occurs. If it does the woman reapplies the squeeze technique. Eventually the man controls his orgasm for a suitable interval.

Treating male impotence requires reducing performance anxiety. As the partner stimulates the man during the sensate focus exercise, an erection will occur. Instead of immediately attempting intercourse at this point, the partner stops stimulation so that the man loses his erection. The partner repeats this process again and again so that each person learns without panic that the erection can come and go. Eventually the couple tries intercourse but in low-key non-vigorous positioning. Gradually, as the erection is maintained, direct thrusting will lead to orgasm.

Additional Treatment

As Masters and Johnson wisely noted, in sexual dysfunctions the relationship is the patient. Often couples who require focused sex therapy also require standard marital counseling to work on relationship problems beyond the sexual ones. Most therapists agree that many aspects of a relationship affect sexual functioning and vice versa. Even if sexual functioning improves, marital satisfaction may not. Without improvement in marital functioning the probability of relapse in the sexual area remains high. In some cases the sex therapist and marriage counselor are the same person. In some cases they may differ, as when a pastoral counselor is the marriage counselor who refers to a sex therapist for specialized treatment. The referral contract might require follow-up marriage counseling.

Pastoral Care and Sexual Problems

In more than 10 years of teaching psychopathology courses to pastoral counselors and ministers, many of whom have had extensive pastoral experience, I am struck frequently by the lack of knowledge many have about the field of sex therapy. Their knowledge often relies on distorted media reports, sensational films, or judgments of moral authorities who object to controversial components. Such distorted views create barriers for referral so that some couples in need will not avail themselves of treatment. Or, alternatively, the pastoral counselor may take a head-in-the-sand attitude and refer without knowing or wanting to know the components of sex therapy. Neither position serves our clients. Clients have a right to bring their questions and concerns to their religious advisors.

For these reasons I have risked providing considerable detail about modern sex therapy practices. Such information should facilitate appropriate referral. Credentialed therapists include licensed or certified psychiatrists, psychologists, social workers, marriage and family counselors, pastoral counselors and the like. The sexual problem may require treatment from a certified sex therapist. Any legitimate professional will acknowledge the possession of such certification. Interested parties may call the local professional associations to request members who are certified sex therapists.

Pastoral care workers need to understand the components of sex therapy so that they may prepare couples. Sex therapy may evoke concerns about values, morality, shame and guilt. The minister may need to remain in touch with clients after referral. This area provides an opportunity for holistic collaboration between pastoral counselor and the mental health professional. A couple may question the ethical acceptability of a treatment procedure. If the pastoral counselor does not appreciate the context and treatment philosophy, a specific technique may sound inappropriate or even bizarre. If the counselor does not understand a strategy, calling or meeting the therapist to discuss its rationale is appropriate. The therapist should welcome the counselor's involvement as a means of enhancing client adherence to the treatment regimen.

The complexity of normal sexual behavior along with paraphilia, gender identity disorders, and sexual dysfunction should challenge all of us in the helping professions to focus on the prevention of sexual problems. The challenge is complicated for religious leaders and counselors. On the one hand excessive religious prohibitions and distorted notions of sexuality are highly correlated with both paraphilia and sexual dysfunction. On the other hand, the assault on family life that occurs regularly from community breakdown in modern society pulls many of us toward conserving traditional sexual norms. Pastoral leaders must struggle to maintain a balance in coping with both pressures.

The contribution religion can make to sexual health is through communicating positive messages about personal sexuality. Sexual dysfunction is most likely if children are prevented from discussing their sexuality, if parents treat the topic as taboo, if early sexual exploration is brutally punished, if adults rape children, and if religious educators give mixed messages about the "goodness" of sexuality in God's plan contradicted by terroristic discussions of pregnancy and sexually transmitted diseases. Those of us in the mental health profession who honor religious experience feel pain when we see religion vandalizing lovemaps rather than nurturing healthy ones. Yet we also know that our traditions have exemplary views of human sexuality, e.g. The Song of Songs (Nelson, 1978). Research quoted at the start of this chapter highlights the relationship between religious commitment, conjugal prayer, and sexual satisfaction (Greeley, 1991).

We must conclude that religion is a force which can free believers to embrace their sexuality joyfully and responsibly, or assist in vandalizing their lovemaps and shape them toward shame and fear about sex. Leaders and teachers in church and synagogue must choose which practices best support sexual health and are consistent with their own traditions. But as leaders strive to balance sexual health with sexual responsibility, information about sexuality from medicine and psychology should assist that search.

Chapter 9

Personality Disorders

  I. Personality as a Disorder
 II. Classification of Personality Disorders
III. Anxious or Fearful Disorders
 IV. Odd or Eccentric Disorders
  V. Dramatic, Emotional or Erratic Disorders

Personality as a Disorder

Standard American English uses the word personality in a positive sense. To say someone "has personality" is a compliment. Indeed, to tell someone that he or she has no personality is an insult. If personality is a positive quality, how can it also be a disorder and the object of psychological treatment?

Some compare personality to nutrition (Tavris, 1989). Both are essential to life. Just as an unbalanced diet may impair physical health, so too an extreme personality style will impair psychological health. We know that, within limits, people adjust to an infinite variety of diets across cultures, customs and food groups. Personality also adjusts through a variety of cultures and developmental experiences.

Personality is elusive to define despite its use in everyday language. Personality is not a thing, though we tend to view it that way; rather it is a construct, a summary label. Personality is a construct for the individual's predisposition to perceive reality, respond emotionally, and behave across a wide range of environmental situations. The definition assumes that this predisposition is resistant to change, predictable and consistent.

In the late 1960s a strong debate occurred in personality psychology which questioned the supposed consistency of human behavior. Research emerged which challenged how consistent we are when circumstances change. Studies of honesty, for example, found that children who consistently told the truth might regularly cheat on school tests and vice versa.

Psychologists conducted many studies and spilled a lot of ink before they salvaged the term personality as meaning something consistent and predictable (Mischel, 1968; 1977). We cannot possibly summarize that 15 year debate here. However, researchers learned that people are behaviorally *inconsistent* with regard to broad *traits* (e.g. honest, warmhearted, assertive, etc.) but highly *consistent* behaviorally within the person's *own definition* of specific classes of behavior. For example, as an "honest" person I might not come to a full stop at every stop sign (my dead end street at 3 A.M.). Yet I will consistently fill out my income taxes honestly (given the mind's limited ability to comprehend the tax code).

If personality is now an acceptable term for experimental psychology, what does a personality *disorder* mean to the field of psychopathology? According to the DSM-III a personality disorder exists when behavioral or emotional responses attributed to these generalized predispositions result in significant distress to the person or in significant dysfunction (American Psychiatric Association, 1987). This definition has important implications. First it suggests that personality itself may be the source of the disorder, not just distressing symptoms such as anxiety, depression or hallucinations. A core organizing principle such as a strong need to rely on others may result in either personal distress or life impairment. Second, unlike most classified mental disorders, individuals with a personality disorder may experience little or no subjective distress. In these instances clinicians infer a personality disorder from the amount of dysfunction in an individual's life.

Psychologist T. Millon provides a useful framework for understanding personality disorders (Millon, 1986a; 1986b). Millon describes the sources of emotional disorders on a continuum. At one end environmental situations influence a disorder's development, and he calls this class of problems behavior reactions. Post-traumatic stress is an example of environmental stress generating a disorder. At the other end of the continuum are personality disorders which are independent of environmental influences. In between are symptom disorders which result from an equal interaction of person and environmental variables. Social anxiety is an example in which the person's vulnerability/diathesis (genetic, biological or learned) combines with a specific situation (evaluative social events) to result in a specific disorder. Millon's model provides a useful tool for locating personality disorders within psychopathology although reality is often less tidy.

The exact impact of personality disorders on society is more difficult to gauge than alcoholism or schizophrenia. We have no epidemiological survey to rival the Epidemiological Catchment Area (ECA) survey. The ECA surveyed only antisocial personality disorder (lifetime prevalence 2.5 percent of U.S. population). This leaves us with little information about the extent of personality disorders in the general population.

The impetus for learning more about personality disorders derives from clinicians and researchers as they treat psychological disorders with specific therapies (e.g. cognitive, interpersonal, brief psychoanalytic) and grapple with treatment failure. Research suggests that failure is more likely with persons diagnosed with a personality disorder. Large-scale studies confirm that personality disorders frequently co-exist in persons with other mental disorders. Depression research, for example, reveals that 30–70 percent of unipolar depressed persons have a personality disorder. This has implications for treatment because a personality disorder will interfere with adherence to a treatment program. How, for example, will a severely dependent person learn to cope with depression through assertive social action when his world view is "others should take care of me"?

Personality disorders have an impact far beyond the realm of psychotherapy. We cannot measure the "aggravation quotient" which personality disorders generate. How can we measure the impact of a passive aggressive individual on the efficiency, productivity or harmony of a workplace? Or the impact of a self-centered person on a committee task? Random selection suggests that personality disorders will exist in typical synagogues and congregations. The role they play in clergy burnout needs investigation. For this reason I refer to this group of disorders as saboteurs of community. Yet, as I have pointed out elsewhere (Ciarrocchi, 1990), the basic stance of empathy, charity, and unrequited giving common to most religion professionals actually creates a barrier for effective management of individuals with personality disorders.

Classification of Personality Disorders

The DSM-IIIR (American Psychiatric Association, 1987) describes eleven official personality disorders. The DSM clusters personality disorders in three broad groups: 1) anxious or fearful, 2) odd or eccentric, and 3) dramatic, emotional or erratic. We will use these labels to describe each personality disorder but appreciate that they exist for convenience. We will discuss the pastoral implications for each disorder separately rather than as a chapter summary since the disorders require distinct strategies.

The problems inherent in diagnosing personality disorders are gargantuan. To appreciate the difficulty we need recourse to the concept of *reliability*. Reliability for a measuring instrument means that it repeatedly measures an event, person or object in the same way. A bathroom scale which registers 150, 140 and 160 pounds for the same person on three trials in the same minute is unreliable. Psychological measurement also requires reliability of instrumentation. An IQ test which measures your IQ today as 130 and tomorrow as 85 is not reliable. Diagnostic reliability requires that the criteria are so specific that several clinicians can independently agree on the diagnosis for a person. The current APA diagnostic manual improved reliability over earlier editions. However, this holds true for categories other than personality disorders. Personality disorders, by contrast, have weak reliability (except for antisocial personality disorder).

This fact resulted in a schism between researchers and clinicians. Clinicians believed that personality disorders existed and directed their energy toward treating them. Research oriented clinicians (e.g. behavior therapists) spoke little about personality disorders. Improved diagnostic reliability eventually healed this split, and most clinicians appreciate the importance of considering personality disorder variables in treatment planning.

The poor reliability of these diagnostic classes, however, should alert the reader to the imprecision of assigning diagnoses to personality problems. The major problem is the overlap among groups. A severely dependent person, for example, will usually have avoidant as well as passive aggressive characteristics. Indeed, in clinical work, multiple diagnoses are the rule rather than the exception.

Anxious or Fearful Disorders

Avoidant Personality Disorder

Avoidant personality disorder describes persons who worry excessively about social evaluation and as a result restrict their social activities for fear of negative evaluation. Millon (1986a) describes these individuals as extremely sensitive to pain (i.e. rejection by others) and yet have a diminished capacity for pleasure. Most people are sensitive to rejection, but this is usually counterbalanced by enjoying positive attention. The avoidant person freezes socially since the pain of rejection far outweighs the desired positive attention. Relationships are problematic since they are shy, reserved, and avoid intimate relationships.

Avoidant persons will present in ministry as shy or even withdrawn. They differ from other withdrawn personality types in that they prefer social relationships but their fear of rejection prevents them. They may appear good-hearted and conscientious yet require an inordinate amount of coaxing to accept positions which will place them in the limelight. They may volunteer for behind-the-scenes projects and make good workers but refuse leadership positions.

The avoidant person is likely to feel dependent on the counselor or minister, particularly if he or she has received abundant empathy. The pastoral counselor may use this positive transference (Frances, 1987) to encourage the person to take risks, to venture out and try new behaviors. Many of the strategies useful in treating anxiety disorders (cf. Chapter 4) are effective for avoidant personalities as well. In particular, gradual desensitization to threatening situations often works. For example, if the person fears social gatherings, one could suggest attendance at a congregational function where acceptance is virtually guaranteed. Repeating these successes will build confidence for taking bigger steps.

Counselor problems (Frances, 1987) revolve around either pushing them too quickly or else nurturing them into paralysis. Pushing too quickly runs the risk of scaring them. Overprotection, on the other hand, reinforces their fears and gives the message that they should never experience anxiety. In reality the path for growth involves coping with anxiety, not eliminating it. The pastoral counselor must keep a wary eye on attachment behavior and maintain appropriate boundaries. In particular the pastoral counselor must give careful consideration and planning to termination. Gradual detachment through spacing out sessions is preferable to a sudden ending.

Dependent Personality Disorder

In Millon's framework a dependent personality sees others as the source of their gratification and as responsible for reducing their pain. They do not see themselves as the source in either case. As a result there is an "anxious attachment" to others. Dependent people feel lost when others are not caring for them. A second feature of this dependency is submission to others. The dependent person passively submits in relationships, deferring to others. Readers familiar with the popular concept of "codependency" may notice echoes of these characteristics (Cermak, 1986).

Men and women may have culturally influenced expressions of this disorder (Frances, 1987). Some dependent women may exhibit the disorder by deferring all major decisions to their husbands while they passively tend to what they perceive as their "domain." Some dependent men give an appearance of autonomy in a relationship but fall apart when the relationship ends. This commonly happens to outwardly self-sufficient men when they become widowers. They are liable to react with unremitting depression since they now feel emotionally helpless.

Writers and the media have taken a special interest in some features of this disorder as it relates to women staying in relationships in which they are mistreated or even abused. The titles alone in the self-help sections of book stores bear witness to this (*Women Who Love Too Much; Men Who Hate Women and the Women Who Stay with Them*).

The persons described in these books often believe that if they were not submissive others would not like them. Still others accept the belief that they cannot manage their own affairs. Dependent persons will try to thrust decisions onto the counselor. As members of congregations they go along with decisions or situations rather than express their own viewpoint, thereby depriving the community of a wider perspective. They complain to leadership when others mistrust or ignore them, yet will not face those who mistreat them.

They may seek help when relationships end, e.g. separation, divorce, widowhood. A distinguishing feature of dependent persons is that they do not bounce back from such events and loss may trigger major depressive episodes.

The pastoral counselor may feel pulled toward total giving and guilty that he or she is not giving enough. Pastoral counselors may also feel flattered that the person requires so much from them. However, this becomes tiresome as counselor or minister feels emptied by the person and is asked for still more. If the counselor vents frustration on the client, the likely effect is to decrease the client's self-esteem still further, rather than to instigate positive change. The client experiences this as one more example of being "a burden to everyone."

Many of the strategies discussed under avoidant personality disorder are effective with dependent personalities. Assertiveness training may ease requesting equality in relationships. Also, cognitive approaches (e.g. Burns, 1980) are useful for challenging assumptions of helplessness. Couples' therapy may help the dominant partner to see the impact of assuming too much responsibility and help balance the relationship.

Obsessive Compulsive Personality Disorder

Obsessive compulsive personality disorder is distinct from obsessive compulsive disorder. The two conditions may co-exist in the same person, but they are not variants of the same condition. Obsessive compulsive disorder is primarily an anxiety disorder characterized by obsessions and compulsions (cf. Chapter 4). The obsessive compulsive personality disorder is primarily a drive toward a rigid perfectionism without obsessions or compulsions.

This rigidity manifests itself in a preoccupation with trivia, an inability "to see the forest for the trees," to get the "big picture," to be "more Catholic than the pope." In bureaucracies they are the workers who reject forms not filled out perfectly. Their style is to focus on trivia and expect everyone else to conform in lock-step fashion. Work is their only source of satisfaction—without it they feel empty and devoid of purpose. Their range of effect is usually restricted and they often lack a sense of humor except perhaps for sarcasm. Some resemble the "Type A" personality—excessively driven by work and unable to relax. With a penchant for taking working vacations, doing nothing almost creates panic.

In the congregation or synagogue they may volunteer for the most undesirable detail work and show intense loyalty to the organization. Despite their loyalty they have an uncanny ability to generate consternation in their fellow workers due to their rigidity. If they teach religious education, colleagues complain how they always "go by the book" and are unable to adapt their faith to the times for fear of compromising eternal truths. They often have difficulty distinguishing morality from moralism.

Obsessive compulsive personalities rarely seek treatment with a desire for personality change. Their interpersonal style may generate conflict with others and someone in authority may "suggest" that they seek help. Another precipitant is procedural changes such as in office routine, filing systems, staff organization, or new members arriving in the work environment. Periods of cultural change which challenge theological tradition may also cause a crisis. The massive changes in the Roman Catholic Church during the Second Vatican Council in the 1960s exemplify this.

When entering treatment the obsessive compulsive personality typically blames others for his or her predicament. If only other people were more logical or followed the rules their troubles would be few. Treatment approaches might aim at deliberate attempts to program mild disruption. If they drive to work by the same route daily, suggest that they take a different route. Setting goals of mediocrity for non-essential tasks may generate anxiety but help them discover the possibility of accepting ordinariness. Positive countertransference issues occur when we need their attention to detail for our project. Negative feelings toward them include boredom or desiring to argue them down intellectually.

Passive-Aggressive Personality Disorder

The essence of this personality disorder is the passive resistance which greets efforts to motivate a person to conform. When given assignments they resist *indirectly*, which is the hallmark of the disorder. They procrastinate, "forget," go slowly, become unavailable, or complain and whine about how much they are put upon. Millon sees this disorder as wavering between seeing oneself versus seeing others as the source of reinforcement. At one moment they conform to achieve the good will of others but almost simultaneously regret their loss of autonomy and try subterfuge to regain it. Their ambivalence about autonomy prevents them from asserting their own needs or facing others. They resort to an indirect style which is synonymous with the disorder, namely passive-aggressive.

The pastoral minister encounters passive-aggressive persons in several situations. They may take doctrinal positions which make worse normal tensions accompanying any change. For example, they will resist liturgical changes through delay tactics. Passive-aggressive styles occur when individuals or groups feel powerless or have little input to the decision process. Many people naturally resist change and not all who resist change are passive-aggressive. For those with the personality disorder it represents a pervasive response style to demands for conformity.

As a psychology trainee, I once worked in a publicly funded outpatient clinic which closed at 4:30 P.M. The two receptionists never answered phone calls after 3 P.M. This allowed them to leave work an hour early unencumbered by last minute business. I was mildly amused to see an agency of psychiatrists, psychologists, social workers, and nurses along with more than 900 patients conform to the receptionists' needs. I was grateful that my wife went into labor while I was not at the office. Passive-aggressive persons are the bane of all committees or small working groups. If they do not fully support the project they fail to pull their weight or miss deadlines. They package their hostilities with a smile. Asking them to speak their mind directly gets little response but they complain as soon as the offending party is out of earshot. If they must communicate they have an affinity for written messages, electronic mail, or notes attached to bulletin boards: anything that avoids face-to-face confrontation.

The passive-aggressive person vacillates between wanting others to be their source of reinforcement versus wanting to depend on themselves. As a result, they appear at times to reach out for relationships while at other times they pull back and sabotage them. As Allen Frances suggests (1987), at times the minister may want to act in an authoritarian manner—simply to compel the passive-aggressive individual to perform. In hierarchical situations the minister may resort to "pulling rank" to force compliance. In the counseling situation the therapist will feel a strong urge to direct the individual or engage in power struggles to ensure a course of action. An alternative response is to combat passivity with passivity to see if the passive-aggressive person will squirm as a result of having no guidelines from the counselor. Pastoral care requires walking a fine line between engaging in constant battle and watching the person flounder.

Change involves at least two dimensions. At the behavioral level learning direct communication skills will improve interpersonal functioning. Assertiveness lies between passivity and aggression and promotes direct expression of needs without hostility. Often people do not feel they can survive interpersonal conflicts and thus resort to passive-aggressive behavior to protect their autonomy. The second change dimension involves cognitive traits. Various therapeutic approaches including psychodynamic, cognitive, and rational-emotive therapy work on altering the passive-aggressive person's structural outlook. This outlook involves feeling thoroughly put upon by the universe. This viewpoint believes that direct conflict will result in annihilation.

An effective pastoral stance involves dealing directly with them without rancor. An imaginary intervention might take the following format:

> This is the third time you said your report would be in. You have said repeatedly that you believe in this project, but your tardiness is making it extremely difficult to accomplish.

Is there some problem in getting your work done that you haven't told me about?

Another model for dealing with a complainer might be as follows:

People on this project have worked quite hard. Yet you seem to complain the most about the work load. Your frequent complaints are having a demoralizing effect on the team and I'm wondering if there is some other way for you to deal with your frustration.

This approach describes the annoying behavior in concrete terms through its effect on others but does not attribute motives to the individual. This allows him or her to save face and use the feedback constructively. This is more effective than unloading on the supposed motives; for example, "I can see you're really interested in sticking it to the rest of us." Also, dwelling on the pain and suffering may reinforce the aggressive intent motivating the behavior in the first place.

Odd or Eccentric Disorders

Paranoid Personality Disorder

The non-specialist (and even the specialist) may find it difficult to distinguish the paranoid personality disorder from paranoia in a delusional disorder or in schizophrenia, paranoid type. The main distinguishing factor is that the paranoid personality disorder lacks the overt psychotic features of the other disorders (cf. Chapter 7). The paranoid personality, while exasperating to deal with due to the illogical beliefs and hostility, often functions normally. The quality of life, however, for self and others suffers due to this disorder.

The characteristic feature of this personality style is a generalized expectancy that others intend to threaten or demean them. To appreciate the disorder's behavioral responses one could imagine how a totalitarian regime alters people: one is always on guard wondering whom to trust, taking nothing at face value but scrutinizing all behavior for hidden meanings, noting all previous wrongs and keeping careful records for an "enemies' list." The resultant emotional state is one of heightened anxiety, irritability, and suspiciousness. The only difference between the paranoid personality and the individual living under a totalitarian regime is that the latter has acquired paranoia honestly. With this disorder no threat exists which warrants the degree of defensiveness. Otherwise the behavioral, cognitive, and emotional responses are similar.

Ironically, the paranoid personality often gravitates toward clergy and religious groups. Just as church or synagogue is often a safe haven under persecutory regimes, the paranoid personality sees these same institutions as relatively trustworthy and places of refuge in an otherwise threatening world. Whether ministry leaders feel honored by this trust is another matter, since the paranoid personality generates considerable disruption. They may present as members whose concern for religious orthodoxy is excessive by the reference group's norms. This concern may take on a vindictive tone with such individuals seeing heresy everywhere. They are zealous in poring over religious education curricula or theological writings to assure others are as orthodox.

The major defense of paranoid personalities is projection. They judge harshly in others what they feel or experience. So well defended, they seldom seek counseling for their own personal growth. They would not say to themselves, "My suspicions toward others are dysfunctional. I'd better seek counseling to become more trusting." Rather, they seek counseling because of others' problems or because of what others have done to them. They may seek consultation because of "mistreatment" by a boss or co-workers, or for marital or family problems. In their mind the problems are external to themselves. The spouse is the problem, or if a child is in difficulty, the school is the cause. The nature of the disorder results in extreme sensitivity to criticism.

Working with the paranoid personality in consultation or for extended periods requires considerable skill. First, the pastoral counselor must appreciate the intractable nature of this personality disorder. One expert in this area (Millon, 1986b) describes the disorder using such descriptors as "unyielding, fixed, tenacious, immutable, and irrevocable." Rapid change, therefore, is not a reasonable goal. The minister must first use the trust projected onto him or her by the paranoid personality to develop a working relationship. Once trust develops, the client may develop tolerance to hear constructive criticism.

Countertransference feelings may occur in two spheres (Frances, 1987). Paranoid personalities trigger anger since we do not enjoy feeling mistrusted or having our motives challenged. We fall into a trap of "protesting too much" which paradoxically makes them more suspicious. The other tendency is never to criticize the paranoid personality for fear of retaliation. This too is not helpful since corrective feedback is essential for change.

When feeling challenged, the best response is to acknowledge to the client the difficulty in establishing a trusting relationship, the importance of time, and the fact that you are willing to put the necessary effort into the relationship to gain that trust. The pastoral counselor delivers negative feedback directly and in a straightforward manner. Direct feedback is also essential so that the client does not have to guess what the counselor thinks. Debating or arguing with the paranoid personality only reinforces his or her hypervigilance and creates more material for disputations. Rather, calm restatement of one's viewpoint works best. The reader may wish to consult Jesuit psychiatrist William Meissner's (1984) extended treatment of dealing with paranoid parishioners.

Schizoid Personality Disorder

In Millon's framework (1986a; 1986b) an indifference to both pleasure and pain characterizes the schizoid personality disorder. Millon does not mean this in an extreme sense. Certainly "if pricked do we not bleed?" is apropos, yet the schizoid personality appears indifferent to positive reinforcement and punishment. This leads to indifference in personal relationships since neither attention nor disapproval from others particularly moves them. When they do interact with others they lack warmth and empathy and actually prefer non-involvement. They seek isolation and are "wallflowers." At a party they will tinker with the host's computer or otherwise distance themselves.

The schizoid personality may resemble the avoidant personality outwardly, but the avoidant person would *like* close personal relationships yet avoids them due to fear of rejection. The schizoid personality, on the other hand, does not crave attention or worry about disapproval.

Schizoid personalities are more interested in things than in people. Some will take an avid interest in animal life or nature to the exclusion of personal relationships. Excessive involvement with material objects may characterize the disorder. They often tolerate long stretches of isolation, e.g. working as a forest ranger or night security officer. They appear emotionally restricted, usually not showing intense feelings such as love, hatred, anger, or joy.

The prevalence of the schizoid personality in the general community is not known. People with depression and other conditions, however, have high rates of schizoid personality disorder as a co-existing condition. Schizoid personalities do not present for treatment due to personality issues, since they are usually comfortable, but seek help for problems such as depression or alcoholism. Marital or family problems may lead to seeking help. In marriage or relationships the non-schizoid partner escalates the emotional intensity in a desperate attempt to stir up *any* feeling in the partner. Since the schizoid person does not respond to normal levels of criticism or praise, the emotional volume gets turned up and this shatters the family's harmony.

The schizoid personality is probably common in the typical church/synagogue community but unless the secondary problems noted co-occur these individuals do not make their presence felt. The minister may see their shy, withdrawn behavior or note how comfortable they are playing behind-the-scene roles to support the congregation. Most attempts to involve them socially are met with resistance and they require coaxing to join social groups.

While respecting their need for privacy the minister should not underestimate the pain of their detachment. Indeed many of the desensitization strategies suggested for the avoidant personality disorder are applicable to the schizoid personality as well. Frequently the attention and the support of a large group will have more influence than any single person, and may motivate them to take social risks.

Schizotypal Personality Disorder

The schizotypal disorder represents one of Millon's (1986a) severe personality disorder types along with paranoid personality and borderline personality. The behavioral and interpersonal aspects of schizotypal personality disorder are identical to the schizoid personality with the addition of cognitive oddities. They may also have unusual mannerisms, peculiarities of dress, poor hygiene, and blunted affect in addition to social isolation.

What distinguishes them, however, is their eccentricities of thought—namely, suspiciousness, feeling that others may be paying particular attention to them (ideas of reference), depersonalization, and non-traditional beliefs within their normative group. They differ from both paranoid delusional disorder and paranoid schizophrenia in that they are not psychotic in their beliefs but rather have the *feeling* that these experiences are true. They often appreciate the illogical nature of these feelings. Many researchers maintain that schizotypal disorders represent a genetic link to schizophrenia. A schizotypal person is likely to have a close relative who is schizophrenic.

In common with other personality disorders, schizotypal personalities do not typically present themselves for treatment. Their suspiciousness and mistrust of relationships result in avoidance of intense interpersonal encounters. For reasons similar to other mistrusting personality disorders the schizotypal personality may seek out religion professionals or pastoral counselors to share their secrets.

Pastors may note that their odd or eccentric ideas place them in concert with unusual ideologies. If not plainly heretical, their beliefs are marginal to the religious institution. They may believe in reincarnation, extrasensory perception (ESP), clairvoyance, telepathy, or channeling. If they are young they may join cults. In mainstream religious organizations they may fade into one of the organizations' subgroups on the left or right. In smaller groups they feel pressured if their beliefs diverge significantly from others. All persons who believe in ESP, reincarnation, channeling, etc., are not by definition schizotypal personality disorders. Some persons believe in these phenomena, but lack the avoidant, withdrawn, and suspicious aloofness of the schizotypal personality.

No universally effective treatment exists for this condition. Psychiatrists sometimes try neuroleptic medication (cf. Chapter 7) but compliance is poor due to physiological sensitivity and the patient's suspiciousness (Frances, 1987). Psychotherapy may stabilize such patients during a crisis or treat co-existing problems, but does not change the personality disorder itself. Treating schizotypal personality disorders is likely to generate feelings of frustration and confusion if one tries to debate their belief system. Verbal persuasion and logic are ineffective. The minister may feel paralyzed if he or she sees them involved with fringe groups, especially dangerous ones (e.g. satanism).

For some the pastoral counselor will represent a safe haven to express feelings or ideas. While the consultations or sessions may appear routine or uninspiring to the counselor they have meaning for the schizotypal personality (Frances, 1987). Guidelines for ministers dealing with these individuals are similar to the guidelines for working with schizophrenia: do not engage in disputes but emphasize a decidedly middle-of-the-road approach to doctrinal and spiritual issues. Presenting them with "novel teachings" only serves to overstimulate a cognitive system already struggling to maintain boundaries.

Dramatic, Emotional or Erratic Disorders

This cluster contains two milder disorders (histrionic and narcissism) and two severe types (antisocial and borderline).

Histrionic Personality Disorder

The histrionic personality disorder in Millon's framework (1986a) focuses excessively on others as the source of pleasure and the protector against pain. Unlike the dependent personality disorder which also has this "other" focus, the histrionic personality does not passively wait for others to provide these goods. Rather, the histrionic personality actively seeks them and employs various strategies including subterfuge and manipulation.

Histrionic personalities are individuals who need to be "on stage" even in everyday life. When they ask someone at table to pass the salt it feels like a scene from Hamlet. Their need to be the center of attention generates a seductive and overdramatic interpersonal style. Their expression of affect is intense but superficial. One moment they will appear deeply moved by sadness, then anger, then joy, but in reality they are shallow and lacking in empathy. People are important to them momentarily as providers of positive affection or as eliminators of pain, but they have little to give in return. As a result they move frequently from relationship to relationship wearing out friends and associates.

As we repeatedly note in this section, these individuals do not appreciate their own contribution to problems in living. They blame failed relationships on others. Psychodynamic therapy has a long tradition with this disorder. Many of Freud's original patients suffered from it, and they influenced his theory of the unconscious. From their ingenuousness and naiveté he speculated to the effects of sexual repression. This disorder has considerable overlap with dependent and borderline disorders and it often co-exists with significant depression. When seriously depressed they may represent a greater than average risk of self-injury or suicidal behavior. Though suicidal intent may not be present when they hurt themselves, this behavior must be taken seriously and referred to appropriate treatment providers.

In the pastoral care setting, the disorder is common. Indeed histrionic personalities are drawn to involvement in church or synagogue. After all, the rituals of many religious traditions have an element of theater including ceremonies marking developmental passages: birth, passing into adolescence, marriage, illness, and death. These events allow the histrionic personality to be at center stage in a socially constructive and adaptive manner.

Intense involvement with the histrionic personality may lead to opposite reactions (Frances, 1987). One response is to defend against the seductiveness and flirtation through indifference. Although some ministers need to defend themselves in this manner, this may wound the person too greatly. The second tendency is to lose track of boundaries. This loss of boundaries is a continuum and ranges from modest social contact to sexual involvement. Psychiatrist Allen Frances (1987) recommends allowing oneself to be "somewhat seduced," by which he means we must like the histrionic personality or he or she will not tolerate therapy. Nevertheless, invitations to cross boundaries require a gentle assertiveness on the part of the counselor followed by exploring with persons what they wish to get for themselves through these invitations. The discussion should include alternative solutions to their needs.

Although no controlled research exists on the treatment of this disorder, clinical reports of psychodynamic and cognitive-behavioral approaches have had selective success. Actually many treatment modalities may work since these individuals are highly suggestible—a trait usually correlated with successful outcome in verbal psychotherapies (Bandura, 1969). At the pastoral level ministers may find two points helpful. First, the minister may wish to give attention or reinforcement "contingently" as the behaviorist would suggest. This means giving attention appropriately—not when the person is putting on a show or being flamboyant. Rather, praise is forthcoming when the individual contributes in quiet, unobtrusive, and thoughtful ways—e.g. visiting shut-ins, doing hidden committee work, and the giving of unseen gifts. Second, the minister should encourage assertiveness. Histrionic persons mistakenly believe that to achieve interpersonal goals they must mask their true intentions. Learning direct methods of communication allows them to drop their masks and stop manipulative behavior.

Narcissistic Personality Disorder

While narcissism is a new diagnostic category with **DSM-III**, the concept played a central part in Freud's theorizing about the development of the id, ego, and superego structure (Raskin and Terry, 1988). The etymology of the term traces to Greek mythology and the story of Narcissus who fell in love with his own reflection in the water and drowned through self-enchantment. There is considerable overlap in this personality disorder with histrionic, borderline, and antisocial personality disorders, with all three having strong narcissistic features. The essential feature of the narcissistic personality is an exaggerated sense of self-worth and self-importance. They appear arrogant and commonly exploit others. In Millon's (1986a) framework they focus excessively on self as the source of pleasure and defense against pain. In popular terminology they are excessively self-absorbed, self-centered, or puffed up. A corollary of this self-centeredness is their lack of empathy for others which means that relationships work for them as long as the other provides enough adoration.

Once a receptionist in my agency tripped over construction material and a staff nurse was tending her bleeding leg wound. In the midst of this minor drama a client interrupted to ask the receptionist subway directions. This narcissistic person assumed that getting directions outweighed tending to a serious injury. Such behavior illustrates their sense of entitlement—an apt description for their behavior and attitude toward life. They believe that they are entitled to privileges, rewards, and special treatment. In colloquial terms they believe that "the world owes them a living."

Psychoanalytic therapists use the phrase "narcissistic injury" to describe the deep wounding when others fail to appreciate them. They enter therapy licking their psychological wounds and bewildered that the slings and arrows of outrageous fortune are aimed their way. They also lack insight into their own contribution to the rejection.

In the initial stage the counselor's task is to build up the narcissistic person's ego to engage him or her in the treatment process. The therapeutic alliance may actually involve praising the client and reinforcing their strengths though their pathology involves an exaggerated sense of self-worth (Frances, 1987). Once engaged, the client faces evidence of self-centeredness in small doses, how it affects others and how others are likely to tire of this behavior. Through therapy they face their sense of entitlement.

Some counselors approach narcissism as development gone awry. In this view narcissism develops from disappointment with parents, and counseling allows the person to work through the resultant rage. Others take a more confrontative approach once the therapeutic alliance is established. I sometimes give to clients the actual diagnostic criteria to read and discuss in the session. Some therapists work with the narcissistic personality through the metaphor of "King Baby" and point out that this internal king needs dethronement before mature relationships can develop.

Borderline Personality Disorder

Borderline personality disorder remains among the most challenging disorders to treat. Within the past five to ten years clinicians have written extensively on this subject, although psychoanalysts were the first to describe the disorder in considerable detail. One reason for the lack of interest by clinicians relates to the poor diagnostic reliability of the personality disorders. Nevertheless, most clinicians agree that no matter how problematic reliability is, the condition itself is real and debilitating.

Meehl's (1989) comments on reliability and validity are germane. Measuring blood pressure, for example, is actually an unreliable enterprise. Measuring the width of a patient's wrist, on the other hand, is highly reliable. Nevertheless, no matter how imprecise reliability is for blood pressure, clinicians will always choose taking blood pressure in an examination over measuring wrist width. In a similar fashion, agreeing on the exact criteria for borderline personality disorder is difficult but few deny its clinical significance.

The three major features of the borderline personality disorder are impulsivity, self-damaging acts, and unstable/intense relationships. Impulsivity includes such behavior as recklessness, excessive spending, anorexia/bulimia, substance abuse, gambling or promiscuity. Instability and intensity characterize personal relationships, with the borderline shifting between rage at others not meeting their needs and desperate clinging. This ambivalence leads to relationships characterized by abuse and counter-abuse. Aggression may turn physical, with partners striking out violently toward each other. Yet the next moment may bring reconciliation because of abandonment fears.

Self-damaging acts are also common. This refers to immediate harmful acts as opposed to long-term self-destructive behavior, e.g. alcoholism or poor diet. Clinicians use the term "parasuicide" to describe behaviors which are self-injurious but do not result in death. Parasuicidal behavior in the borderline includes cutting oneself with a razor or sharp object, ingesting sub-lethal amounts of pills or poisons, head-banging, or other self-mutilating behavior. The usual intention is to hurt oneself but not to die, although when deeply depressed the person stops caring about living.

Psychologist Marsha Linehan has worked extensively with female borderlines and developed a treatment model she calls "dialectical therapy" (Linehan, 1985). She proposes a diathesis-stress model (cf. Chapter 2) in which a biological predisposition to high emotional arousal interacts with an invalidating interpersonal environment. A person who is unable to regulate intense emotions without great effort interacts with caretakers who minimize her difficulty and fail to support the necessary coping skills. As a result intense emotion overwhelms her, she lacks the skills to handle it, and she clings to others as a source of relief. Since no one is available 100 percent to rescue her, she turns to other soothing behaviors for emotional release such as alcohol, drugs, sex, spending, and self-mutilation which releases endorphins (cf. Chapter 6), thereby reinforcing self-injurious behavior.

Ideally the borderline patient needs to develop new coping skills for strong emotion. Linehan illustrates the difficulty through an analogy that the borderline personality is like someone who needs shelter from a tornado, but who tries to build it *during* the tornado. Since the borderline is so often in crisis the therapist spends much of her time attending to disaster control and seldom pursues important long term goals. Parasuicidal behaviors and substance abuse followed by financial problems, health care, and unsafe sex practices all demand therapist attention. The borderline's natural tendency to intensify relationships and demand unusual guarantees of care and concern continually threatens to end therapy. The counselor always keeps a watchful eye on the therapy relationship itself since no progress is possible if the client terminates abruptly. As if this clinical picture needed any further complications, many female borderlines were sexually abused as children.

The range of countertransference toward borderlines is extensive and includes confusion, fear, wanting to rescue them, wanting to run from them, sexual attraction, and quite often anger (Frances, 1987). Therapists who work closely with borderlines seek consultation themselves to remain objective about their care. Counselors are prone to ignore boundaries with this population more than with most and will rationalize counseling "techniques" which disinterested colleagues might label problematic.

If experienced clinicians have problems treating borderlines, non-specialists are apt to have their hands full as well. In this spirit we offer the following guidelines for pastoral counselors working with the disorder.

1. Maintain clear boundaries. Keep the focus of involvement on

the role of pastoral care. If boundaries do blur, admit the mistake and re-establish the original limits.

2. Refer to appropriate specialists. Only trained, credentialed clinicians should have the major therapeutic role in the treatment of borderlines. This is particularly important if any self-injurious behavior is present.

3. Seek consultation. A good check on the legitimacy of a counseling strategy is the clear gaze of the proverbial prudent person.

4. Pick only one problem to help. If the pastoral counselor has developed skills in substance abuse, for example, work on that dimension alone. If spiritual direction is the focus of the relationship, stay within the parameters of that discipline.

5. Suggest abundant use of self-help and support groups. Refer to Alcoholics Anonymous, Narcotics Anonymous, Survivors of Incest Anonymous or similar groups. These groups help build coping skills and dilute the transference often found in individual counseling.

Antisocial Personality Disorder

Antisocial personality disorder, also known as psychopathy, has the most reliable diagnostic criteria of the personality disorders. The hallmark of this disorder is its chronic course, with symptoms present before age 16. The individual must exhibit a variety of antisocial behaviors such as school problems, family problems, running away, substance abuse, and illegal behavior. These outward behaviors allow for reliable diagnosis, but sharp disagreement exists among clinicians who feel that the criteria miss the essential nature of antisocial personality, namely the lack of conscience or guilt feelings.

Recent research (Smith and Newman, 1990) suggests that antisocial personality involves two components: socially deviant behavior *and* callous egocentricity. The social deviance factor includes impulsivity, poor delay of gratification, early behavior problems, high need for stimulation, and parasitic lifestyle. This factor contributes to a criminal lifestyle and nearly ubiquitous alcoholism and/or drug abuse. The callous egocentrism factor includes manipulation, lack of empathy, lack of guilt or remorse, superficial charm, and lying. This second factor accounts for the inability of antisocial personalities to maintain an intimate relationship which involves mutuality. If they marry they cannot sustain fidelity, and the only bond is fulfilling their infantile needs. When that ceases, they end the relationship. Many, but not all, career criminals are antisocial personalities. Incarceration alone does not define the disorder clinically. However, the disorder's characteristics incline the person toward deviant and criminal behavior. For this disorder socially deviant behavior begins in early adolescence. They have histories of school conduct problems and juvenile delinquency. Alcohol and drug abuse start early, and they are likely to have a family history of antisocial personalities. Men with the disorder far outnumber women. Depression in this population is common as well as high rates of suicide.

Physiological theories of the origins of antisocial personality are inconclusive. Some evidence exists that they demonstrate decreased autonomic nervous system arousal so that pain feedback makes no impression on them. This reputedly leaves a person unable to learn from his or her mistakes and explains his or her chronic impulsivity. Recent research discredits earlier ideas that the disorder results from organic brain damage. Controlled studies reveal no neuropsychological differences between incarcerated antisocial personalities and prisoners without antisocial personalities.

The history of antisocial personality treatment is justifiably pessimistic. Due to the immense social cost of the disorder many treatment programs have tried to change these individuals. All have failed. While most clinicians agree that no effective treatment exists, many maintain that some antisocial personalities "mature out" of the disorder as they age. The cynic would suggest that jail is the only "treatment" until the antisocial personality is beyond the capacity to harm society.

Religion professionals are likely to meet antisocial people in ministry to offender populations. Occasionally they meet the "con artist" schemer trying to get money from church or synagogue. The encounters tend to generate countertransference feelings in opposite directions. Some will feel sympathetic and succumb to the manipulation, believing the antisocial person's hard luck story. In this scenario the minister believes that the antisocial personality has never had anyone trust him or her or give unconditional positive regard. The minister believes that with the proper conditions the individual might change. The other response is to counterattack and treat the antisocial personality with hostility.

The antisocial person is an excellent con artist, so one should not harshly judge oneself if fooled. As one of the alcoholism counselors on my treatment team liked to comment about an occasional patient, "He must be antisocial because I really like him." This comment pays tribute to their superficial charm. In the ministry of pastoral counseling, seldom do we hear terms such as "hopeless" or "impossible." Yet with the antisocial person, reality forces us to accept the absence of any known treatment. This fact must color our expectations in ministry. A reasonable strategy is to assist with collateral problems such as substance abuse, depression, marital or parenting issues. Counselors who believe therapy will change the core indifference of these people have set themselves up to experience failure.

We will probably never know the degree to which the antisocial personality disorder impairs free choice. In the absence of an answer to this question a pragmatic strategy interacts non-judgmentally yet firmly. The pastoral counselor must look out for manipulation since allowing that behavior only reinforces the disorder. In addition the pastoral counselor expects and demands appropriate behavior. I have personally known of instances where a creative pastoral counselor became the conscience of several psychopaths. The minister gained their trust and developed informal contracts whereby his clients called to validate the wisdom of decisions rather than impulsively act them out. This did not "cure" the disorder but it brought a measure of stability to a chaotic lifestyle.

References

Ahrons, S.J. (1989). *A comparison of the family environments and psychological distress of married pathological gamblers, alcoholics, psychiatric patients, and their spouses with normal controls.* Unpublished doctoral dissertation, University of Maryland.

Ainsworth, M.D.S., and Bowlby, J. (1991). An ethological approach to personality development. *American Psychologist, 46,* 333–341.

American Psychiatric Association (1980). *Diagnostic and statistical manual of mental disorders* (3rd ed.). Washington, D.C. Author.

American Psychiatric Association (1987). *Diagnostic and statistical manual of mental disorders* (3rd ed. rev). Washington, D.C. Author.

Andreasen, N.C. (1987). The diagnosis of schizophrenia. *Special Report: Schizophrenia 1987.* Rockville: U.S. Department of Health and Human Services.

Backus, W. (1985). *Telling the truth to troubled people.* Minneapolis: Bethany House.

Bandura, A. (1969). *Principles of behavior modification.* New York: Holt, Rinehart & Winston.

Bandura, A. (1986). *Social foundations of thought and action: A social cognitive theory.* Englewood Cliffs: Prentice-Hall.

Barlow, D.H. (1988). *Anxiety and its disorders: The nature and treatment of anxiety and panic.* New York: Guilford Press.

Barlow, D.H., and Cerny, J.A. (1988). *Psychological treatment of panic.* New York: Guilford Press.

Bass, E., and Davis, L. (1988). *The courage to heal.* New York: Harper/Collins.

Beck, A.T. (1991). Cognitive therapy: A 30-year retrospective. *American Psychologist, 46,* 368–375.

Beck, A.T., and Emery, G. (1985). *Anxiety disorders and phobias: A cognitive perspective.* New York: Basic Books.

Beck, A.T., Rush, A.J., Shaw, B.F., and Emery, G. (1979). *Cognitive therapy of depression.* New York: Guilford.

Bergin, A.E. (1991). Values and religious issues in psychotherapy and mental health. *American Psychologist, 46,* 394–403.

Black, C. (1982). *It will never happen to me.* Denver: M.A.C. Printing and Publications Division.

Bowlby, J. (1980). *Attachment and loss (Vol. 3): Loss, sadness and depression.* New York: Basic Books.

Brown, G.W., and Harris, T.O. (1978). *Social origins of depression.* London: Tavistock.

Browne, A., and Finkelhor, D. (1986). Impact of child sexual abuse: A review of the research. *Psychological Bulletin, 99,* 66–77.

Bry, B. (1983). Empirical foundations of family-based approaches to adolescent substance abuse. In T.J. Glynn, C.G. Leukefeld, and J.P. Ludford, *Preventing adolescent drug abuse: Intervention strategies.* NIDA Research Monograph 47. Rockville: Department of Chapter 2. Health and Human Services.

Bufford, R.K. (1981). *The human reflex: Behavioral psychology in biblical perspective.* San Francisco: Harper and Row.

Bunyan, J. (1988). *Grace abounding: To the chief of sinners.* Westwood: Barbour & Co.

Burns, D.D. (1980). *Feeling good: The new mood therapy.* New York: William Morris.

Burns, D.D. (1985). *Intimate Connections.* New York: New American Library.

Callahan, R. (1991). The ministry of crisis intervention. In B.K. Estadt, M.C. Blanchette, and J.R. Compton (eds.), *Pastoral counseling* (2nd edition). Englewood Cliffs: Prentice-Hall.

Cannon, T.D., Mednick, S.A., and Parnas, J. (1989). Genetic and perinatal determinants of structural brain defects in schizophrenia. *Archives of General Psychiatry, 46,* 883–889.

Carpenter, W.T. (1987). Approaches to knowledge and understanding of schizophrenia. *Special Report: Schizophrenia 1987.* Rockville: U.S. Department of Health and Human Services.

Carroll, B.J. (1985). Dexamethasone suppression test: A review of contemporary confusion. *Journal of Clinical Psychiatry, 46,* 13.

Cermak, T.L. (1986). Diagnosing and treating codependence. Minneapolis: Johnson Institute.

Cheston, S. (1991). *Making effective referrals: The therapeutic process.* New York: Gardner.

Christiansen, E.M. (1989, July 15). 1988 Gross Annual Wager. *Gaming and Wagering Business, 10,* 8.

Ciarrocchi, J.W. (1984). Alcoholism. In A.W. Sipe and C.J. Rowe (eds.), *Psychiatry, ministry, and pastoral counseling* (2nd ed.). Collegeville: Liturgical Press.

Ciarrocchi, J.W. (1987). Addiction counseling. In B.K. Estadt, J.R. Compton, and M. Blanchette (eds.), *The art of clinical supervision: A pastoral counseling perspective.* New York: Paulist Press.

Ciarrocchi, J.W., and Richardson, R. (1989). Profile of compulsive gamblers in treatment. *Journal of Gambling Behavior,* 5, 53–65.

Ciarrocchi, J.W. (1991). Counseling with the recovering alcoholic. In B.K. Estadt, M. Blanchette, and J. Compton (eds.), *Pastoral counseling.* Englewood Cliffs: Prentice-Hall.

Ciarrocchi, J.W. (1993). Pathological gambling and pastoral counseling. In R.J. Wicks and R.D. Parsons (eds.), *Clinical handbook of pastoral counseling, Vol. 2.* New York: Paulist Press.

Ciarrocchi, J.W. (1990). Scrupulosity: Religion and obsessive-compulsive disorder. *OCD Newsletter,* 4, No. 3, 1, 4.

Clark, D.M., Salkovskis, P.M., and Chalkey, A.J. (1985). Respiratory control as a treatment for panic attacks. *Journal of Behavior Therapy and Experimental Psychiatry,* 16, 23–30.

Clayton, P. (1983). The prevalence and course of the affective disorders. In J.M. Davis and J.W. Maas (eds.), *The affective disorders.* Washington, D.C.: American Psychiatric Press.

Clinebell, H. (1978). *Understanding and counseling the alcoholic.* Nashville: Abingdon.

Cloninger, C.R. (1987). Neurogenetic adaptive mechanisms in alcoholism. *Science,* 236, 410–416.

Cohen, R. (September 16, 1990). Dark victory. *The Washington Post Sunday Magazine,* Column title: Critic At Large, p. 11.

Custer, R.L., and Custer, L.F. (1978). Characteristics of the recovering compulsive gambler: A survey of 150 members of Gamblers Anonymous. Paper presented at the Fourth Annual Conference on Gambling, Reno, Nevada.

Custer, R., and Milt, H. (1985). *When luck runs out: Help for compulsive gamblers and their families.* New York: Facts on File.

Davison, G.C., and Neale, J.M. (1990). *Abnormal psychology* (5th ed.). New York: John Wiley.

Domino, G. (1990). Clergy's knowledge of psychopathology. *Journal of Psychology and Theology,* 18, 32–39.

Egan, G. (1975). *The skilled helper.* Monterey: Brooks/Cole.

Elkin, I., Shea, T., Watkins, J.T., Imber, S.D., Sotsky, S.M., Collins, J.F., Glass, D.R., Pilkonis, P.A., Leber, W.R., Docherty, J.P., Fiester, S.J., Parloff, M.B. (1989). National Institute of Mental

Health treatment of depression collaborative research program: General effectiveness of treatments. *Archives of General Psychiatry, 46,* 971–982.

Ellis, A., and Grieger, R. (1977). *Handbook of rational-emotive therapy.* New York: Springer.

Farmer, R., and Nelson-Gray, R.O. (1990). Personality disorders and depression: Hypothetical relations, empirical findings, and methodological considerations. *Clinical Psychology Review, 10,* 453–476.

Folsteen, M.F., Folsteen, S.E., and McHugh, P.R. (1975). Mini-mental state: A practical method for grading the cognitive state of patients for the clinician. *Journal of Psychiatric Research, 12* (3), 189–198.

Frances, A. (1987). *DSM-III personality disorders: Diagnosis, and treatment.* New York: BMA Audio Cassettes.

Franklin, J. (1987). *Molecules of the mind.* New York: Dell Publishing.

Gartner, J., Larson, D., and Allen, G. (1991). Religious commitment and mental health: A review of the empirical literature. *Journal of Psychology and Theology, 19,* 6–25.

Gold, M.S., and Morris, L.B. (1988). *The good news about depression: New medical cures and treatment that can work for you.* New York: Bantam.

Goldstein, M.J. (1987). Psychosocial issues. *Special report: Schizophrenia 1987.* Rockville: U.S. Department of Health and Human Services.

Goodwin, D. (1981). *Alcoholism: The facts.* New York: Oxford University Press.

Gottesman, I.I., McGriffin, P., and Farmer, A.E. (1987). Clinical genetics as clues to the "real" genetics of schizophrenia (A decade of modest gains while playing for time). *Special report: Schizophrenia 1987.* Rockville: U.S. Department of Health and Human Services.

Gottesman, I.I., and Bertelsen, A. (1989). Confirming unexpressed genotypes for schizophrenia. *Archives of General Psychiatry, 46,* 867–872.

Greeley, A. (1991). *Faithful attraction: Discovering intimacy, love, and fidelity in American marriage.* New York: Tom Doherty Associates.

Halberstam, D. (1979). *The powers that be.* New York: Knopf.

Hall, C.S., and Lindzey, G. (1970). *Theories of personality.* New York: Wiley.

Heiman, J., LoPiccolo, L., and LoPiccolo, J. (1976). *Becoming orgasmic: A sexual growth program for women.* Englewood Cliffs: Prentice-Hall.

Hogarty, G.E., Anderson, C.M., Reiss, D.J., Kornbleth, S.J., Greenwald, D.P., Jarna, C.D., and Madonia, M.J. (1986). Family psychoeducation, social skills training, and maintenance chemotherapy for the aftercare treatment of schizophrenia. I: One year effects of a controlled study on relapse and expressed emotion. *Archives of General Psychiatry, 43,* 633–642.

Holzman, P. (1987). Recent studies of psychophysiology in schizophrenia. *Special report: Schizophrenia 1987.* Rockville: U.S. Department of Health and Human Services.

Jackson, J. (1954). The adjustment of the family to the crises of alcoholism. *Quarterly Journal of Studies on Alcohol, 15,* 562.

Jacob, T., Krahn, G., and Leonard, K. (1991). Parent-child interactions in families with alcoholic fathers. *Journal of Consulting and Clinical Psychology, 59,* 176–181.

Jacobson, G.R. (1989). A comprehensive approach to pretreatment evaluation: I. Detection, assessment and diagnosis of alcoholism. In R.K. Hester and W.R. Miller (eds.), *Handbook of alcoholism treatment approaches: Effective alternatives.* New York: Pergamon Press.

Kaplan, H.I., and Sadock, B.J. (1988). Sexual disorders. In H.I. Kaplan and B.J. Sadock (eds.), *Synopsis of psychiatry: Behavioral sciences, clinical psychiatry* (5th ed., 358–376). Baltimore: Williams & Wilkins.

Kaplan, H.S. (1979). *Disorders of sexual desire.* New York: Brunner/Mazel.

Keating, A.M., and Fretz, B.R. (1990). Christians' anticipations about counselors in response to counselor descriptions. *Journal of Counseling Psychology, 37,* 293–296.

Keegan, A. (1991). Mental illness, substance abuse cost U.S. $273.3 billion in 1988, ADAMHA Study says. *NIDA Notes, 6,* 26–27.

Kellerman, J.L. (1973). *A merry-go-round named denial.* Center City: Hazelden.

Kinsey, A.C., Pomeroy, W.B., and Martin, C.E. (1948). *Sexual behavior in the human male.* Philadelphia: Saunders.

Klerman, G.L. (1988). Overview of the cross-national collaborative panic study. *Archives of General Psychiatry, 45,* 407–412.

Klerman, G.L., Weissman, M.M., Rounsaville, B.J., and Chevron, E.S. (1984). *Interpersonal psychotherapy of depression.* New York: Basic Books.

Küng, H. (1990). *Freud and the problem of God.* New Haven: Yale University Press.

Kurtz, E. (1979). *Not God: A history of Alcoholics Anonymous.* Center City: Hazelden.

Kurtz, E. (1981). *Shame and guilt: Characteristics of the dependency cycle (An historical perspective for professionals).* Center City: Hazelden.

Kurtz, E. (1988). *AA: The story.* San Francisco: Harper & Row.

Larson, D.B., Hohmann, A.A., Kessler, L.G., Meador, K.G., Boyd, J.H., and McSherry, E. (1988). The couch and the cloth: The need for linkage. *Hospital and Community Psychiatry, 39,* 1064–1069.

Lesieur, H.R. (1984). *The chase: Career of the compulsive gambler.* Cambridge: Schenkman Books.

Lesieur, H.R., and Rosenthal, R.J. (1991). Pathological gambling: A review of the literature (Prepared for the American Psychiatric Association Tasks Force on DSM-IV Committee on Disorders of Impulse Control Not Elsewhere Classified. *Journal of Gambling Studies, 7,* 5–39.

Lewinsohn, P.M. (1974). A behavioral approach to depression. In R.J. Friedman and M.M. Katz (eds.), *Contemporary theory and research.* Washington, D.C.: Winston.

Lewinsohn, P.M., Munoz, R.F., Youngren, M.A., and Zeiss, A.M. (1978). *Control your depression.* Englewood Cliffs: Prentice-Hall.

Linehan, M.M. (1985). Dialectical behavior therapy for borderline personality disorder. *Bulletin of the Menninger Clinic, 51,* 261–276.

Lystad, M. (ed.) (1985). *Innovations in mental health services to disaster victims.* Rockville: U.S. Department of Health and Human Services.

Marks, I. (1985). Stress and other risk factors in anxiety disorders. In H.H. Goldman and S.E. Goldston (eds.), *Preventing stress-related psychiatric disorders.* Rockville: U.S. Department of Health and Human Services.

Maslow, A. (1971). *The farther reaches of human nature.* New York: Viking.

Masters, W.H., and Johnson, V.L. (1966). *Human sexual response.* Boston: Little, Brown & Company.

Masters, W.H., and Johnson, V.L. (1970). *Human sexual inadequacy.* New York: Little, Brown & Company.

Masters, W.H., and Johnson, V.E. (1979). *Homosexuality in perspective.* Boston: Little, Brown & Company.

McDonnell, R., and Callahan, R. (1987). *Hope for healing: Good news for adult children of alcoholics.* New York: Paulist Press.

McKim, W.A. (1986). *Drugs and behavior: An introduction to behavioral pharmacology.* Englewood Cliffs: Prentice-Hall.

Meehl, P.E. (1989). Schizotaxia revisited. *Archives of General Psychiatry, 46,* 935–944.

Meichenbaum, D. (1985). *Stress inoculation training.* New York: Pergamon Press.

Meissner, W.M. (1984). The paranoid parishioner. In A.W. Sipe and C.J. Rowe (eds.), *Psychiatry, Ministry and Pastoral Counseling* (2nd ed.). Collegeville: Liturgical Press.

Melamed, B.G., and Siegel, L.J. (1975). Reduction of anxiety in children facing hospitalization and surgery by use of filmed modeling. *Journal of Consulting and Clinical Psychology, 43,* 511–521.

Meltzer, H.Y. (1987). Biological studies in schizophrenia. *Special report: Schizophrenia 1987.* Rockville: U.S. Department of Health and Human Services.

Miller, W. (1988). Including clients' spiritual perspectives in cognitive behavior therapy. In W.R. Miller and J.E. Martin (eds.), *Behavior therapy and religion: Integrating spiritual and behavioral approaches to change.* Newbury Park: Sage Publications.

Miller, W.R., and Hester, R.K. (1989). Treating alcohol problems: Toward an informed eclecticism. In R.K. Hester and W.R. Miller (eds.), *Handbook of alcoholism treatment approaches: Effective alternatives.* New York: Pergamon Press.

Miller, W.R., and Jackson, K.A. (1985). *Practical psychology for pastors.* Englewood Cliffs: Prentice-Hall.

Millon, T. (1986a). A theoretical derivation of pathological personalities. In T. Millon and G.L. Klerman (eds.), *Contemporary directions in psychopathology: Toward the DSM-IV.* New York: Guilford.

Millon, T. (1986b). Personality prototypes and their diagnostic criteria. In T. Millon & G.L. Klerman (eds.), *Contemporary directions in psychopathology: Toward the DSM-IV.* New York: Guilford.

Mischel, W. (1968). *Personality and assessment.* New York: Wiley.

Mischel, W. (1977). On the future of personality assessment. *American Psychologist, 32,* 246–254.

Mohr, D.C., and Beutler, L.E. (1990). Erectile dysfunction: A review of diagnostic and treatment procedures. *Clinical Psychology Review, 10,* 123–150.

Money, J. (1986). *Lovemaps: Clinical concepts of sexual/erotic health and pathology, paraphilia, and gender transposition in childhood, adolescence, and maturity.* New York: Irvington.

Money, J. (1988). *Gay, straight, and in-between: The sexology of erotic orientation.* New York: Oxford University Press.

Myers, J.K., Weissman, M.M., Tischler, G.L., Holzer, C.E., Leaf, P.J., Orvaschel, H.A., Anthony, J.C., Boyd, J.H., Burke, J.E., Kramer, M., and Stolzman, R. (1984). Six-month prevalence of psychiatric disorders in three communities: 1980–1982. *Archives of General Psychiatry, 41,* 959–967.

Nelson, J.B. (1978). *Embodiment: An approach to sexuality and Christian theology.* New York: The Pilgrim Press.

Nolen-Hoeksema, S. (1987). Sex differences in unipolar depression: Evidence and theory. *Psychological Bulletin, 101,* 259–282.

O'Leary, K.D., and Wilson, G.T. (1987). *Behavior therapy: Application and outcome* (2nd ed.). Englewood Cliffs: Prentice-Hall.

Ornstein, R., and Sobel, D. (1987). *The healing brain: Breakthrough discoveries about how the brain keeps us healthy.* New York: Touchstone.

Peele, S. (1989). *The diseasing of America: Addiction treatment out of control.* Lexington, MA: Lexington Books.

Politzer, R.M., Morrow, J.S., and Leavey, S. (1985). Report on the cost-benefit/effectiveness of treatment at the Johns Hopkins Center for Pathological Gambling. *Journal of Gambling Behavior, 1,* 131–142.

Propst, L.R. (1988). *Psychotherapy in a religious framework: Spirituality in the emotional healing process.* New York: Human Sciences Press.

Propst, L.R., Ostrom, R., Watkins, P., Dean, T., and Mashburn, D. (1992). Comparative efficacy of religious and nonreligious cognitive-behavioral therapy for the treatment of clinical depression in religious individuals. *Journal of Consulting and Clinical Psychology, 60,* 94–103.

Rachman, S.J., and Hodgson, R.S. (1980). *Obsessions and compulsions.* Englewood Cliffs: Prentice-Hall.

Raskin, R., and Terry, H. (1988). A principal-components analysis of the Narcissistic Personality Inventory and further evidence of its construct validity. *Journal of Personality and Social Psychology, 54,* 890–902.

Regier, D.A., Myers, J.K., Kramer, L.N., Robins, L.N., Blazer, D.G.,

Hough, R.L., Eaton, W.W., and Locke, B.Z. (1984). The NIMH Epidemiological Catchment Area program. *Archives of General Psychiatry, 41*, 934–941.

Renshaw, D.C. (1990). Sexual medicine 1939 to today. In B.T. Taylor and I.J. Taylor (eds.), *Psychiatry: Past reflections—future visions.* New York: Elsevier.

Rimmele, C.T., Miller, W.R., and Dougher, M.J. (1989). Aversion therapies. In R.K. Hester and W.R. Miller (eds.), *Handbook of alcoholism treatment approaches: Effective alternatives.* New York: Pergamon Press.

Robins, L.N., Helzer, J.E., Croughan, J., Williams, J.B., and Spitzer, R.L. (1981). *NIMH Diagnostic Interview Schedule:* Version III. Rockville: U.S. Department of Health and Human Services.

Robins, L.N., Helzer, J.E., Weissman, M.M., Orvaschel, J., Gruenberg, E., Burke, J.D., and Regier, D.A. (1984). Prevalence of specific psychiatric disorders in three sites. *Archives of General Psychiatry, 41*, 949–958.

Rogers, C.R. (1951). *Client-centered therapy.* Boston: Houghton-Mifflin.

Royce, J.E. (1989). *Alcohol problems and alcoholism: A comprehensive survey* (rev. ed.). New York: The Free Press.

Sadock, B.J., Kaplan, H.I., and Freedman, A.M. (eds.) (1976). *The sexual experience.* Baltimore: Williams & Wilkins.

Sapolsky, R.M. (1988). Lessons of the Serengeti: Why some of us are more susceptible to stress. *The Sciences, 28*, 38–42.

Sarason, I.G., and Sarason, B.R. (1984). *Abnormal psychology* (4th ed.). Englewood Cliffs: Prentice-Hall.

Seligman, M.E.P. (1975). *Helplessness: On depression, development, and death.* San Francisco: Freeman.

Shea, M.T., Elkin, I., Imber, S.D., Sotsky, S.M., Watkins, J.T., Collins, J.F., Pikonis, P.A., Leber, W.R., Krupnick, J., Dolan, R.T., and Parloff, M.B. (1990). *Course of depressive symptoms over follow-up: Findings from the National Institute of Mental Health treatment of depression collaborative research programs.* Manuscript submitted for publication.

Sheehan, D. (1982). Current concepts in psychiatry: Panic attacks and phobias. *New England Journal of Medicine 301*, 156–158.

Siegel, R.K. (1989). *Intoxication: Life in pursuit of artificial paradise.* New York: Pocket Books.

Smith, S.S., and Newman, J.P. (1990). Alcohol and drug abuse-dependence described in psychopathic and nonpsychopathic criminal offenders. *Journal of Abnormal Psychology*, 99, 430–439.

Strub, R.L., and Black, F.W. (1985). *The mental status examination in neurology* (2nd ed.). Philadelphia: A. Davis Co.

Sullivan, H.S. (1953). *The interpersonal theory of psychiatry.* New York: Norton.

Tavris, C. (1989). *Anger: The misunderstood emotion* (rev. ed.). New York: Touchstone.

Tollison, C.D., and Adams, H.E. (1979). *Sexual disorders: Theory, treatment and research.* New York: Gardner.

Toole, E.M. (1991). *Study of stress influences on women religious children of alcoholics.* Unpublished doctoral dissertation, Loyola College in Maryland.

Truax, C.B., and Carkhuff, R.R. (1967). *Toward effective counseling and psychotherapy.* Chicago: Aldine Press.

Tsuang, M.T. (1982). *Schizophrenia—the facts.* New York: Oxford University Press.

Tyrer, S., and Shopsin, B. (1982). Symptoms and assessment of mania. In E.S. Paykel (ed.), *Handbook of affective disorders.* New York: Guilford Press.

U.S. Department of Health and Human Services (1990). *Seventh special report to the U.S. Congress on alcohol and health.* Rockville: U.S. Department of Health and Human Services.

Volberg, R.A., and Steadman, H.J. (1989). Prevalance estimates of pathological gambling in New Jersey and Maryland. *American Journal of Psychiatry*, 146, 1618–1619.

Wicks, R.J. (1983). Passive-aggressiveness within the religious setting. In R.D. Parsons and R.J. Wicks (eds.), *Passive-aggressiveness: Theory and practice.* New York: Brunner/Mazel.

Wicks, R.J., and Parsons, R.D. (1990). *Counseling strategies and intervention techniques for the human services* (3rd ed.). St. Louis: The Catholic Health Association of the United States.

Wolpe, J., and Lazarus, A.A. (1966). *Behavior therapy techniques.* New York: Pergamon Press.

Wolpe, J. (1978). *The practice of behavior therapy* (3rd ed.). New York: Pergamon Press.

Wright, L. (1988). The type A behavior pattern and coronary artery disease: Quest for the active ingredients and the elusive mechanism. *American Psychologist*, 43, 2–14.

Wysowski, D.K., and Baum, C. (1989). Antipsychotic drug use in the United States, 1976–1985. *Archives of General Psychiatry*, 46, 929–932.

Index